LEADING ACROSS CULTURES IN PRACTICE

A guide to understanding the logic of culture values in a globalized world

Fernando Lanzer

Published with the support of
LCO Partners BV
Meester F. A. van Hallweg 23
1181ZT – Amstelveen
The Netherlands

Translated from the original in Portuguese: *Cruzando culturas sem ser atropelado: gestão transcultural para um mundo globalizado*, published by Editora Évora, São Paulo, 2013.

Leading Across Cultures in Practice: A guide to understanding the logic of culture values in a globalized world

First printing November 2017
ISBN-10: 1977620574
ISBN-13: 978-1977620576

Text copyright © 2017 Fernando Lanzer Pereira de Souza
All Rights Reserved

Back cover photography by Jussara Pereira de Souza

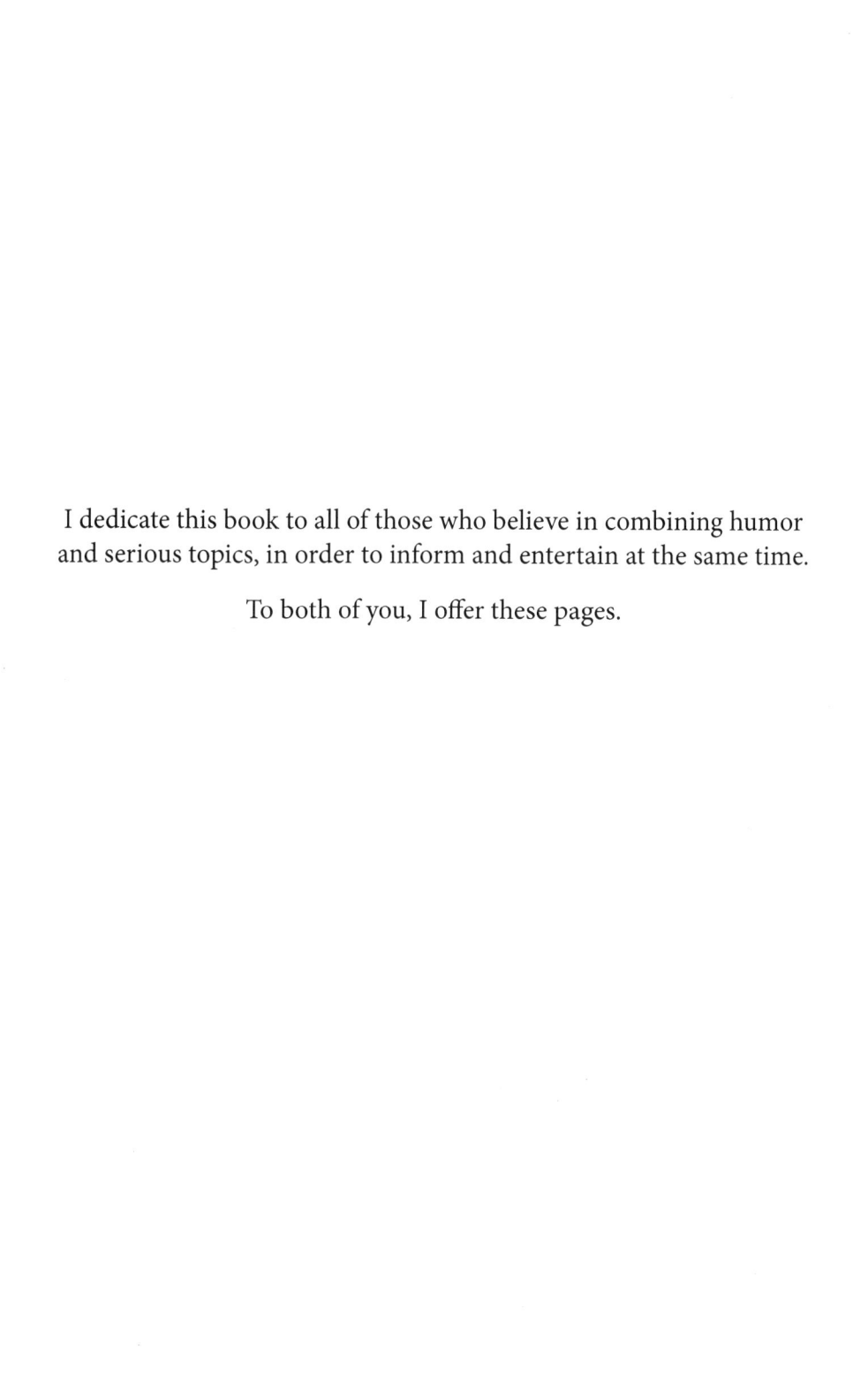

I dedicate this book to all of those who believe in combining humor and serious topics, in order to inform and entertain at the same time.

To both of you, I offer these pages.

Acknowledgments

I am profoundly grateful to:

Professor Geert Hofstede, a genius of our times, for having taken the study of culture to a new level. Thank you for your support, inspiration, and for being an example of a curious and open mind.

Bob Waisfisz, for having welcomed me as if we were old friends the first time we met, and taking me to have lunch in Muiden to begin a friendship that lasts for over 20 years. Thank you for sharing your knowledge of organizational culture and for welcoming me into the ITIM network where I made many other friends.

Huib Wursten , for contaminating me with an incredible enthusiasm about national cultures and sharing everything you know about Mental Images and culture clusters. Thank you also for the partnership in writing several articles.

Juanita Wynands, for the Foreword and for our everlasting friendship.

Contents

Acknowledgments, v

Foreword, ix

Introduction, xi

Part I – Basic Concepts About Culture, 1
    A bit of history, 1
    National Cultures, 5
    Will globalization bring about a single culture for the whole world?, 10
    The culture "iceberg", 11
    Culture bias, 13
    Stereotypes and prejudice, 13
    It all begins in childhood, 14
    Culture as an onion, 15
    Relative and general comparisons, 16
    Human beings in 4D, 17
    My encounter with Hofstede and Freud, 23
    Culture dimensions, 24

Part II – The Culture Dimensions Model, 27
1. Power Distance (PDI), 29
    Main differences between high/low PDI cultures, 34
    Information flow, 36
    Decision-making, 37
    Delegation and empowerment, 38
    Managing by Walking Around, 38
    The open door, 39
    Power Distance in Government and Politics, 43

CONTENTS

    Power Distance outside organizations, 46
    Family, 48
    Education, 48
    Conflict, 49
    Does egalitarianism increase when people's income increases?, 52

2. Individualism versus Collectivism (IDV), 53
    Shame or guilt?, 55
    Relationship versus task, 56
    Personal space, 57
    Privacy, 59
    Belonging to a group, 61
    Direct and indirect communication styles, 63
    The British visit Brazil, 65
    Too much context or not enough of it?, 67
    International political negotiations, 72
    How each side perceives the other side, 73
    Body language, 77
    The notion of family, 81
    Education, 82
    Feedback at work, 82
    Contracts, 83
    Nepotism, 84
    Beer, 85
    Is the world becoming more individualistic?, 86

3. Performance Orientation (PER), 87
    Live to work or work to live?, 89
    Competing to win, 90
    Winning is not everything, 91
    Competitive spirit, 92
    Fast food and slow food, 93
    The cook as a hero, 95

4. Uncertainty Avoidance (UAI), 97
    Planning and/or organizing, 97
    Religiousness and/or superstition, 99
    Expressing emotions, 100

Extensive, detailed and abundant legislation, 101
Contradicting Indicators, 102
Curious correlations, 103
Other ways of expressing UAI, 103

5. Long-Term Orientation, 104
What is it all about, after all?, 105
Practical Implications, 106
Opposites may coexist, 107
Analysis and synthesis, 107
How and why, 108
Relationships, 110
Special Chapter on Traffic, 111
Physics Lesson, 113
Driving Lesson, 114
What is "a Good Driver" like?, 115
Long Term, 115

6. Indulgence versus Restraint (IVR), 118

Part III – A Few Countries, 121
1. United States of America, 123
Overview, 123
The land of the free, 125
Freedom to be exploited?, 126
A culture of competition, 127
Crazy for money?, 129
Only what can be measured has value, 130
The bigger, the better, 131
The cult of heroes, 132
Employee of the month, 134
The American Challenge, 136
The free market culture, 137
The contract culture, 138
Litigation culture, 140
Black and white, 141
Conflict culture, 142
My favorite enemy, 143
Who is "number one?", 145

Optimism and arrogance, 146
Lay an egg and sing like a rooster, 148
Privacy, 149
Short Term, 149
When norms are taken literally, 151
Crime, punishment and revenge, 152
A management Guru in the States, but not elsewhere?, 153
The American's challenge, 154
Running away from the lion, 156
The ideal leader, 156
Hero dependency, 157
Work-life balance, 158
Men at work (and women too), 159
American feminism, 160
Gender wars, 161
Dealing with sex, 162
Emmanuelle in New York, 163
Carl Rogers versus B. F. Skinner, 164
What irritates most Americans?, 165
Pro and anti-Americanism, 167
An American outside-in point of view, 168
Working with Americans in America and elsewhere, 169

2. United Kingdom, 171
Overview, 171
Communication, 172
The class system, 173
Working with the British, 175

3. Germany, 176
Overview, 176
Curtains and plants, 177
Cars made in Germany and in other places, 178
The expert is more important than the boss, 180
Participative management, 181
Planning and implementation, 183
Work is more valued than quality of life, 184
Martin Luther and the Protestants, 185

Stopping on the sidewalk, 187
Children at the toy shop, 187
No, means no. Do not insist., 188
Double parking means jail, 188
Respecting speed limits, 189
Merkel and the proposals for the EU, 190
Breath analysis at the bar's restrooms, 193
Economic austerity, 194
German original better than American remake, 196
The autonomy of the *"Lander"*, 197
Working with Germans, 198

4. The Netherlands, 200
Overview, 200
Similarities and differences, 200
Performance, yes; but not as a priority, 202
Business can wait, 203
The secretaries and the beach, 204
The world's most communist country, 205
The Chairman trying to leave the building, 205
The only BMW on this street, 207
One cookie, one potato, 208
Giving birth at home, 209
Ambition? What for?, 210
Competition to avoid losing, 211
Punctual from start to finish, 212
Sense of urgency? What do you mean?, 213
Low service quality, 214
The ten-week sofa, 215
Treating the client badly when he is trying to pay, 216
One client at a time gets full attention, 216
German on the outside, Brazilian hidden inside, 217
Extreme Individualism, 219
Re-discussions, 220
Refugees, 222
Tolerant, except with loud noises, 223
Exclusive or inclusive?, 224

Social Control, 226
Working with the Dutch, 227
Dutch Summary, 229

5. Brazil, 230

The scores, 230
Paternalism, 231
ABN AMRO in Brazil, 232
Pros and cons of paternalism, 233
Hierarchy, 233
Sanctioned Initiatives, 234
The *mutirão* culture, 235
Privacy is relative, 236
Whoever is on top gets the blame, 237
Work and fun at the same time, 238
Joint Venture in Germany, 239
Vale in Canada, 241
Uncertainty Avoidance in Brazil, 241
Long Term Orientation in Brazil, 243
Some popular notions about Brazilian culture, 244

6. China, 251

Overview, 251
Differences and similarities with American culture, 251
Differences from other Asian countries, 253
Power Distance (PDI) in China, 254
Democracy in China, 256
Guanxi, 258
The foreigners' illusion, 259
Invasive intimacy, 259
Chinese contracts, 261
Mistaken notions about China, 262

Part IV – The Big Issues, 265

Does Culture Change?, 265
Is it possible to change culture deliberately?, 266
Are we putting people in boxes?, 269
Is happiness a cultural value?, 269
Does religion precede culture or it the other way around?, 271

Are multicultural teams better or worse?, 272
Society's Great Dilemmas, 273
Skepticism, 279
The spinning onion, 286
In conclusion, 290

Bibliography, 293

About the Author, 297

Foreword

Our world, will most probably never go back to homogenous cultural groups and tribes. At least not in the foreseeable future. Apart from diasporas that took place centuries ago, the displacement of large groups of people in our times means that our world, looking from the cultural perspective, is becoming ever more complex. The same is true for the corporate business world, national and international.

In the last decades, a Transnational Professional Nomad Tribe has come into being. This is a new type of tribe, formed by people who work and live abroad for a shorter or longer period of their (working) lives.

Nomads are tribes that roam the world. Their most important characteristic is that, as a group, they stay together and they develop values, behaviour and communication patterns that are stable. That is the constant in their lives. Their environment may change, however their culture stays intact. Precisely that element is what corporate nomads nowadays do not have. To survive, they need to form or enter a new group every time they move to a new location. Not only that, they need to understand the cultural context of their new environment quickly, to be able to function effectively, at whatever level of the organisation. They must learn new behaviour and communication skills, often without understanding the drivers behind them. Behaviour and communication are the only two competencies that people possess to connect with each other. These skills are not yet an integral part of the educational system in the Western world.

How do these contextual and people competencies work? That is precisely the subject and theme of this book. Using the scientifically validated and reliable 5-D model of Professor Geert Hofstede, Fernando Lanzer explains and gives in-depth insight into **how** culture impacts people personally, **how** cultural dynamics impact international cooperation, and **how** culture can be used strategically for effective management decisions. Fernando, himself a professional nomad, weaves a lot of examples from all walks of life: cinema, books, and especially his own life's experience. Fernando is a born story-teller, it makes a fascinating read. The book bridges the gap between academic research and **how** cultural encounters happen and work in practice.

Another reason for my warm recommendation is the fact that there are not a lot of Interculturalists who are able to paint the intercultural business picture with so much clarity and with so many colourful nuances.

Juanita Wijnands
Interculturalist by life-experience and vocation

Introduction

Culture is a subject that began getting the attention of the corporate world around the 1960's and 1970's, when the international image of Japan shifted from being a "brand X" country, maker of trinkets and low-quality goods, to being a sophisticated producer of highly valued consumer electronics. Japanese products (first electronics, then cars and other goods) began to be exported all over the world and gained market share from American and European brands. The Japanese products were more innovative, of better quality and lower price.

This was a wake-up call for business leaders in the West, and soon management specialists were filling all flights to Japan trying to uncover what the "Japanese miracle" was all about: what were they doing in the Far East in order to become so successful?

The first response they got was: "it's the Quality Circles!" And many companies all over the world started copycatting the Japanese quality control processes and procedures. Subsequently, however, they found that the resulting quality was not the same as in Japan, even though they were basically following the same procedures. Besides, these processes had been created by an American consultant, W. Edwards Deming... Why was it that they did not enjoy the same success in the United States?

The second response was: "it's the Japanese culture". The Japanese have a culture of discipline and dedication that maximizes the procedures invented by Deming. Therefore, it became logical that what was needed was to understand, diagnose and measure this phenomenon of "a different national culture" and its consequences for people performing on the job.

Around this time, the first research studies by Professor Geert Hofstede were published. He was a Dutch engineer turned psychologist who became a pioneer in measuring what he called "culture dimensions" thereby making it possible to compare, more objectively, the concepts until then intangible of national cultures.

As a Human Resources executive in large banks and also as a management consultant, I became involved with the practical applications of corporate culture and national cultures. My own job was at the crossroads of these two concepts, as I was constantly dealing with multinational organizations. Our daily work involved these two issues constantly.

I've led countless workshops on corporate culture, both as an HR executive as well as a management consultant. When I got to know Hofstede's 5D model in 1993, I found the answer to many of the questions my team was facing then at ABN AMRO. We used the model to understand the differences in management and leadership styles between the bank's Head Office and its Brazilian branch (initially) and among the dominant styles in the different ABN AMRO offices throughout the world. When the Dutch bank acquired Banco Real in Brazil in 1998, we again used the Hofstede model as a reference to merge the two different bank cultures. The good results we obtained in that process made that merger an international benchmark.

The underlying values of national cultures influence everything we do: both in our private lives and at work. They influence politics, the economy and even management theory. If we don't understand national culture issues, we will be condemned to live our lives based on a distorted vision of reality, each of us with a bias coming from the culture in which we were brought up since childhood. It's impossible to manage effectively in a global market without an understanding of national cultures.

When I left ABN AMRO in 2007 and returned to my work as a consultant, which I had interrupted in 1992, I went deeper into the practical applications of the culture model and its concepts. I've always positioned myself as a practitioner in the field of leadership and organization development; however, since most of my clients were multinational companies, their demands invariably involved a combination of national culture and corporate culture issues. Even if I wanted, I would not be able to avoid national culture issues when addressing management themes in these organizations.

INTRODUCTION

Often people asked me to suggest books where they good read further about national cultures. The subject of corporate culture is well served with plenty of available literature, mainly by American, Canadian and British authors. I cannot say the same about national cultures: there are few good books available on that topic.

Corporate culture books, however, suffer from an Anglo-Saxon bias influencing their approach. They need to be considered with a critical view, in order to avoid applying American concepts in cultures that work better using different values.

Many times I suggested Professor Hofstede's books; yet they are more technical and academic works, not always easy to digest by readers interested only in the practical application of those ideas.

Therefore, I decided to write a bit of material myself, trying to fill that gap. At first I wrote a series of articles, published in 2012 as "Take Off Your Glasses". After that I wrote the Brazilian version of this book, "Cruzando Culturas", in 2013.

My intention here was to summarize my own experience in applying the 5D framework in practice. I've used a simple and direct language whenever possible, as is usual in the workplace. I've re-written the whole book in "International Business English," targeting people who use English as a "lingua franca" in their work, whether it is their native language or not.

I trust that this book will be useful to readers as a reference, above anything else. I also hope to provide a pleasant read, perhaps even a fun read. I believe very much in combining work and pleasure, in any culture. That is probably due to my own Brazilian culture bias…

Part I – Basic Concepts About Culture

A bit of history

Up until a few years ago, the term "culture" was understood as referring to "art" and whatever was considered to be "beautiful". This concept of beauty was determined by the elite, in every country, and was linked to history, to whatever was considered beautiful in the so-called classical periods. By the way, the concept of "classic" applies both to Western and Eastern civilizations. In the West we refer to classical music, paintings, sculpture, literature, and those references equally are found in the East, among Muslims, Chinese, Japanese, etc.

I've been working with organizational culture since 1974 and with national cultures since 1993. From the very beginning I had to face the issue of defining "what is culture".

The term "culture" has been used with many different meanings. In the more popular sense it conveys the idea of education and experience as in "Susan is a cultured individual". In this sense we are trying to say that Susan knows a lot, from her formal education and or experience.

Another meaning of the word "culture" is conveyed when using it in reference to anthropology. Culture is used as the total set of knowledge and artistic output typical of a certain people or of an era. Anthropologists study "Greek culture" of the 5th Century B.C. or "the French Culture" of the 18th Century.

Around the second half of the 20th Century a third meaning became more popular: the term "popular culture" began to be used, referring to contemporary arts. Up until then, culture was used as synonym of sophistication, something for the social elite. Classic music was "culture";

popular music was not. Culture in the historical sense was acknowledged and studied by anthropologists and historians. Contemporary culture was not taken seriously.

This all changed in the 1950's and 1960's. Margaret Mead published her books "Coming Of Age in Samoa" and "Growing Up in New Guinea"; studies on how tribal cultures in distant parts of the planet were very different from the habits of people in the so-called "Western World". Psychologists like Erich Fromm started debating whether it was modern culture or genetics that determined how people developed their personality. The term "culture" started to be used in its sociological sense, as the set of norms that guided people's behavior in society.

"Pop culture" became a concept used all over the world, referring to present-day habits, likes and dislikes of people in general. No one summarized this better than Andy Warhol with his painting of a can of Campbell's soup. With this work, and with all of his work, Warhol was saying: "art is not something for the elite and about elitist subjects; art is also about everyday things and for the common folk." Therefore, culture is not just about sophisticated education, it is about how we do things, how we behave, what we make and what we hold valuable.

The concept of culture became more democratic. Intellectual leaders hijacked the concept of culture from the traditional elite. They valued modern art, rather than classic art; modern jazz rather than classic music; and so forth.

In the sixties the hippie revolution took this process further and crossed a new frontier. The term "counter-culture" was coined to describe a popular concept of opposing whatever was hitherto considered beautiful by the elite. The hippies contested all kinds of norms by proclaiming: "I do my thing, you do your thing. And it's all good!" General norms were no longer accepted: what is appropriate or not became a matter of preference or personal taste.

This whole process opened the concept of culture to encompass everything that is considered to be "beautiful" or "appropriate" by any given group of people. A group of people could be a bunch of friends, a tribe, a town, a country, a certain region within a country or a region spanning two or more countries. The notion of culture freed itself from the elites.

The media started dedicating space and time for popular music, films and TV.

In the seventies business leaders started talking about corporate culture and national cultures. In companies, managers were interested in factors affecting productivity. How come certain organizations were more effective than others? What kind of things affected performance?

Surely productivity was affected by the behavior of leaders and managers; the concept of leadership styles was developed trying to define and describe this aspect. Other, broader aspects were discovered, and almost simultaneously the concepts of corporate climate and culture were identified. Subsequently these two concepts were differentiated: corporate climate is linked to, yet different from, corporate culture.

Many concepts and definitions were created, became fashionable, and disappeared with the times; some were rather complex, others were quite simple. I always had a preference for the latter and I specially liked the definition that "culture is the way we do things around here". The more complicated version says that "culture is the set of unwritten norms and values that guide people's behavior in a given group, at work, in an organization or nation."

Professor Geert Hofstede, a Dutch engineer turned psychologist who worked at IBM and left the company to dedicate himself to academic research on culture, has coined a provocative definition: "culture is the collective programming of the human mind."

What he meant was that we are all "programmed" by our parents, our family, our school and our community, which all teach us what is considered to be "right" and "wrong", "beautiful" and "ugly". Culture is that notion of what is considered appropriate or inappropriate, acceptable or not. Different groups have different cultures, and the most basic aspects of culture are rooted in childhood, when first learned what is adequate and what is not.

Hofstede was the pioneer in measuring culture differences. Thanks to his work, culture became no longer "just another of those 'vague', indefinite subjects" and is now regarded as something that can be described and statistically measured.

Taking the definition of culture as "the set of (unwritten) behavior norms of a given group", we come to the conclusion that each group has its own culture. There are as many cultures as there are groups

Depending on how we organize people into groups, we can observe different cultures, according to these groupings.

Hofstede noted that gender is one of the most basic forms of grouping people and observing the norms that guide their behavior. Therefore we can speak of a "feminine culture" and of a "masculine culture", since in all societies we can find different norms for masculine behavior and feminine behavior.

That is precisely the central theme of feminist movements all over the world: the differences between the norms dictated by society regarding to what is acceptable for little boys and little girls, since early childhood.

Up until the middle of the last century, most people still gave greater weight to genetic differences between men and women (the president of Harvard University believed in this until the 21st Century, until he was fired…). The feminist movement showcased the fact that yes, genetic differences do exist, it is obvious that women are different from men, but there are many differences that have been culturally determined and that are not innate. The classic examples are that "boys don't cry" and girls must be delicate and graceful. These behavior norms are taught by each culture to children since an early age and they have a deep effect on everyone's personality. These notions are very difficult to change, even in adulthood.

Hofstede started by dedicating himself to the study of the differences among national cultures. It is true that there are different cultures for boys and for girls, and it is also true that in certain countries girls are expected to behave differently from what is expected in other countries, and the same applies to boys, that is: from one country to another, the norms for the same gender are different.

National culture is also learned in childhood and is also difficult to change.

As we become adults, we become members of other groups and become part of other cultures. We observe that there are "corporate cultures" that differentiate one company from another; and professional cultures that differentiate departments within the same company. We talk about how the culture of Engineering is different from the Sales Department culture.

Yet another difference lies among the nature of organizations: the culture of the private sector is different from the culture of the civil service; hospitals have a different culture compared to banks, and so on.

Corporate cultures are easier to change, since their values are learned by their members as adults, not as children. People conform to those values only while they are part of the company. When they change jobs to work in a different organization, people can adopt this new organization's values much more easily than they can adopt different national values when they move to another country and must confront values that are very different from those that they learned in childhood.

Hofstede developed different models to describe organizational cultures and national cultures. His earlier and better-known work refers to national cultures and began in 1971. The organizational culture model is much more recent and was developed with Bob Waisfisz from 2005 onwards.

This book will focus on national cultures and the impact of such cultures in organizations dealing with different national cultures. The organizational culture issues mentioned here are related to the national culture differences. Organizational culture is the subject of a different book I have written, complementary to this one.

National Cultures

The concept of national cultures became the object of attention for corporations as they realized that this is a crucial factor for a company's (or an individual's) success or failure.

A survey published by Price-Waterhouse in the nineties revealed that among the biggest challenges faced by expatriate managers, culture differences were the second most-often mentioned, referred to by 65% of respondents. It was right behind "changes in own behavior" (mentioned as a challenge by 69% of respondents), well ahead of things like "working too far away from Head Office" (52%) and "accounting and tax differences" (36%).

Actually, we know that it all began in the eighties, when Japan's rapid economic development spurred the West's curiosity. European and American companies rushed to Japan in order to discover the secret of Japanese success.

They discovered the "quality circles" and a series of management practices used in Japan to ensure the constant improvement of quality in manufacturing all kinds of goods. Foreign companies tried to learn the Japanese ways of working and kept asking them "how did you manage to implement all these processes?"

The Japanese would say: "it is a matter of culture..." And that response would leave the visitors blank-faced. What do you mean, "culture"? What the hell is that?

The responses were then rather elaborate and did not clarify the issue. Some people said that this was all rooted deeply in the Japanese culture and could not be reproduced in any other country. Others spoke of a very strong "organizational culture" in large corporations such as Toyota, Mitsubishi or Sony.

Part of the difficulty in understanding what was happening in Japan derived precisely from cultural differences between the people asking and the people responding to their questions. Today we know that the Japanese culture is more geared towards pragmatic synthesis, while the visitors came from analytic cultures. The Americans and the British tried to break down the Japanese quality processes into their smaller components, and attempted to establish cause and effect relationships among these various parts. These researchers examined each part of the process and asked "why?"

That is: "why is it that you obtain this effect under these circumstances?" "What is the underlying principle causing this to occur in this process?" The basic idea is that it is possible to isolate a component of the process and handle it in such a way in order to recreate the desired effects in other situations. The ultimate goal is to replicate the process in order to control everything that happens, from start to finish. By decomposing the process it should be possible to make it even more efficient, minimizing the need for input and maximizing results. That is how "Western" thinking works.

The Japanese culture, however, values synthesis more than analysis. The central question to be asked is not "why?". The central question is "how?"

The attitude that is most valued in Japanese culture is one of trying to understand the process as a whole, respecting its integrity. What is valued is respecting reality as it is. Virtue lies in accepting reality and trying to understand it, rather than intending to control each part of the whole process. Decomposing the process is considered something invasive and pretentious, a destructive interference. People must show humility in their scientific approach, they must understand processes in order to be able to reproduce them with no changes (or with minimal interference).

From these international conversations about the culture behind the Japanese quality processes a growing interest developed over culture differences in general and the implications for managing businesses and people.

It was no coincidence that one of Hofstede's early books was titled "Culture's Consequences". Up until then culture studies were dealing with peculiar habits of Australian aborigine tribes compared to Europe, or fertility rites in South Pacific islands. None of this seemed relevant for the business world. It was all just interesting for academic conversations among anthropology professors when they met for tea in large universities.

The Japanese miracle shifted the attention of researchers. Culture differences (they discovered) were linked to ways of working and to differences in productivity in different countries. The subject gained relevance as more and more companies were becoming "multinational", with manufacturing plants located in different countries, often managed by expatriate staff members coming from a different culture. It was the beginning of "globalization" and with it "culture shock" as something companies had to deal with.

Of course there had already been people born and raised in one country, but working as adults in a different culture. This had been happening for centuries. However, these were the exceptions, not the rule. The vast majority of populations, until then, grew up and worked in the same culture. Contact with different cultures occurred through leisure activities: traveling on holidays, watching plays in the theater, watching films and TV programs, reading about other cultures in novels.

Globalization brought culture differences to the workplace of people in general. Now common folk found products in their daily life coming from other cultures; they worked for a company whose main office was from abroad; they had a boss who came from another culture, their own careers now included the possibility of traveling for business or even relocating abroad for two or three years. Foreigners were not just occasional visiting tourists; they were business colleagues, clients, and providers. And they all did things differently, in a rather "strange" way.

Each nationality had its own peculiar habits. Each culture had a different way of greeting, different etiquette, sometimes opposite ways of doing things. These differences in behavior were very visible.

When visiting another country on a business trip, the first thing anyone noticed were differences in business greetings: the Japanese bowed, the Indians shook hands rather loosely, Americans would crush your fingers in a handshake and spoke loudly, and so forth. Soon there were many little books on "do's and don'ts" becoming popular. They dealt with these superficial aspects of culture differences: how to greet people, things to avoid in certain countries, gestures that had different meanings across cultures.

Unfortunately these little books spread the mistaken notion that it was enough to know how to greet someone from a different country and all barriers were removed; this was all it took in order to do business across borders. It got even worse, because half the content in such books was utter nonsense. In their eagerness to identify little anecdotes and habits that they could classify as "typical" of each country, the authors frequently exaggerated and included in their findings some obscure regional outdated superstitions that were no longer practiced and not at all typical of that culture. This did not add value in trying to bridge gaps and foster better understanding among cultures, on the contrary: it helped to build stereotypes that completely missed the mark.

As an example, I've found books that mentioned some absurd "pearls of wisdom" about Brazil, such as:

- *Never pour wine holding the bottle with your right hand and tilting it towards another person's glass by twisting your hand towards your right side: this is a symbol of death.*

Actually, if you do this, you will probably end up spilling some wine out of the glass, because it's much easier to hold the bottle with your right hand and twist it towards your left side… This whole idea of "symbol of death" must have been a misunderstanding by whoever was doing the research, or perhaps just a specific superstition found somewhere deep in the Brazilian hinterland; you cannot say that this is something typical of Brazilian culture.

- *Never give someone a knife as a gift; this means that you are wishing the death of the person to whom you are presenting the gift.*

This is a superstition from gaucho folklore, very specific to the South of Brazil, not known outside of that part of the country and not known by most of the younger generations. People from the Brazilian South are generally meat lovers and it is common to give friends a finely decorated meat knife as a gift. Those who know about the superstition would typically do the following: upon presenting the knife, they would ask the receiving person to give them a coin; upon receiving the coin, the person would explain: "I'd like to give you this knife as a gift, so in order to avoid the negative connotation known to gaucho folklore, let's pretend that you just bought the knife from me with this coin!" This is all about gaucho traditions originated in the 18th Century, and it is a long way from representing something typical of Brazilian culture in general, today.

In the fifties, American anthropologist Margaret Mead wrote "Growing Up in New Guinea", and "Coming Of Age In Samoa", books that became landmarks in anthropology literature, describing typical habits of youngsters in the South Pacific, in contrast with what was customary in America. This work had the merit of revealing that "the American Way of Life" was not universal: there were other cultures elsewhere in the world where habits were totally different from the United States.

Many years later, when Professor Mead had already passed away, a journalist decided to visit the islands and interview the youngsters who had been mentioned in the books and provided the material featured in them. These youngsters were now middle-aged ladies, with their own children and grandchildren, still living in the same villages 40 years later. To the journalist's surprise (and to the astonishment of the scientific community in general), one of these ladies revealed that at the time Professor Mead had visited their village, the local youngsters made fun of her (as youngsters often do in any culture). The teenagers in those days decided to pull a prank on the naïve scientist and made up all kinds of weird things pretending that they were "typical of our village culture". They were actually later surprised to hear that their tall tales had been taken seriously and published as scientific fact, translated to many other languages throughout the world.

Therefore, do be careful when trying to understand the customs and habits of a foreign culture! Never take anything at face value; and do not mistake certain specific ancient superstitions as something really typical of that culture, today.

Will globalization bring about a single culture for the whole world?

Imagine the following scene: a young man is driving a Japanese car on a busy avenue. On his car's radio, an American pop song is playing. He wears jeans and an Italian sweatshirt. He parks his car in front of a fast-food outlet where he orders a hamburger and a Cola.

The question is: where in the world is this imaginary scene taking place?

The answer is that this scene could happen in almost any country in the world, because these products and brands are all present in at least one hundred different nations.

However, the global presence of the same products and brands does not mean that we are heading towards a single culture. These products and brands are just a superficial part of what we call culture. The way you dress, the kind of food you have, the means of transportation, these are just appearances. Culture runs much deeper than that. Let us recall, once again, the working definition of culture that we employ here.

We call "culture" *the set of norms (generally unwritten) that guide the behavior of a group of people, giving them a notion of what is "right" and "wrong", acceptable and appropriate or unacceptable and inappropriate.*

This set of norms is defined by underlying values, not apparent, not easily seen, but that actually determine people's behavior, the way they relate to each other, at work and in their private lives.

The more superficial aspects of culture are indeed gradually tending towards uniformization through the proliferation of global brands and standard habits. However, research has shown that this uniformization of the visible and more superficial aspects of culture causes an inverse reaction of the underlying values, which are strongly linked to local traditions in opposition to globalization.

This strong feeling of identification with local tradition has caused a rebirth of separatist movements all over the world, threatening the integrity of the "nation-states" that were born in the 19th and 20th Century. More and more people are identifying themselves with local values and rejecting what they perceive as "foreign" and "standardizing". Idiosyncrasies are increasingly valued all over the world.

The culture "iceberg"

We can consider that culture is like an iceberg: the visible part, that can be seen above the water line, is people's behavior and the products people make. This is the smaller portion of the iceberg. The more significant portion, much larger, lies beneath the surface, unseen. This corresponds to the underlying values of culture. These values are the most important aspect of culture, because they determine the logic that drives the behaviors, habits and traditions you can see above the surface. In order to understand a culture it is necessary to look beneath the surface and get to know the underlying values.

Not observed

Values

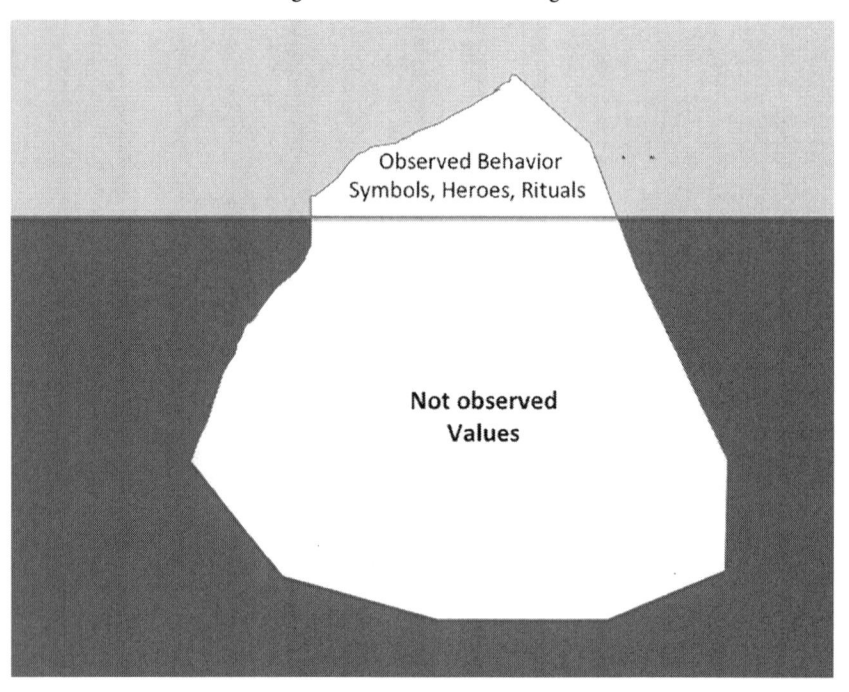

Figure 1: The culture "iceberg"

[Iceberg diagram: above water — "Observed Behavior, Symbols, Heroes, Rituals"; below water — "Not observed, Values"]

This is specially difficult because we are all immersed each of us in our own culture and we are normally not aware of just how much our culture influences the way we perceive the world around us. There is an Arab proverb that says, "We don't know who invented water, but it certainly was not a fish!"

This proverb emphasizes that we do not see what is all around us and has always been around us. A fish is not aware of the water around it because it is the only environment that it knows. Perhaps it will only be aware of water's very existence when it is removed from it… When there is no water the fish is painfully aware of its existence and of how it is needed for its own survival.

In a similar way, we become aware of our own culture when we travel abroad and visit another culture. When we find ourselves in a different country we suddenly realize that there are other behaviors and habits different from our own, based on values that are different from the ones we have learned.

Culture bias

We all have a culture bias, a prejudice that affects our perception and our value judgments. Everything that is different from our culture we perceive as being "wrong" or "bad". Everything that is similar to our culture we consider to be "right" or "good". However, in terms of culture there is no "right" or "wrong": there is just "different". There is no culture that is better than others. All cultures work, all cultures can be effective. And all cultures are different.

We all wear a sort of "tinted culture sun glasses", of different colors, that affect the way we see the world, acting like a filter.

If we want to understand other cultures that are different from our own, we must first become aware of our filter, we must get to know our own "sun glasses" in order to be able to take them off and see the world as it is, without filters.

Stereotypes and prejudice

When we fail to remove our glasses, we have the tendency to form culture stereotypes and make generalizations about people of other nationalities. This is the source of general statements such as: all Germans are well organized, all Brazilians love parties, the Scots are stingy, Americans are aggressive and so forth.

The danger in adopting stereotypes as a reference is that they affect our ability to see individuals as they really are, with all the intrinsic richness of a human being. The less we know a foreign person, the more stereotyped our vision tends to be. As we get to know more about the specific person, we are able to leave the stereotype aside.

Stereotypes affect our value judgment of others both in a positive and in a negative way, depending on how they are similar to or different from our own values.

Our tendency towards using stereotypes as a reference also increases in proportion to our level of stress. When we feel somehow under pressure, being threatened, in order to defend ourselves we regress and use stereotypes as a reference. The greater the feeling of being threatened, the greater the use of stereotypes.

This phenomenon is emphasized in war situations, in which the enemy cultures are completely "demonized". This was clearly visible during World War II, when each side in the conflict demonized the others. It was also seen more recently when the 9/11 attacks brought about an attitude, among Americans, of perceiving all Muslims as their enemies.

The feeling of being under threat was soon extended to the French, when their government questioned the legal and ethical validity of invading Iraq. What ensued was a nice example of stereotyped perception, as all Frenchmen were perceived as being anti-American and there was an outcry in the US to stop calling "French fries" as such, calling them "Freedom Fries" instead.

Another issue linked to the use of cultural stereotypes is that when we verify that one characteristic of a stereotype is true, we readily assume that they must all be true. Keeping the French as an example, let's consider the stereotype that all French people are romantic; they like wine and enjoy discussing philosophical issues. When we meet a French person who likes wine, we assume that she must be romantic and enjoy discussing philosophy… when it may very well be that this person hates philosophy and is not romantic at all.

It all begins in childhood

The reason why our culture filter is so deeply rooted and difficult to remove is that it is developed in early childhood, before we are ten years old. It is in childhood that we learn our values, the notion of what is "right" and "wrong", the notion of "good" and "evil".

In this aspect Geert Hofstede's research meets Sigmund Freud's principles of psychodynamics. According to Freud, it is in childhood that we form "the superego", the part of our mind that contains the notions of right and wrong. A child's character is formed before she reaches ten years of age and it is difficult to change during adult life. All behavior as an adult is strongly linked to childhood and to how we learned to deal with emotions and values as we coped with situations that life presented us with.

In a similar fashion, Hofstede found that culture values are very difficult to change in time. Culture is something quite perennial, lasting for centuries with but small superficial variations and very little change at its core, which are values.

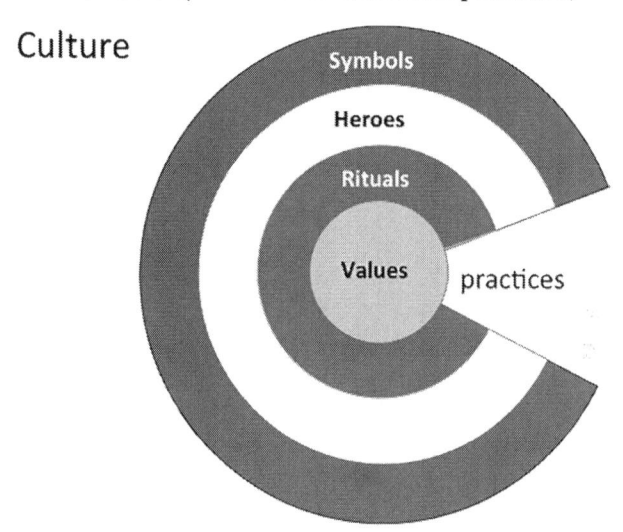

Figure 2: The culture "onion"
(Created by Geert Hofstede, used with permission)

Culture — Symbols, Heroes, Rituals, Values, practices

Culture as an onion

Another way of looking at culture is to consider it as an onion, with several layers (Figure 2). The outer layers correspond to the things I mentioned previously as being on the surface part of the iceberg: the rituals, the symbols, and the heroes. At the core of culture we find the values, which change very little and determine people's practices and behaviors.

The rituals of a culture include ceremonies, such as weddings, graduations, the way birthdays are celebrated, how to organize and behave at funerals and burials. The word "burial" in itself has a cultural connotation, since in many cultures the deceased are not buried, but rather they are cremated. In some cultures the deceased may be thrown into rivers or into the sea.

Rituals also include the way to greet others, habits observed during meals, the kind of food people eat, the schedules kept regarding eating and sleeping.

All these superficial aspects are easily observable in any culture.

Another aspect of culture that lies on the surface layers regards symbols, such as flags, banners and coats of arms, ways of dressing and fashion statements, anything that shows status and prestige, housing styles, architecture, internal decoration, car styles, workplace furnishings.

Yet a third aspect of culture lying on the more superficial parts regards the heroes of that culture. Who are the characters cited as a culture's heroes? What sort of personal characteristics led these people to be regarded as heroes? How did these individuals differentiate themselves from "normal" people in that same culture? What we can see is that there are underlying values that help us understand how these heroes, symbols and rituals came into being adopted and remain in use in the present days.

The relevance of Hofstede's research is that he achieved a breakthrough in identifying the underlying values, situated at the core, that determine the more superficial layers of culture and influence the way people behave.

Relative and general comparisons

A couple of disclaimers are in order, before we go further in describing the deeper layers of different cultures. Whenever we speak of culture, we are always referring to phenomena that are *general* and *relative*.

They are general in the sense that we refer to research that has been done on a group of people, or on a sample of a region or a nation's general population. We are not speaking of specific individuals. Therefore, we may say that in the German culture people value structured processes; however, it is quite possible that there are certain German people who as individuals do not value structured processes. When speaking of culture we are speaking of characteristics that have been observed on the average behavior of a population, but not necessarily in every individual.

We speak of culture in relative terms in the sense that we always compare a given culture with another. There are no "absolute" scores of any aspect of culture; all research scores were obtained by comparing one culture with others. There are certain cultures that are more "hierarchical" than others, but there is not an absolute score for "hierarchy" as "the maximum possible score" nor one for "the minimum possible".

A few years ago, in a social psychology experiment, a group of Mexicans were asked to describe a typical American. The traits mentioned by the Mexicans described the typical American as being serious, reserved, always in a hurry, averse to risk, methodic, polite and restrained.

Subsequently, a group of Japanese was asked to describe a typical American. The Japanese described the typical American as being friendly, relaxed, spontaneous, reckless, uninhibited, impulsive and emotional. In summary, the Japanese described the typical American very differently from the way the Mexicans had done.

As we've seen before, this happened because the "culture filter" of the Mexicans is different from the "culture filter" of the Japanese. Each nationality compares other nationalities according to their own culture standards, thereby making all comparisons relative. There are no absolute standards.

Human beings in 4D

It is also important to note that a person's behavior is not determined solely by the underlying values of that person's culture.

If we look at individuals through a simplified model (Figure 3), we can recognize four vectors: Spiritual, Physical, Emotional and Rational.

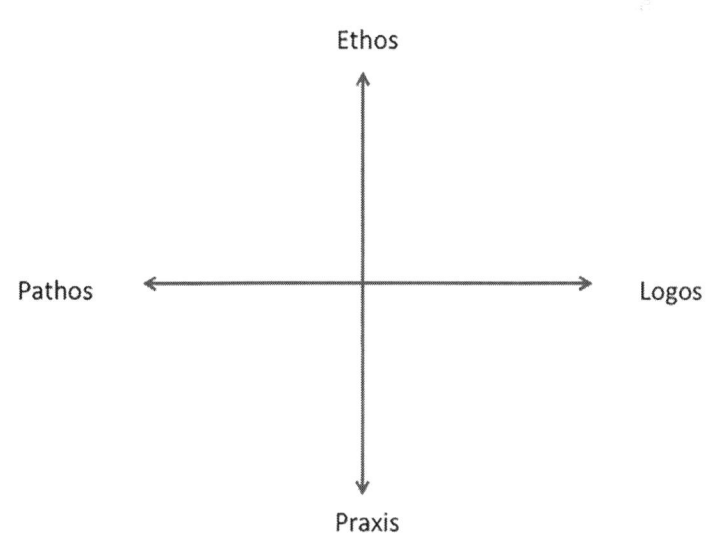

Figure 3: Four dimensions of a human being

```
              Ethos
                ↑
                |
  Pathos ←─────┼─────→ Logos
                |
                ↓
              Praxis
```

This model is archetypical, with equivalents in many different cultures and in different models created by different psychological and philosophical disciplines.

I believe the human mind can be seen as composed by three dimensions: the spiritual, emotional and rational dimensions.

The spiritual dimension contains our values and everything we believe in. As such, it includes the notion of "right" and "wrong"; culture, or what is considered to be appropriate or inappropriate, adequate or inadequate. It also contains ethics and moral principles; and it includes aesthetics and the notion of what is considered beautiful or ugly.

The spiritual dimension furthermore contains everything we believe in as a matter of faith. That includes religion, superstitious beliefs, the belief in another life after death, or the belief that nothing more exists after death, except funeral expenses and inheritance transmission taxes.

This whole concept is not something that I have created: many authors have written about this and have received greater or lesser consideration, depending on the respective beliefs and values of those who read them and heard them speak.

Freud called this spiritual dimension the Superego, the seat of a person's values; the rational dimension is the equivalent of what he called Ego and the emotional dimension corresponds to the Id, the seat of primary impulses and of the pleasure principle. Eric Berne, in Transactional Analysis, mentioned three "ego states": the spiritual dimension is the equivalent of what he called parental state; the rational dimension is the equivalent of the adult state, and the emotional dimension is the equivalent of what Berne named "the child" or "the infantile state of the ego".

For those who prefer a more erudite perspective, we can use terms taken from Ancient Greece: the spiritual dimension is what the Greeks referred to as *Ethos*, the rational dimension is what they called *Logos* and the emotional dimension is what they called *Pathos*. Aristotle used these terms to classify rhetorical arguments, thus referring to them:

"There are, therefore, these three ways of effecting persuasion. The man who commands them must, it is clear, be capable of (1) reason logically (*Logos*), (2) understand human character and kindness in its various forms (*Ethos*), and (3) understand the emotions—that is, to name them and describe them, know their causes and the way they are excited (*Pathos*)" (MCKEAN, 1941).

It seems to me quite evident that Aristotle was referring to reasoning, values and emotions. When trying to persuade someone using rhetoric, a person may appeal to each of those aspects of the human mind in the arguments employed.

However, a misconception has spread to many parts of the world, stating that Aristotle was referring to Logos as Reason, Pathos as Emotions and Ethos as Behavior (a big mistake!). This can only be explained by a culture bias originating in the pragmatic philosophy of David Hume (himself a product of the Anglo Saxon culture), in which ethical considerations actually are placed as having less importance than "just doing it." Pragmatism and "a bias for action", typical of the Anglo Saxons, has used a distorted interpretation of Aristotle as justification for "shooting first and asking questions later."

It is also ironic that Nike, one of the better-known brands of the 21st Century, has a name inspired by Greek-Roman mythology but uses as a slogan ("just do it") this pragmatic attitude that supports the misinterpretation of Aristotle.

In our globalized world, I have found scholars (not worthy of that name), even in far away Brazil, quoting this distortion, stating that Ethos refers to Behavior, and forsaking Ethics as an important dimension that must be considered with at least the same relevance as Reason and Emotions.

According to the New Oxford Dictionary, Ethos refers to "the characteristic spirit of a culture, era, or community as manifested in its attitudes and aspirations." This reinforces the interpretation that Ethos refers to values and the spiritual dimension, rather than to behavior per se, as something devoid of morals and ethics.

This division of the human mind, of course, is merely an academic argument used in order to make it easier to understand the complexities of a human being.

In practice, these three aspects of the mind are always interconnected and they express themselves simultaneously. There is no such thing as purely rational thinking, devoid of values or emotions. All human behavior is equally influenced by rational, emotional and value judgment considerations. This division in three aspects is just a didactic gimmick, in itself influenced by culture values.

They say that the Dalai Lama, in an interview, once expressed a degree of ironic amusement with this Western tendency towards dividing people in pieces... To the Tibetans a human being is a single whole integrated entity, impossible to separate into parts! However, the so-called Western cultures show a preference for analyzing everything in parts, rather than appreciating the whole. As we will see further ahead, this is a matter of cultural preference, a value judgment that is manifested differently from one culture to another. Certain cultures value analysis, while other cultures value synthesis and maintaining the integrity of the whole. Culture and culture values in its core influence the philosophy of great thinkers, who are all also a product of their respective cultures.

Philosophical thought is not only logical; it contains in itself, always, value judgments; and it also contains an emotional aspect. Philosophical stupidity lies in denying this integration of reason, values and emotions, which are always together in a human being.

Therefore, when I talk about culture, I am referring to one aspect of human beings (values) but not to the totality that constitutes human beings; I'm talking about one of the aspects of personality, but not about personality as a whole. There are many other things besides culture to explain people's behavior.

In a conversation we had together in Amsterdam in 2008, Doctor V. Chockalingam explained that these three vectors (Emotional, Spiritual and Rational), to the Hindus constitute the mind (CHOCKALINGAM, 2010). The Physical vector corresponding to the mind is the brain, often confused with the mind by cultures in Europe and in their colonies throughout the world.

In the mind we have thoughts, feelings and beliefs (respectively: reasoning, emotions and spiritual values). In the Physical vector we have the nerve cells that constitute the brain and the expression of the mind: language and behavior.

Everything we can see occurs through the Physical vector. By the physical expression (language, behavior, actions, electrical impulses in the brain that can be measured by sophisticated instruments) we infer what happens in the mind in terms of thinking, feeling and values.

We do know, from the so-called behavioral sciences (Philosophy, Psychology, Sociology, Economics, Politics) is that human behavior is determined by the mind. Human behavior is determined by the interaction of values, emotions and rational thoughts inside the mind.

One of the most important "discoveries" of our times, at the turn of the 21st Century, was the notion that the human mind is not just rational, it is also emotional and spiritual (in terms of values and beliefs).

NOTE: The spiritual dimension, in certain cultures, is commonly associated with "life after death" or "life in another dimension". What we mean here is values and beliefs in a very broad sense, and that includes (but does not restrict itself to) religious beliefs. The spiritual vector encompasses all values and beliefs, the notion of "right" and "wrong", of "good" and "bad". It is in the spiritual vector that we find culture: "the norms of conduct for a group that determine a preference for one state of affairs over another, to which strong emotions are attached" (HOFSTEDE, 2010).

It is increasingly acknowledged, as we go further into the 21st Century, that the human mind not only includes emotional and values aspects in addition to the rational aspect, but also that reason is not "superior" to the other two aspects.

The "cursed legacy" from the cultures of Northern Europe is the notion (now forlorn) that Reason is more important than Emotions or Values, that reason dominates and should dominate over the other two vectors. This notion is in itself determined by a values judgment, a cultural paradigm that says that Reason is somehow "better" than Emotions. Acknowledging this cultural/ethical/moral paradigm in itself should suffice to argue that it is the Spiritual (values) vector that dominates the other two, rather than Reason being the dominant vector...

Actually, one could equally argue that, thanks to discoveries made in the neurological sciences over the past 50 years, supporting what psychologists have also been telling us, it is the Emotional vector the one that dominates the others. Advancements in the study of the brain have convinced even the hard-nosed scientists of the Anglo-Saxon world that the neural zones linked to emotions are activated even when an individual is acting in a purely "rational" way, solving math problems or merely waving his arms.

Freud explained around 100 years ago that our behavior is not determined only by conscious and rational factors; there are emotional factors at play, often unconscious, determining our behavior without us being aware of it. There are also moral and ethical factors (values) that influence how we behave, also sometimes unconsciously.

Science has not yet been able to measure how much "weight" does each of these factors have in influencing what we do. In practice, I find it more useful to consider that there is balance, the three vectors are equivalent and none of them dominates the others.

The economic crisis that occurred on the latter half of 2008 served to destroy the myth that was still predominant among American and European economists that the financial markets behave in a rational form "as if guided by an invisible hand" as Adam Smith said in the 19th Century. It became evident that emotional and ethical aspects determined the behavior of the main economic agents involved in generating that crisis. The existing rational analysis models were found to be insufficient to explain what was going on and to manage the risk factors embedded in the global economy.

In terms of Individual Psychology one can easily recognize the equivalences with the Freudian model (Id corresponding to emotions; Superego to values and Ego to reasoning). In Transactional Analysis, the equivalences are with the "ego states": child, parent and adult, respectively. There are actually important technical distinctions in these comparisons, but in a practical sense, in broad terms, the analogies are valid.

What should interest us the most, specifically, is to better understand the values vector (spiritual) to the extent that the notion of what is "right" and "wrong" forms the basis of national and organizational group cultures, determining which behaviors are considered to be "efficient" and "productive" and which are deemed to be "inefficient" or "unproductive".

What we know today, thanks to Hofstede's research and to all subsequent studies on values and culture, is that there is no single "right" or "wrong" way to manage people or businesses. There are different versions of management, each of them congruent to a pre-existing values-system in the culture of a social group (national or organizational).

My encounter with Hofstede and Freud

In summary, we can say that a person's behavior is due to that individual's personality, which in turn is composed of the rational, spiritual and emotional experiences accumulated by a person over time. Part of that personality is determined by the notion of "right" and "wrong", which is learned in childhood from the family and the environment surrounding a child (including school and community).

This notion of "right" and "wrong" is also influenced in adult life by the values of organizational cultures (behaviors accepted or rejected in an organization). The values at the core of organizational culture originate in the national culture enveloping that organization.

Thus we see that "the circle is complete." National culture values determine the values of the organizations belonging to that culture and they determine the values of families that educate new generations. Each new generation of children, as it is educated according to the values of that culture, tends to perpetuate those values through their behavior inside and outside organizations.

It is no wonder that culture core values are very stable and change very slowly, according to research. These core values will only change when the education of children is also changed.

Hofstede stated that culture values are acquired in childhood, before you are ten years old. This coincides with Freud's statements regarding the formation of the Superego. All that we learn and develop after that age are surface layers added on top of a very stable core that is difficult to change.

Hofstede has always emphasized that culture should never be confused with personality. What he researched and measured refers to collective preferences (values). Hofstede is a rigorous researcher and very careful in his approach.

As a psychologist interested in people's behavior as individuals, I dare to take another step and link Hofstede's work to that of Freud and Jung.

Jung spoke of the "collective unconscious", of unconscious aspects of personality that would be common to many people belonging to the same community. In my view, culture represents a sort of "collective Superego".

If Jung's collective unconscious was formed by portions of the Superego (values) and also aspects of the Id (emotions, impulses), then culture as measured by Hofstede is precisely the expression of these shared value sets that constitute the common Superego of an organization, community, region or country.

In terms of culture, what we know is that the external layers of culture are represented, for example, by its rituals, heroes and symbols. These external layers change more easily and those changes are also more easily perceived.

I'm talking about observed behavior, fashion and fads, idiomatic expressions, slang, music, food habits, ceremonies, interior decoration and similar aspects. All this is commonly known and talked about as "culture"; the breakthrough came when Hofstede looked deeper and tried to identify the core of culture, the underlying values that determine the superficial layers.

We all know that people have different ways of greeting each other in different cultures, different ways of celebrating weddings and different food habits. We also know that people work differently in other cultures, they set different priorities and have different styles of communication. Why is that so? What are the underlying values that determine these differences in the way we work?

Culture dimensions

In his attempt to understand this, Hofstede researched how people in different cultures responded to the same questions posed to them in questionnaires about employee satisfaction within the same company, but with branches in different parts of the world. Perhaps the most valuable aspect of his methodology is the fact that he did not set out to prove a pre-existing hypothesis, but rather he took pre-existing surveys from a data base and did extensive factor analysis to find out if there was something that could explain how certain people from certain countries had consistently responded differently from other countries regarding the same questions.

Initially he identified three basic dimensions of culture values using this method. Subsequently he identified a fourth dimension and published his conclusions as forming a four-dimensional model of culture values.

A different research study carried out by Michael Harris Bond (later reviewed and endorsed by Hofstede) revealed the existence of a fifth culture dimension, which was included to build the "5D Model" used as a base for most culture studies throughout the world.

In 2008, the Wall Street Journal surveyed the CEO's of top American companies and asked them who were the major management thinkers that had most influenced them throughout their careers. Out of the top 20 most mentioned authors, there was one Englishman (Sir Richard Branson), eighteen Americans and only one was not either American or British: Professor Geert Hofstede, who came out at number 16 on that list.

Research on culture value dimensions continues to this day, carried out by Hofstede himself, his associates and by numerous others. Recent developments include the introduction of six "types" of culture by Huib Wursten, in order to make the model more easily assimilated and applied in practice, in work situations. These culture "types" have been used by many multinational corporations to manage multi-cultural teams, to operate in different markets and in merger and acquisition integration processes.

In 2010 the identification of a sixth dimension was announced, based on research carried out by Michael Minkov and Gert Jan Hofstede, son of the pioneer. To incorporate these studies into the model, Hofstede's bestseller "Cultures and Organizations: Softwares of the Mind" was totally revised and expanded. Its third edition was signed by the three professors together.

Hofstede himself has said that there is no way to determine *a priori* the number of existing dimensions. There may be a seventh or an eighth dimension, everything should be examined and researched. The ultimate limit lies in the usefulness of the results.

A six-dimensional model is indeed useful to understand culture differences and especially the implications of such differences in business and people management. If an author some day identifies ten other dimensions and makes a model composed of sixteen dimensions in total, I don't think such a model would be very useful, in practice. It might be scientifically robust and valid from a statistical point of view, but using a model with that many dimensions would prove to be cumbersome.

All social psychology models are just didactics tools used with the purpose of helping people to understand, in a simplified way, a complex reality. If a model becomes almost as complex as the reality itself that it seeks to represent, than it is defeating the purpose of having a model in the first place.

Therefore, let´s look at Hofstede's framework before it becomes too complex to be useful in practice.

Part II – The Culture Dimensions Model

The six culture dimensions according to their underlying values:

1. Power Distance (PDI)
2. Individualism (IDV)
3. Performance Orientation (PER)
4. Uncertainty Avoidance (UAI)
5. Long Term Orientation (LTO)
6. Indulgence (IND)

1. Power Distance (PDI)

This dimension explains the source of most difficulties managing people when one compares the management practices of North America and Northern Europe with the practices found everywhere else in the world.

In its original definition, this dimension represents "the extent to which the less powerful members of organizations or institutions expect and accept that power is distributed unequally."

An important implication of this dimension is the fact that it is the less powerful members of society who define whether power distance is high or low. When people consider that in effect power is distributed in the world in an unequal fashion and that is just a fact of life, that needs to be accepted as such, then such societies have a higher score.

When people consider that power should be distributed more evenly and that everyone should have more or less the same amount of power, such a society scores lower, or has a low power distance score.

Figure 4: The Prime Minister of Thailand

1. POWER DISTANCE (PDI)

"Figure 4", a clipping from a magazine, shows to the left, dressed in white, the Prime-Minister of Thailand.

If he is the Prime Minister, why is he sitting on the ground? Because the other person in the picture, behind the small desk, is the King of Thailand!

Thailand is a country with a high PDI culture. In such cultures, the difference in power is clearly demonstrated, even among people who hold high positions in its hierarchy. The power distance between each rung and the next is explicitly shown through symbols, rituals and behaviors.

This happens both in the higher levels of the social structure hierarchy and in the lower levels as well. The power distance is always unequivocally expressed.

Figure 5: The Prime Minister of Sweden patiently waits in line for his turn at the ATM

"Figure 5" shows the Prime-Minister of Sweden… waiting in line to use an ATM on the sidewalk. Sweden is a low Power Distance culture. Prominent political figures do not have a much higher status than other ordinary citizens. This is a very different situation compared to what we see in high PDI cultures.

In Sweden the fact that the Prime Minister is standing in line at an ATM is hardly newsworthy… In this specific case (the picture is from a

CULTURE DIMENSIONS

newspaper clipping) the "news" is the fact that the Prime Minister is now feeling much better after his accidental fall while playing tennis; he is now able to use the ATM by himself, with the aid of a walking stick.

When I was part of a bank's management team in São Paulo, I never had to go to the ATM to get cash… All I did was ask my secretary to get me some cash and she would produce it as if by magic bringing it to my desk. All I needed to do was sign a receipt slip. It goes without saying that Brazil is a high Power Distance culture.

Figure 6 shows the Princess of Denmark, also a low PDI culture. Why is she being received on a red carpet and having flower petals thrown at her feet?

Because she is visiting Thailand. The people of Thailand are used to treating royalty in this way, even when the royals are coming from other countries.

The fact is that it is the people with less power in a society who determine whether a culture has high or low Power Distance. If the people consider it "normal" or "natural" that some people have much more power than others, then we say that this culture has high PDI.

Figure 6: The Princess of Denmark

LEADING ACROSS CULTURES IN PRACTICE | 31

1. POWER DISTANCE (PDI)

This means that a dictatorship is not determined by the dictator, but rather by the people subjected to the dictator… When a people accept the existence of a strong, authoritarian style of government, or when they even wish for that, then a dictator will retain power. There may, sometimes, be a revolution to oust a dictator, but typically he will be replaced by another dictator, or by an equally strong style of government.

When a culture scores low on Power Distance, there is no dictator capable of securing power, no matter how powerful he may be. The people in such a culture simply do not support any kind of dictatorship.

This is something independent of the political regime: it might be a monarchy or a republic, presidential or parliamentary, communism or capitalism.

There are democratic monarchies such as England and Holland where the monarch has little or no power at all. The monarch serves as a symbol for the nation, but does not rule in reality. And there are other countries with high power distance cultures where an elected president or prime minister might have more power than the king of a low Power Distance nation.

One can better understand, then, the history of China, with its Emperors who enjoyed absolute power of life and death over their subjects. In the 20th Century there was a revolution, including a cultural revolution, but it only affected the more superficial layers of culture. The core values remained the same, the Power Distance remained the same, and soon the Communist Party leaders enjoyed the same kind of absolute power that the ancient Emperors used to have.

Now, China has gone from communist to capitalist, the leaders are other people, but the Power Distance is still the same and the new leaders continue to have absolute power over the people. This is not so much because the leaders have decided to be authoritarian (as most Westerners seem to think), but rather because the people of China allow it and expect it as part of their cultural values. It is a whole cultural system at work and not just something coming from a few individuals at the top (see also "Democracy in China" in my book "Take Off Your Glasses", 2012).

In Russia there were the Czars, equally absolutely powerful, within a high Power Distance culture. There was the great communist revolution of 1917 and soon the communist leaders had the same absolute power enjoyed by the Czars.

Today Russia has opened its borders, has turned to capitalism, has dissolved the Soviet Union... and its government continues to be as authoritarian as the Czars used to be, for the culture is still one of high Power Distance and this has not changed much in three hundred years.

Why didn't it change? Because these values are learned in childhood, when people are under ten years old. Throughout all these years, children have continued to be educated in a very similar way regarding these values.

This is a typical scene set in any country with a high Power Distance culture: in a home, the owners are in the living room, entertaining neighbors who have dropped by for a visit. The couple's two children run into the living room playing, interrupting the conversation. Their parents say: "Children, go play outside, we're having an adult conversation here!"

These kids soon learn that, in this world, some people have more power (for instance, adults) and some people have less of it (for instance, children). That's life, they learn, and you just have to accept it as such.

Popular sayings are always a reflection of culture and many of them reflect the PDI dimension, such as: in Brazil, they say "*cada macaco no seu galho*", meaning "each monkey on its own branch", that is to say: everyone should remain in their place in the hierarchy. Another Brazilian saying goes: *manda quem pode, obedece quem tem juízo*, which means: if you can, give orders; if you're smart, obey them!

By contrast, let's look at what happens in The Netherlands, a low Power Distance culture, like the Scandinavian countries, which are all low-PDI cultures.

Whenever I visit my neighbors in The Netherlands and their children run into the living room to play, their parents interrupt our conversation and include the children in it, speaking to them on an equal basis. The children learn that, in this world, all people have more or less the same amount of power, with subtle differences.

> *A few months after I first moved to Holland, in 1996, there was a knock at my door. It was someone from the local county office who introduced himself and said:*

> "We are doing a survey in this neighborhood's home, because the municipality is going to refurbish the public playground at the end of this street, we're going to put in some new toys for the kids. We want to make sure that the new toys are the ones that are preferred by the children who live around here. Do you have kids at home?"
>
> "Yes I do," I replied. "I have two girls, they are four and five years old and they like the slide, the see-saw, the..."
>
> "Sorry to interrupt," said the civil servant. "We would like to talk to them. Are they home?"
>
> I had a "culture shock." I had never seen a public survey done directly with the children, foregoing me as a parent! These children, in this culture, certainly learn from an early age that they are respected as individuals and that everyone has, more or less, the same amount of power in society!

Main differences between high/low PDI cultures

In low PDI cultures, people in general are more autonomous and independent. They enjoy working without direct supervision and tend to take initiative more often, making decisions on their own about different aspects of their work. Supervision by the boss is seen as interference and, as such, is avoided and not welcome. People appreciate getting a certain degree of delegated authority, so that they are allowed to resolve certain issues without having to consult their superiors.

By contrast, in high PDI cultures people tend to be more dependent. Supervision from the boss is actually desired, for it is seen as a sign of appreciation for what the subordinate is doing. People ask for instructions more often and sometimes, even though they know what must be done, they still seek confirmation from their superior: "Hey boss, do you want me to review the week's cash flow like I do every Friday?" When facing an obstacle of any kind, or an unforeseen situation, they tend to do nothing and wait for instructions.

In low PDI cultures, hierarchy exists in organizations as a mater of convenience. That is, someone needs to play the role of managing a team; therefore that role is assigned to some person. Outside of the work environment, that person is treated as a colleague, a fellow worker. If you meet your boss at a restaurant on the weekend, or standing in line to buy movie tickets, you treat him as a work colleague.

In high PDI cultures, hierarchy is existential. The boss is always seen as being the boss, within and outside of the work environment. If you meet him some place outside of work, you should treat him with the same deference that his position deserves, or even more. You might even let him have your place in a queue. After all, as the saying goes, "the path to success goes through your boss's success!"

Wherever there is high PDI, subordinates expect to get instructions from their superiors. Whenever they fail to get instructions, they tend to remain waiting for said instructions. Wherever PDI is low, subordinates expect to be consulted before a decision is made. If decisions are made without previous consultation, subordinates feel betrayed in the process: "How could the boss make that decision without even talking to us beforehand?" This sort of challenge rarely ever occurs in a high PDI culture.

In low PDI cultures the manager knows that he/she can rely on the experience of his/her subordinates. In high PDI cultures, it is the subordinates who rely on the boss's experience and on the rules that come down from the top.

From the subordinates' point of view, in a high PDI culture, an ideal boss is a kind of paternal figure; he may be a benevolent parent or a strict one, but definitely a parent. They expect the boss to "take care of them" like a parent would and to look after everything that happens in the organization: the business, sales, production, and administration.

In a low PDI culture, subordinates consider the ideal boss to be a kind of coach, someone to motivate and encourage them to give their best as a contribution to the organization's objectives. The boss is respected for knowing what should be done and how to motivate the team to obtain optimal performance, using the talent available.

In low PDI cultures, those who occupy the higher positions in the hierarchy of organizations have the same rights and similar privileges that their colleagues enjoy at other levels in lower positions. In high PDI organizations, senior managers are entitled to differentiated privileges and this is endorsed by all organization members as a whole.

1. POWER DISTANCE (PDI)

> *Many years ago, when I first visited ABN AMRO headquarters in Amsterdam, I was impressed to learn that all head office staff were on the very same health plan, with no differentiation between the lowest and the highest level in the hierarchy.*
>
> *When I returned to my post as Head of Human Resources for Brazil in São Paulo, I proposed in a Management Team meeting that we change our existing medical plan in that country. At the time, our plan had four different levels of coverage; my proposal was to streamline it into just two levels.*
>
> *Nobody at the meeting supported my proposal. The argument against it was that, in Brazil, people had the expectation of getting slightly increased benefits as they progressed to higher positions in the hierarchy, throughout their career. When someone is promoted from administrative assistant to supervisor, the first level of management, that person expects to get, aside from an increase in compensation, certain privileges reflecting an improvement in status: a larger desk, a better health plan, a desktop calendar with the company logo.*
>
> *When that person is promoted to manager, the next higher level in the hierarchy, the expectation is to get again other improvements in status: a private office, a health plan entitling you to a private bedroom at the hospital, and so forth. Removing these privileges would be very frustrating for whoever already had those expectations. In other words, equalizing benefits would be demotivating.*
>
> *That's when I realized that there were fundamental culture differences underlying the different management policies used in two different countries, within the same company. This incident ignited my interest in cross-cultural management and that is when I began to study the subject.*

Information flow

In high PDI cultures, information tends to flow from the top down, in the form of instructions and orders from bosses to subordinates. The flow in the opposite direction, from subordinates to bosses, is more difficult and occurs less frequently, because subordinates are fearful of the enormous power that they themselves attribute to bosses.

One often finds that mistakes and "bad news" are hidden from the boss's view, for subordinates fear a negative reaction. It's the old story of "shooting the messenger", when the messenger is the bearer of bad news. Nobody wants to play the role of being the bearer of bad news, so bad performance and mistakes are hidden from the boss.

Many times this ends up causing even bigger problems, because it becomes hard to identify issues as they are beginning to sprout and tackle them at the root. Problems tend to be hidden and are only discovered when it is already too late.

The case of a Korean airliner became famous when hundreds of people died in a plane crash. The recording of the conversation between the commander and the other crewmembers in the cockpit revealed that the navigation officer identified that the plane was on the wrong course and warned the captain. He in turn responded that he knew what he was doing and disregarded the warning from the officer. The navigator decided not to insist and refrained from confronting his superior. The plane crashed on a mountaintop, killing all of its occupants.

As a result of the investigation report following the accident, the airline carried out extensive training programs to all its airborne staff, emphasizing that respect for hierarchy should not come to the point of stopping people from taking corrective action in emergencies that threatened the lives of all involved. The program also stressed that commanding officers needed to be more open to hearing the observations of their subordinates.

In low PDI cultures, information flows occur naturally in all directions, top down, bottom up or sideways.

Decision-making

In high PDI cultures, organizations tend to be more centralized and decisions tend to be made at the top. The boss decides about everything and seldom consults other people. When he/she does, it involves consulting a few trusted advisors who are closer to the boss and part of an inner circle.

1. POWER DISTANCE (PDI)

In low PDI cultures organizations are more often decentralized; decisions are delegated and bosses consult more people, more often, before making them. Many times decisions are made at a meeting, together with a management team, for instance, rather than by the boss alone as an individual.

Delegation and empowerment

Delegation is usually more extensive and happens more frequently in low PDI cultures. The now popular expression "empowerment" is a typically American management term, created in a low PDI culture.

When this concept is applied in a high PDI culture it may be perceived in a wrong way. Too much delegation in such cultures may be considered as an attempt by the boss to forego his/her responsibilities inherent to the position in the hierarchy. Rather than resulting in motivation, subordinates may feel that they are unduly burdened by an irresponsible superior.

It is important to very carefully consider such aspects before simply transplanting a certain management practice from one culture to another, for this can have devastating effects, much different from those intended.

This is not to say that delegation cannot happen in high PDI cultures. What it means is that in such cultures you have to explain the situation in greater detail to the person to whom you are delegating. It does not happen so naturally. It is necessary, also, to supervise more frequently, in order to create the feeling that the boss has delegated, but no abandoned the subordinate. Frequent control shows that the boss in interested in what the subordinate is doing.

Managing by Walking Around

In the 1950's the expression MBWA, Managing By Walking Around became popular in the United States. The idea is that the boss should approach the subordinates informally, coming closer to them by walking around the office from time to time, rather than only seeing them at formal meetings. He should talk to them informally here and there, on the shop floor or by the water cooler. By doing so, the concept goes, the boss demonstrates that he is "people like us", treating staff members as colleagues and promoting a climate of equality around the company.

This may work beautifully in a low PDI culture, such as the one in America, but it may cause more harm than benefit when used in a high PDI culture.

In these cultures bosses are perceived as being very powerful, as having the power of life and death over their subordinates. They are perceived as almighty gods and therefore are highly feared.

When the boss decides to "take a stroll around the office", his secretary immediately phones everybody to warn them: "run, the boss is coming!"

Everybody then pretends to be very busy and they breathe a sigh of relief after the boss has passed them.

What is a boss to do, then? Should he remain closed off in his office in order to avoid scaring away the staff? That's not what we mean.

He should, indeed, walk around the office or plant, chatting with staff members. Not only that, in some high PDI cultures his absence might be perceived as being a sign of lack of interest for what is going on in the company. Staff members are afraid of the boss, but they appreciate the attention.

What is important is to be aware that in these cultures the boss's presence inspires fear. Whatever he/she says, no matter how small a remark, will be amplified by the employees of the firm. Being aware of this, the boss can and should go ahead with his strolls among the staff, but knowing that others do not see him as "a colleague" and will be extremely careful with what they say in his/her presence. The boss, in turn, must also be careful with his/her own choice of words, due to the fact that his position has this huge amplifying effect on anything that is said.

The open door

In low PDI countries bosses are often proud to have "an open door policy". In high PDI cultures, even when the boss leaves the door open, no one dares to cross the threshold...

1. POWER DISTANCE (PDI)

> *Once I was visiting a branch of my company in the Caribbean. As I chatted with the local Head of Human Resources, he complained that his boss, the regional line manager, was very inaccessible. I remarked that I found that odd, since the Head of HR's office was right next door to the region head's office, and I also noticed that he always left his door open. In fact, the door was open at that very moment, while we chatted in the next-door office.*
>
> *—Yes—responded my colleague indignantly—, but he never invites me to go into his office!*
>
> *Later I also chatted with the regional line manager. He felt he was being very open and accessible, just by leaving his door open. He could not quite figure out why nobody took the opportunity to go into his office and talk to him. He assumed it was because "people here are just lazy and not interested in talking about work…"*
>
> *Meanwhile, the local Head of HR, one of the top 5 most senior officers in the region, still considered that he could only go into his boss' office when he was explicitly invited to do so. The open door did not convey an invitation, in his mind.*

The fact remains that in high PDI cultures people are afraid of the boss, basically because of his/her position, not because of the person's actual behavior. The boss may behave in a way considered to be "open and accessible" in his/her original culture; but in the destination culture that same behavior (leaving the door open) does not signify accessibility per se.

Inviting someone into the office explicitly is perceived by the low-PDI boss as being condescending and patronizing, so he/she does not do it. Yet, this is exactly what the high-PDI staff expect a boss to do, and they will criticize the boss for not doing it.

In low PDI cultures there is also hierarchy, but it exists as a matter of convenience. Someone needs to play the role of team boss at work, so companies assign people to that function. Outside the workplace that person is treated as a colleague. If you run into your boss when you go to the movies, or at a restaurant, you treat him as a fellow co-worker.

In high PDI cultures, hierarchy is existential. The boss is always considered the boss, whether within or outside of the work environment. If you run into your boss at a restaurant or standing in line to buy tickets for a movie, you are supposed to treat him/her with the same deference that his position demands, or even more. You might even let him/her take your place in the queue… After all, in these cultures "brown nosing" is seen as the way to find your path to a higher position in the social ladder.

In high PDI environments the subordinates expect that they will get instructions from their superiors. If they do not get such instructions, they tend to remain waiting for them. In low PDI environments subordinates expect to be consulted before bosses make decisions. If decisions are made without previously consulting the people involved, subordinates feel betrayed in the process. "How could the boss make that decision without consulting us?" This sort of questioning rarely happens in high PDI cultures.

In low PDI cultures superiors know that they can rely on the experience of their subordinates. In high PDI cultures it is the subordinates who rely on the boss's experience and on the norms coming from above.

The ideal boss, from an employee's point of view in a high PDI culture, is a "father figure", whether a benevolent or strict parent figure. Employees expect the boss to "take care of them" like a parent would, and they also expect the boss to take care of everything in the organization: the business, sales, production, and administration.

On the other hand, in low PDI cultures, employees consider that the ideal boss is a kind of coach, or trainer. He/she is a motivator above all else, able to get the best out of what everyone has to offer. The boss is respected for knowing what needs to be done and knowing how to motivate the team to obtain top performance, using the talent available among team members.

In low PDI cultures, incumbents of top positions in organizations' hierarchies have the same rights and obligations as their colleagues occupying positions lower in the hierarchical structure. In high PDI cultures, incumbents of top positions are entitled to privileges and this is endorsed by all members of the organization.

Years ago, at Banco Real Headquarters in São Paulo, a staff team were working in a meeting room next to the CEO's office, preparing a presentation that he was due to deliver a week later at an meeting with investors.

At a certain moment, they engaged in a discussion about the sequence order of certain slides in the presentation. One of the staff members said that the CEO usually preferred a specific order, while another member of staff argued that for this specific upcoming meeting the sequence should be different than usual, that this would be better received by the target audience. In that team there was a young Dutch trainee, recently arrived from Amsterdam; she was handling the computer and designing the slide layouts.

At one point she asked simply: "Why don't we just ask him what he prefers for this meeting?" The others looked at each other and smiled, thinking that she was kidding. Nobody would even think of bothering the CEO with such a trivial question.

She simply stood up and walked into the CEO's office next door (as usual, his door was open; he would only close it when meeting someone). The staff members felt like hiding under the table, in shame! How could this young girl, a mere trainee, dare to enter the CEO's office without an appointment? And to disturb him with such a trivial question!

She just said: "Excuse me, may I ask you a question? For the presentation to the investors next week, would you prefer the slides in this order or in that order?" The CEO, a Brazilian executive greatly admired for his simple manner, always trying to make others feel at ease, responded directly: "For this meeting I prefer this other sequence, it will be better that way."

She thanked him and skipped back to the adjoining meeting room, where the staff team awaited her with amazement. Since she was coming from a low PDI culture, she was used to accessible bosses. She knew that she could simply walk into their offices and ask them a direct question.

The Brazilian team, even though they had frequent contact with the CEO and knew of his informal way of working with those who were part of his advisory team, were conditioned by a culture that lends enormous respect to the figure of "supreme boss"; they always maintained a certain distance, despite the fact that he never required them to do so.

Power Distance has an impact also on organizational structures. Wherever PDI is higher, organization structures are more vertical, with many more levels in hierarchy between the top level of a structure and the bottom. In cultures with low PDI, the opposite is more commonly found: organization charts tend to be flatter, with fewer levels separating the bottom of the structure from the top.

Similarly, culture affects salary structures. Whether there is a very formal pay structure with published tables and standards, or not, the fact is that in high PDI cultures salary differences are much more significant between the bottom wages and the compensation packages of top management.

In low PDI cultures one usually finds companies in which the top executive earns fixed compensation that is 10 or 12 times more than that of the incumbents of bottom level positions. In high PDI cultures this difference in fixed pay easily reaches 80 times or more. The top levels are higher and the bottom levels are lower, when compared to what you see in low PDI cultures.

Power Distance in Government and Politics

Government structures, for instance, tend to be more centralized in high PDI societies. Typically, the national government concentrates power and tax revenue than state and municipal governments. On the other hand, in low PDI cultures, we see the opposite: the organization of government is more decentralized, with more revenue and authority allocated to provinces and municipalities.

There is also a tendency to find more corruption in government when looking at high PDI societies, compared to low PDI cultures. There is government corruption in every culture; no society is free from it. But since it is true that power corrupts, and absolute power corrupts absolutely, it should not come as a surprise that there is more corruption to be

1. POWER DISTANCE (PDI)

found in high PDI cultures. The concentration of power eventually leads to this.

In high PDI cultures it is more common to see revolutions as a way of changing the political situation. Since power is more concentrated at the top, it becomes more difficult to influence change; often this only happens through force, ousting the incumbent through a revolution. In low PDI cultures it is more usual to see change happening through democratic elections, whether through different political factions alternating in power (like in the US), or by successive coalitions of different political parties (such as in Germany and the Netherlands).

Wherever there is high PDI, one finds that power, business and professional competence, social prestige and wealth are closer together. These aspects reinforce each other mutually, so that whoever has more money tends to have more status, is more influential, has higher education level and is perceived as being more competent.

In lower PDI cultures, one can more easily find people who are competent and influential (from an intellectual point of view, for instance), but who may not have great wealth or enjoy outstanding social prestige. These factors are more independent among themselves. You may find very rich people with very little influence, and so forth.

> *Example: when the so-called "Arab Spring" came about, one could observe different behaviors from different leaders in North Africa and the Middle East.*
> - *The leaders of the United Arab Emirates (UAE) were not challenged by revolutions. They had traditionally ruled as "benevolent patriarchs," holding supreme authority but handing out many benefits to their people. As long as the people enjoyed a good standard of living, there was no widespread dissatisfaction.*
> - *In Saudi Arabia there were a few rather timid protests against the government. The leaders responded by announcing a few decisions that involved greater liberties and additional benefits, and the protests were deflated. There was no significant revolt.*
> - *In Egypt, Nasser and Sadat, previous authoritarian military leaders, deceased long ago, are still idolized to this very day. Although they were both strong rulers who did not tolerate any*

kind of opposition, they kept the people happy through several different sorts of benefits. They cared for the people as benevolent father figures. Mubarak had started with the same style and was initially popular. As time went by, the economic situation began to deteriorate: food became more expensive, unemployment increased, health and education became less accessible to everyone. The government held on to power through fear, violently repressing dissidents while the economy continued to deteriorate. The poor economic situation is what unleashed the revolution. The Egyptian people concluded that their leader was no longer taking care of them, and dissatisfaction turned to revolution until he was toppled. In the Parliament elections that followed, the winning parties were the salafites and the Muslim Brotherhood: both these political movements had been very active with social assistance, distributing food and health care to the poor, plus education. They were taking care of the people, by providing what the government was not. Eventually, the first elected president of Egypt (Modi) was also toppled after a year, because he failed to improve the economic situation (it actually became worse). The military returned to power, backed by the middle class, with the promise of economic recovery. They will remain in power for as long as they are able to "take care of the people;" otherwise there will be yet another revolution.

An American leader is not expected to "take care" of his/her followers, but rather is expected to make decisions, show the way forward and let the people go on with their lives enjoying freedom and autonomy. By contrast, in Egypt the culture will topple a leader who does not "take care" of the people, and will replace the leader with someone who can provide better care for the nation. It is important to understand that an "Egyptian style of leadership" would never work in America, just as an American style of leadership would never work out in Egypt. The purpose of the "Arab Spring" revolutions was not to implement an American style of democracy in any of the countries involved.

1. POWER DISTANCE (PDI)

Power Distance outside organizations

This dimension is not only visible in work situations, in companies and organizations in general; it can be seen in all kinds of social relations.

> *When I was in Amsterdam looking for a rental home, having just arrived from Brazil, I went with my wife to see an apartment that had been advertised for rent. When we got to the address on the ad, a lady who appeared to be in her late 50's, the apartment owner greeted us and explained that the apartment for rent was actually across the hall, on the same floor. It was being painted and should be ready in a week; we were welcome to see it now, if we did not mind the mess.*
>
> *She took us there and rang the bell. A man appearing to be of similar age answered the door, wearing overalls covered in paint. "My name is Piet," he said. "Please come in. Would you like some coffee? I've just made it!"*
>
> *We thanked him and politely declined.*
>
> *"I will have some coffee, yes!" said the lady. She went into the kitchen with him and they started chatting. My wife and I looked around the apartment for a few minutes; it was very spacious and charming.*
>
> *When we finished, the gentleman took us all to the door and said good-bye. On the building hall, I asked the lady: "Was that your husband?"*
>
> *"Oh, no," she replied. "That is a painter I hired. He will finish the job in a few days."*
>
> *My wife and I were quite surprised. We had assumed the man was the owner's husband, by the way he had acted welcoming us into the place, offering coffee, chatting cheerfully with her... To our Brazilian eyes he did not look like a hired worker, he looked like a peer. We knew that the Dutch do a lot of home renovation on a "do it yourself" basis to save money, so we assumed this was the case.*

That was our first "culture shock". In Brazil, a hired painter would never behave that way, totally at ease, inviting the lady who hired him to have a cup of coffee in the kitchen, at a time when he was supposed to be working on the job he was hired to do. In the Netherlands this is normal, since there is not a pronounced social hierarchy such as the one found in Brazil.

You only become aware of your own culture standards when you experience a different culture first hand. I realized, for instance, that in Brazil I had the habit of talking to waiters at a restaurant without looking them in the eye. I did as most people (in Brazil) did: I called for the waiter/waitress and ordered food and beverages looking at the menu or at my fellow guests at the table, maybe looking at the waiter's notepad, as if checking to see if he was taking down everything we were ordering.

In the Netherlands I saw that people talk to waiters in the same way that they talk to the people at their table: looking at the other person's face, making eye contact. It's a matter of attention and respect.

What I did in Brazil was not intentionally offensive. Everybody behaved the same way, that's the way we all learned to behave. And no Brazilian waiter ever feels offended by clients acting this way. It's just the "right" way to behave in the Brazilian culture.

The problems always arise when you cross cultures. In the Netherlands waiters are annoyed with the way they are treated by foreigners (from high PDI cultures), which they perceive as being arrogant snobs. It's no wonder that service is often of bad quality, delivered slowly and with a certain visible disdain! When I changed my own attitude and started to treat waiters as equals rather than as "mere service people", I could see that the quality of service and attention I got was much better.

In high PDI cultures clients put themselves in a higher position than the people who provide them with service, in restaurants, shops, everywhere. When service is delivered with a careless attitude, people complain: "Terrible! It's as if he's doing me a favor! Actually, I'm paying for all this, I demand respect! He should be thanking me!" In the Netherlands it is quite the opposite. People who render service consider that they are, indeed, doing you a favor. They regard themselves as equals to the clients, and not their subordinates. They expect to be treated in the same way as you would treat a next-door neighbor, with kindness and respect.

1. POWER DISTANCE (PDI)

Family

Family life, of course, is also influenced by culture differences in terms of the PDI dimension.

In low PDI cultures, children are encouraged to be independent from an early age and to express themselves, developing their own ideas and opinions. In high PDI cultures children are encouraged to be obedient. They are allowed to ask questions, but the answers they get should not be challenged. Children should show respect towards their parents and their elders in general. By contrast, in low PDI cultures respect must be earned, rather than simply awarded because of position or age.

In high PDI cultures, respect for elders is seen in the forms of treatment in communication: it is customary to address the parents as "sir" or "ma'am", as in: "Father, can I stay out late this Saturday evening, Sir?"

In low PDI cultures the forms of treatment in communication reflect the lower hierarchical difference. Often a son might address his father using his first name, as in: "Hey, Pete, can I stay out late on Saturday?"

Education

In low PDI cultures, teachers expect that children will take initiative in class and engage in group discussions. In countries with higher PDI, it is up to the teachers to take initiative and to use a lecturing style of giving class. In such cultures, there is an expression saying that college professors "spill" their knowledge over their fortunate pupils, who are expected to enjoy the opportunity of drinking from this source ok knowledge. In low PDI cultures, college professors play the role of coach and facilitator of group discussions. Their main contribution is to teach pupils how to research the subject at hand and to develop critical thinking.

In high PDI cultures, federal governments tend to concentrate their investments and education policies towards fostering the development of universities and post-graduate institutions. In low PDI cultures, federal governments tend to focus their policies and investments in primary schools and basic education.

Conflict

It is worth noting that a high Power Distance does not mean that authority figures are never challenged in such cultures. What actually happens is just that they are challenged less frequently than in low PDI societies. In high PDI societies, respect for hierarchy is more valued than challenging authority; in low PDI cultures, the opposite is true.

In practice, this dimension has implications on how people are expected to behave in situations where there is not an evident hierarchy, such as in certain informal social situations or in business events that are open to the public in general.

In low PDI societies, people consider themselves equal to each other, so the natural behavior is of mutual respect, since unconsciously people assume that the distribution of power among that group is more or less equal.

In high PDI societies, the unconscious assumption is that power is distributed unequally, in a hierarchy; therefore, the standard behavior is to try to find out where does each person fit in the hierarchy, since that is not self-evident in such situations. The assumption is that a hierarchy exists, since this is considered to be natural; it is necessary to find out exactly what is the specific hierarchy in the specific situation.

What follows is a kind of "power struggle", generally very subtle and civilized, attempting to determine who has more power and who has less, in the specific situation. Each person tries to "find their place" in the pecking order, until it becomes clear, for all those present, what is the actual hierarchy in place in the situation.

Those who really do have power need to make it visible, so that their authority may be respected and accepted. That is why it is expected that authority figures should wear power symbols and should demonstrate their authority through rituals.

This explains what is known in many high PDI cultures as "the hand-kissing ritual": in a social meeting with someone who is generally respected as a power holder, all those present should greet this individual in person and "present their respects." (The name derives from a 19th Century habit of actually kissing the back of the host's hand.) This happens even when the gathering is quite informal, in someone's home, for

1. POWER DISTANCE (PDI)

instance. In high PDI cultures the host/hostess should always be greeted in person; in low PDI cultures this is not always considered to be necessary, and if you fail to shake hands with the host this does not mean that you are being impolite.

Turning to a less ordinary situation, let's look at what happens when there is an important political discussion or even a revolution. In low PDI cultures, the assumption is that there is a more or less equal distribution of power; therefore, we can observe heated debates, but eventually a discussion may actually result "in a tie" with both parties acknowledging the points that they agree on and the ones about which they disagree.

In high PDI societies there is a tendency towards one of the parties involved trying to overpower the other party by whatever means possible, until a power hierarchy is established, in which it should be clear who has more power and who has less. It is no wonder, then, that the vast majority of political revolutions throughout history have happened in high PDI societies, from the Middle Ages to current days. When government is challenged, the opposition tries to topple those who are in power, and establish a new hierarchy in which the revolutionaries become the ruling authority up until they are also overthrown, in turn.

It is no coincidence, also, that when we see on TV newscasts that congressmen somewhere in the world are actually fighting physically and exchanging punches at the height of a discussion, invariably this is happening in a high PDI culture. It's not that these cultures are "backwards" or "less civilized". What must be understood is that their underlying values lead to that kind of behavior, regardless of how "civil" that society might be.

There is also another type of situation in which hierarchy is not immediately clear to all those involved: it is in those situations in which, for instance, a client meets a civil servant.

Civil servants, in high PDI cultures, are power holders; even if they are just a clerk at a counter, at some agency of the local City Hall. In that position, they may consider themselves as being in a higher position within the local town's social hierarchy, relative to the common citizens with whom they interact on a daily basis.

Imagine a situation in which a local citizen, a businessman owning a medium-size company, approaches the civil servant's counter to submit an application for some legal documentation. This businessman is used to being treated with reverence by every employee in his company and also by his business' providers. As he meets the civil servant at the counter, it is not immediately clear, to both of them, what are their respective positions in the hierarchy pertaining to that specific situation. They might both, initially, consider themselves superior to the other, and they will make that visible to each other by their attitude.

It is quite common to see discussions and conflicts developing in such situations, as each party attempts to demonstrate to the other that power lies with one, and not with the other. Each will try to exert power over the other. Statements will typically be made such as "Do you know who you are talking to?" or "Who do you think you are?" The meta-message is: "I have more power than you, therefore you must submit to what I want!"

Because of all this, in high PDI societies people use symbols that are externally visible to show their power and authority. The businessman will wear a suit and tie, the more expensive-looking, the better, to convey to all those around him "I have power, you must respect my authority!" Usually these symbols are quite effective: people who come to the Town Hall well-dressed are given better service than those who arrive dressed like slobs. The same thing happens in any social interaction situation in high PDI cultures, much more visibly than in low PDI cultures. Those who are well-dressed command respect.

The most important aspect of all this is simply the following: in high PDI cultures it is important that the hierarchy should be clearly evident. Clear hierarchy is respected, and there is no problem. When the hierarchy is not clear, there is conflict among the people involved, trying to clarify the hierarchy for the specific situation, and trying to establish their own position in that hierarchy. Conflict will continue until the hierarchy becomes clear to those involved.

Does egalitarianism increase when people's income increases?

In the 1990's, Hofstede compared PDI scores with *per capita* income in different countries. A correlation was found: the lesser the scores in PDI, the greater the *per capita* income. However, one cannot necessarily conclude which of these is the cause and which is the effect.

Could it be that a culture that is less hierarchical and more egalitarian ends up generating greater GDP (Gross Domestic Product) and a higher *per capita* income? Or is it that an improvement in income leads a society to adopt more egalitarian values, improving the distribution of wealth?

More research is needed on this subject. Many economists and sociologists are quick to conclude that an egalitarian society is more efficient and generates a higher GDP *per capita*. However, they are not aware of their own cultural bias towards egalitarian values. As usual, their conclusions are influenced by their underlying culture values, without them realizing it's happening.

2. Individualism versus Collectivism (IDV)

This dimension is very connected to matters of communication and to how the members of a culture might perceive the members of a different culture with mistrust, due to "cultural bias."

Hofstede's definition is: "In **individualistic** societies people should only look after themselves and their immediate families. In **collectivistic** societies people belong to groups that take care of them in exchange for loyalty." (Hofstede, 2003)

Wherever Individualism (IDV) is high, cultures value that people take individual responsibility for their actions. Having an individual opinion, whatever the subject, is also considered important. Therefore, people learn, from a tender age, to express their opinions in a very assertive fashion.

Strong discussions, in which neither party makes concessions, are frequent. It's important to "stand your ground", an expression that is even used to denominate a state law in the United States (this law determines that a person has the right to confront someone who challenges their opinion and to not back down). It is hard to reach consensus, since disagreeing with someone else is actually seen in a better light than reaching an agreement. In these societies, if you easily change your point of view, in order to agree with another person, you are deemed to "lack personality." In The Netherlands, for instance, this comes to such a point that "lack of assertiveness" is officially labeled as a mental illness and is recognized as such by the government-funded official health service, to be the subject of medical treatment.

The Dutch also learn in high school how to make public speeches. It is a common custom for people to stand up and make speeches whenever friends get together for dinner, as a tribute to the host, who is expected to reply by also making a speech expressing his thanks. In wedding ceremonies, many guests make speeches saluting the bride and groom, and they also respond by making speeches of their own.

Since the expression of an individual's point of view is highly valued, often discussions do not come to a conclusion; the discussion ends with one of the parties saying, "then we agree to disagree." Following that, they change the subject and go on to discuss a different topic.

It is worth noting that disagreement does not mean that people cannot continue to be friends; on the contrary, there are frequently friendships that develop among people who are constantly disagreeing with each other. Disagreement means no offense. It exists as a way of establishing mutual respect, without necessarily people feeling hurt or resentful towards each other.

In collectivistic societies, it is important to belong to a group, and the group will take care of you in exchange for your loyalty. This is all happening at an unconscious level, people are not aware of it; they are not doing it deliberately. In practice, what you see is that they are concerned with maintaining a certain harmony within the group they belong to. Confrontation is avoided, so that there are no ill feelings among group members.

Mind you, people belong to many groups simultaneously; and some of these groups may get into strong conflicts with other groups. It is just within each group that conflict is avoided. When conflict does arise in a group, there are usually two related outcomes: in the first place, the confronting individual leaves the group or is asked to leave; in the second place, that individual typically forms another group, a dissident gathering, and the two groups become fierce rivals, though still avoiding conflict within their respective ranks.

Group opinion is more important than the individual opinions of each person. Because of this, from an early age people learn to "read" the predominant trends in the groups of which they are part. In these societies people develop a greater sensitivity to perceive body language and the nuances of communication: they are more aware of differences in tone of voice, facial expression, and gestures.

In individualistic societies people focus on message content and explicit communication. In collectivistic societies the emphasis is on message formats and on implicit communication. In collectivistic cultures people are better able to "read between the lines" and "see the writing on the wall". There is a common expression in Portuguese that conveys this very well: *para bom entendedor, meia palavra basta*, which means: to someone who understands well, half a word is enough.

When mixed groups meet, in which there are people coming from individualistic cultures and others coming from collectivistic cultures, what is frequently seen is that the collectivistic have a better sense of group dynamics and of the meeting's overall climate. Individualists many times "have no clue" of what is going on, because they fail to perceive the rich trove of non-verbal details exchanged among the meeting attendants. Individualists have not been trained to value these aspects.

In order to maintain group harmony, in collectivistic cultures people frequently agree by "paying lip service" to certain ideas; that is: they pretend to agree, simply to avoid confronting someone with a dissenting opinion. A person's actual opinion about something is often expressed only in small sub-groups, rather than in front of everyone else.

Disagreements, when unavoidable, are often taken as personal offenses; people feel hurt and groups may split between the allies of one party and the allies of another, forming sub-groups.

People do belong to many groups simultaneously, and their sense of identity is strongly linked to these groups, who reinforce this by trying to help there members in all kinds of situations, including getting jobs, managing stress, overcoming illnesses and handling adversity of all kinds.

Shame or guilt?

In individualistic cultures self-esteem and guilt are important feelings when facing a mistake or inappropriate behavior. The person feels badly vis-à-vis the person's own personal standards. Guilt feelings are quite pronounced in such societies.

In collectivistic cultures the stronger feeling when facing a mistake or inappropriate behavior is shame. The most important thing is how the person is seen by others, by the person's reference group.

When someone is criticized for behaving badly, often the person tries to justify him/herself by comparison to others. If there are more people behaving in the same way, that behavior is perceived to be more acceptable. In any society, one could argue that "if everyone else is behaving badly, that does not justify that you behave in the same way." However, this argument is stronger in individualistic cultures, in which you also see this used more often, since they value individual responsibility to a greater degree. In collectivistic societies, the argument "I'm not the only one doing this, you cannot criticize me for doing it" is used more frequently and carries more weight.

Relationship versus task

In collectivistic societies, relationships are considered more important than tasks. In situations in which people are asked to choose between preserving a relationship and completing a task, the tendency is towards focusing on the relationship. In individualistic societies, tasks have priority.

In collectivistic cultures it is important to develop a relationship before discussing business issues. When business people meet, they first try to get to know each other, before getting down to business. First, they need to establish a trusting relationship, verify to which groups they relate to, before they are ready to discuss a commercial deal or any work-related subject. This process does not last just a few minutes; it may last for months, throughout several different meetings, until both parties feel comfortable enough to discuss business. Mutual trust is very important and may take quite a while to be developed.

Once trust is established, however, everything becomes much easier for both parties involved. Caution is set aside and million-dollar contracts may be agreed upon with nothing but a handshake. Complex projects may be quickly implemented in these cultures, once mutual trust is in place.

It is easier to mobilize people when the reference group is mobilized. People enjoy being part of a group dedicated to a task. The motivating aspect is not the task itself, but the fact that it is being carried out as a group; this reinforces the relationship among people.

In individualistic cultures we see the opposite. Teams put their energy on the task itself, not on relationships. They tend to begin working on tasks directly, dedicating little time to get to know the other team members.

In business, the people involved come to the point sooner, right after introducing themselves. Talking about personal issues that have little to do with the business at hand is considered a distraction, something to be avoided.

This aspect is frequently mentioned as the cause of misunderstandings in cross-border negotiations. Typically, business people from an individualistic culture want to discuss business issues immediately upon meeting their collectivistic counterparts. The latter consider it rude to immediately start talking business, when they "hardly know each other."

Often both parties leave such a meeting feeling frustrated. The collectivists complain that the individualists were rude and tried to force a business discussion before establishing mutual trust. This behavior actually increases any latent mistrust and reinforces the suspicion that the other party must be up to something; that they are trying to hide something and therefore are trying to close a deal quickly, before the collectivists find out what they are up to. Therefore, the collectivists drag their feet and detach themselves even further from the process.

On the other hand, the individualists complain that the collectivists do not seem interested in making the deal. They spent the whole time talking about all kinds of other stuff like sports, the economy and whatever, avoiding focus on the meeting's objective, which was to discuss business. They even talked about their families, to take the focus of discussion away from the deal on the table. This behavior is perceived with a lot of suspicion by the individualists. They think the collectivists are trying to hide something about the deal, which must be why they keep avoiding the business discussion. Therefore, the individualists get impatient and detach themselves even more.

Personal space

This difference in values also influences the concept of personal space. People from all cultures have a notion of what they consider to be their "own" personal physical space, unconsciously. Each individual has a certain distance from another person that he/she feels comfortable with.

2. INDIVIDUALISM VERSUS COLLECTIVISM (IDV)

Certain people, when talking to other people, move closer to them and allow the others to move closer too. Other people feel uncomfortable when people get too close, when the distance between them is too small. Typically, such people take a slight step backwards to maintain a certain distance from those they are talking to.

In collectivist cultures this optimal distance tends to be shorter than in individualist cultures. This is easy to observe in the way people greet each other, and how they subsequently engage in conversation. Those coming from individualist cultures tend to keep a greater distance when extending their arm to shake hands. Those coming from collectivist cultures feel more comfortable with a shorter distance between themselves and the people with whom they are talking. The outstretched arm is slightly flexed, shortening the distance, and the handshake may be accompanied by a hand touch on the other person's arm, with the other hand. It is a gesture to convey "almost a hug."

In collectivist cultures people often stand closer to each other while talking and may also touch each other slightly in the arm to emphasize a certain aspect during conversation. In individualistic societies this may be perceived as offensive or even sexual harassment. In these cultures the distance between people is bigger and people deliberately avoid touching each other unless it is absolutely necessary to get the other's attention for a matter of personal safety (to avoid someone falling, for instance).

> *A friend of mine once witnessed an amusing situation some years ago in the Middle East. In a luxury hotel conference room, a team of American businessmen discussed a large project with a team of Arab businessmen. During the formal business meeting there seemed to be little progress towards closing the deal. The Americans made a Power Point presentation and the Arabs listened intently but showed no reaction.*
>
> *They went for a small break and people dispersed to go to the men's room, get coffee, go for a short walk. The leader of the Arab delegation decided to take the opportunity to get closer to the American team leader, addressing him in the corridor that led to the conference room. In the Arab culture, deals are only made when the leaders of two teams talk in private, informally.*

This appeared to be a good moment for the Arab leader to show his American counterpart that he was really interested in doing the deal and that discussions about it would be taken seriously.

In the Arab culture, such an interest is often shown by physical proximity. Someone approaches the other person and whispers in the other's ear, over his shoulder. It is a way of demonstrating intimacy and trust. It is a posture that means: "let's talk in private, just the two of us; we trust each other and we can commit to something together."

The American, in turn, knew nothing about Arab customs. At each step that the Arab took in his direction, trying to whisper in his ear, the American took a slight step back, to maintain the physical distance between the two with which he was comfortable. My friend observed them at a distance, trying to suppress a smile.

In a few minutes they were almost at the end of the corridor and going into the Men's room, for at each of the Arab's steps, the American retreated another step. If not for the meeting's mediator call to both, for them to resume the meeting, the Arab would continue chasing the American all over the hotel... These small things often stop great business and political deals from getting done, because of people's ignorance regarding the culture differences involved.

Privacy

In individualist societies, privacy issues are deemed to be very important. People value their privacy very much and react aggressively when they feel that their privacy has been invaded. This is more about the psychological aspect than the physical aspect just mentioned above.

The simple fact of requiring every citizen to carry an individual identity document is something controversial in individualist cultures. The idea of government keeping a data base with records of all its people and a number assigned to each person, is perceived as a breach of the right to privacy enjoyed by each individual, in these cultures.

2. INDIVIDUALISM VERSUS COLLECTIVISM (IDV)

In 2010 there was a big row in the United States when the state of Arizona passed a law allowing police to demand identity documents from people on the street, from people suspected of being illegal immigrants. The whole debate reached large proportion because in the American culture (highly individualist) individual freedom is so highly valued that the simple act of a policeman asking for ID is perceived as something invasive and offensive.

In collectivist cultures this is considered normal and natural. Everyone should carry identity documents and it is regarded as natural that police might ask to see them in any given situation; this is not perceived as offensive. They find it odd that in individualist cultures the whole issue of privacy is valued to the extent that it there is, and that any threat to privacy is taken so seriously.

> *Once, a few years ago, my wife had just arrived to The Netherlands as an expat and she saw that an old lady was leaving the local supermarket carrying large shopping bags with some difficulty. Acting like the Brazilian that she was (collectivist culture) my wife reached out her hand to help the old lady carry one of the bags, saying "let me help you carry this."*
>
> *To her surprise, the old lady yanked the bag away from her and hissed: "I know how to take care of myself!" My wife was shocked and hurt by her reaction, when she was merely trying to help. But she soon realized what had happened, as she was already researching culture issues at the time.*
>
> *The old Dutch lady greatly valued her individual responsibility, her ability to take care of herself. She did not want somebody else taking care of her. My wife's gesture was interpreted as an invasion of privacy and as a way of calling her incompetent.*

In a collectivist culture the same gesture is a way of getting closer to other people. Helping others is a way of looking after the harmony within a group. It never occurs to a collectivist that helping others might be seen as an invasion of privacy.

What can be done, then? Let the old ladies look after themselves? My wife found a way to bridge the gap between the two types of culture. In similar situations, she approaches elderly ladies and starts by asking permission. "Excuse me, madam: may I help you?"

Only after the old lady has given permission (they usually smile and agree to the request for permission) is that my wife then extends her hand to carry the shopping bag. This physical act of offering help must be preceded by a request for permission. Once permission is granted, the gesture is no longer ill perceived.

It's worth noting that other Latin American friends of ours went through similar experiences: they tried to help little old Dutch ladies and were brushed off rudely... Nowadays they always ask permission before offering help.

In a similar way, it is usual to ask for permission before asking a question to a stranger on the street. "Excuse me sir, please: may I ask you a question?" This procedure may seem like an exaggeration to a collectivist, but it allows the individualist to feel that his/her privacy is being respected and gives the person some time to prepare for the question that is about to be asked (a couple of seconds will suffice). "Could you tell me which bus I should take to get to the train station?"

Once these little etiquette habits are observed, people are very nice and polite. What happens is simply that each culture has its own (unwritten) norms of communication. These are not just superficial habits. These behaviors are anchored in the core values of each culture.

Belonging to a group

There is a group dynamics exercise called "Value Preferences" (Souza, 1971) that I have used several times in Brazil and in The Netherlands.

The exercise consists in handing out to participants a set of statements about value preferences, such as "making friends is the most important thing in life" or "a job well done gives me the most satisfaction". Participants are asked to rank the statements in order of preference, individually, according to their personal opinion. Subsequently, they are asked to find the people that made a ranking equal to their own, and form groups. By doing this, everyone who made the same ranking choices will sit in one corner of the room, and others who made coinciding choices will each sit in a group of people who have all made the same choices.

2. INDIVIDUALISM VERSUS COLLECTIVISM (IDV)

The number of statements used in the exercise allows for six groups to be formed, and their size depends on how many people made exactly the same values ranking. If the overall workshop group is made of around thirty participants, typically there are one or two sub-groups with eight or ten members, and there might be a group with just one or two people whose value preferences were the same.

The facilitator asks each subgroup to discuss among themselves what were the reasons behind the choices they have made and how they feel about their choices and the motives expressed by their fellow members of the same sub-group.

The striking difference between the collectivist Brazilians and the individualist Dutch was that, when I did the exercise every time in Brazil, those who ended up in a large subgroup, with many others sharing the same ranking, expressed joy in being part of such a large group sharing similar values. On the other hand, those who found themselves in a small sub-group, with just two people, or maybe even alone by themselves, said that they felt uncomfortable for discovering that their values were different from everybody else, and that made them feel lonely.

When I ran the same sessions with Dutch groups, their reaction was exactly the opposite. Those who found themselves in a large group said that they felt uncomfortable as they found out that their choices were so similar to those of other people. "I'm not as unique as I thought I was", complained a participant.

And those who found themselves in a small subgroup with just one other companion, or even were alone by themselves, had a great big smile of satisfaction on their faces. "I have unique values, I'm different from everybody else," said a participant, proudly.

In individualist cultures, people feel better showing their individuality. Belonging to a group means losing a bit of your individual originality, their uniqueness. In collectivist cultures we see the opposite: belonging to a group brings with it a feeling of being safe, secure and taken care of; being alone elicits feelings of abandonment and loneliness.

Direct and indirect communication styles

In individualist cultures communication is explicit and people come directly to the point. Subsequently they may add context aspects that surround that central point. If we considerer the communication of a message as represented by a spiral, then in individualist cultures it is usual to begin communicating by the central point in that spiral, and then continue moving along the spiral towards the external part of the spiral, by adding information about the context.

In collectivist cultures the communication of a message usually begins by the external part of the message, conveying information about the context and gradually coming to the point at the spiral's center, usually reached only towards the end of the message.

Let us look at an example to clarify this process. Suppose that the manager of a department has the unpleasant task of telling a group of employees that the department will be extinguished and that, as a result of that, they will all be fired at the end of the month.

In an individualist culture, typically this manager would call everyone together for a general meeting and would deliver the message more or less like this:

"Ladies and gentlemen, I've called you all here to inform you that unfortunately you will all be dismissed from the company by the end of this month. The department you are working in will be extinguished and there is no other way that we can keep you on the payroll. In the last six months our sales have been going down and the company is making a net loss instead of a profit. This has been happening for many reasons, the main one being the overall economic recession that has affected the whole country and especially our industry has been hit very hard. We tried different sales strategies, but none were successful. After considering several alternatives, we concluded that the only remaining option is to close down this department and make all your jobs redundant, dismissing all of you."

The unconscious logic behind this direct approach is that you are avoiding suspense and reducing people's anxiety by coming straight to the point. Once the main point is communicated, you can add further

2. INDIVIDUALISM VERSUS COLLECTIVISM (IDV)

considerations about the context, but the main task (to communicate the dismissal) has been accomplished at the beginning of the session.

In a collectivist culture, the manager would typically call everyone for a meeting and address the issue as follows:

"Ladies and gentlemen, I've called you all here to tell you that, unfortunately, our country's economy is going through a deep recession. This recession is affecting our industry most severely, and because of that our sales have been going down in the last six months, and we are now making a loss instead of a profit. We've tried different sales strategies, but none of them was successful. After considering several alternatives, we concluded that the only remaining option is to close down this department and make all your jobs redundant. We cannot keep you on the company payroll any longer. Unfortunately, you will all be dismissed from the company by the end of the month."

The unconscious logic behind this indirect approach is that you are avoiding the shock of communicating bad news in an abrupt and rude manner, which might hurt people. You need to prepare them gradually to receive the bad news, for the relationship you have with them is more important than the task of communicating the dismissal. It is important to show that the manager is sensitive to the feelings of those present, and a gradual approach conveys that sensitivity. As the manager speaks, he/she is attentive to people's non-verbal reactions to the words being spoken. The manager's own tone of voice, deep, solemn and sad, reveals to everyone that the outcome of this message is likely to be something terrible, and allows people some time to prepare for the worst. This time period also allows people to look at each other and sense the group's reaction as a whole. If someone starts crying, others can come to their aid. There is a whole group process going on while the manager slowly makes his way from the external part of the spiral towards its center.

Both styles of communication are valid, within each culture. None of them is in essence better than the other. They are simply different.

Problems arise when the manager employs a communication style that is inappropriate for a culture that is different from his/her own, and the audience therefore has a different expectation.

If a manager is coming from an individualist culture and uses an individualist style of communication in a collectivist culture, this manager is likely to be considered insensitive and rude. "How could he say those terrible things, just like that, right to our faces, he was so cold and inconsiderate! And only later he explained what led the company to make this decision!"

If the manager comes from a collectivist culture and uses the collectivist style in a group of individualist culture employees, people are likely to be very impatient. "When is this guy coming to the point? Why doesn't he just tell us what he needs to say, instead of running around in circles, talking about the economy and whatnot? This suspense is killing me!"

The British visit Brazil

Once I had the chance to be one of the facilitators for a senior executive workshop, in which a group of British venture capitalists visited Brazil as part of their international program.

The course design included several simultaneous visits to large Brazilian organizations, allowing the participants, divided in smaller subgroups of five or six people, to engage in dialogue with Brazilian businessmen. After these visits, which happened in the morning, the whole group would come together in the afternoon to discuss and share what they had learned, plus the faculty would add aspects of management theory that were relevant to the observations they had made about their morning visits.

You might say that the program design was typically individualist: it started with the center of the spiral (the practical application), at the beginning of the day, and then expanded on the subject towards the underlying academic theories (the external part of the spiral), at the end of the day.

Anticipating that there might be some communication aspects highlighting the culture differences involved, with the possibility of some misunderstandings and frustrated expectations from all parties, right at the start, before the visits, I ran a short session on Brazilian culture and how it contrasted with the British one. I put extra emphasis on those aspects related to styles of communication, including the different spiral approaches: centrifugal (from the center to the outside) and centripetal (from the outside to the center), as just described above.

I joined a sub-group of five participants to visit the head office of a large construction company. One of the senior vice-presidents hosted us for a two-hour visit, consisting of a company presentation and an open discussion with the visitors.

The Brazilian executive began by recounting the history of the organization since its founding, over 60 years ago. He narrated in detail the personal biography of the founder, since his childhood, and how the way he had been educated shaped his personal development and how that influenced his decision to start a company when he became an adult. He also stressed how the founder's personal values influenced the company's corporate culture and how that shaped the way the company was managed to this very day, in all its projects, all over the world.

His approach was clearly collectivistic, rich in context, beginning from the external part of the spiral.

After about fifteen minutes of this monologue, still describing the personal history of the founder, the host made a short pause and said: "if you have any questions, please interrupt me and ask."

One of the British took the opportunity and fired away: "What's the company total assets today?" (A typical individualist culture question, going straight to the center of the spiral!)

"Whooa!" exclaimed the host, throwing his hands back. "If you want to discuss finance, then I'd better call my finance director! He is better suited to address this kind of detail."

The British participant realized immediately the "faux pas" and remembered the presentation I had made on the previous evening. He apologized.

"No, please, that won't be necessary. Sorry for the interruption. Please continue with the story you were telling us, let's leave the financial aspects for later." The meeting continued normally. Eventually, the Brazilian came to the financial aspects and to the present situation of the company. He answered all the questions easily and there was no need to call anybody else into the meeting.

Returning from the visit to the hotel where we would later meet the other sub-groups, the British participant confided in me:

"I immediately realized, right after making that question, that it was the wrong moment to make it, but it was already too late! What happened was exactly what you had told us before, the host was following the spiral from the outside to the center and I was impatient, I wanted to get to the financial aspects, which are my main interest."

This little case illustrates another important aspect of culture differences: **the main usefulness of the culture dimensions model is that it helps people understand what is happening in a given moment, and not, necessarily, predicting what is going to happen, in advance.**

No matter how much we may be prepared to cope with another culture, we cannot predict exactly what will happen. Many times something very unpredictable, unexpected, happens. Knowing the model, however, helps me to understand what is going on, or something that has just happened, and allows me to correct a mistake or to reinterpret what has just happened, in time to change my behavior and make communication more effective. Otherwise, I might continue insisting with the wrong approach, causing a misunderstanding to turn into something worse, aggravating a frustrating situation for both parties to the point of causing some kind of rupture.

Too much context or not enough of it?

Direct or indirect communication has also another aspect, in addition to the centrifugal and centripetal spirals that were mentioned. It pertains to the amount of context used in communication messages.

In collectivistic cultures, the tendency is towards providing a lot of context information. The message senders feel compelled to include data about the context and the receivers expect to get that data as an important part of the message. Understanding the context helps to understand the message, since it allows people to know the interpersonal relationships affecting the situation, the positioning of different stakeholders, how much power they hold, the degree of urgency attached to the issue, etc.

In individualist cultures the tendency is to focus on the essence of the message and leave context aside. Contextual information is regarded as less relevant and reducing efficiency. Too much information is a nuisance, it distracts and causes confusion. Just focus on the essence, the rest is not needed and it simply complicates and slows down the whole thing. The important thing is to be objective.

As usual, everything works fine within the same culture, but it can work quite badly when you need to cross cultures and communicate with someone from another culture.

Here is another real and simple example:

Individualist Steve: "Joe, during my absence you can lead the project, with the client, until next month. Since Irene is also going on holidays, if you need support, talk to Mary Trishford."

To another individualist, this message is perfectly clear and complete; there are no doubts and no need for anything else. However, Collectivist Joe sees the message in a different light. He thinks:

Collectivist Joe: "Initially, everything seems to be OK, but... who is this Mary Trishford that I never heard of? Is she a temp or a new staff member? Does she know our company routines? How can I trust her if I don't know her? How will she respond to a request from me if she doesn't know me? Does she know who I am? Does she know the project and our client?"

To the collectivist, Steve's message lacks information. It was not enough, it was incomplete. Joe concludes that Steve is not a good manager, because his communication is lacking, he seems uninterested in the project, he is leaving on vacation and "leaves everything up in the air."

Let's consider the opposite example, in which Collectivist Joe is going on vacation and he talks to his subordinate Individualist Steve.

Collectivist Joe: "Steve, in my absence, you lead the project with the client, until next month. Since Irene is also going on holidays, if you need support, talk to Mary Trishford. She is a Colombian who was hired a month ago in Paul's department; she will cover for Irene's vacation and for a lot of other people's holidays in our department during the summer. If she does well, we might keep her on board afterwards, as long as Paul agrees to let her go from his team, because she seems to be very efficient, he might want her back there with their department. Anyway, she knows the project and the client, because she used to work for them until a few months ago, but she had to leave because she got married to a colleague and they don't allow couples to work together in the company. So they asked us if we could take her on. Paul had an opening in his unit, she started over there and she did really well, she did a great job. I told her you are also South American, so she will enjoy working with you on the project.

To a collectivist, this is a good, complete message, providing all relevant context information pertinent to the situation. Individualist Steve, however, has a different view on this...

Individualist Steve (thinking): "My God, how can my boss be so confusing? I did not need all that information, thank you very much! I don't need to know all that crap about Mary's personal life! He lost me halfway through all that gibberish; I was not paying attention any more... I've got work to do and he keeps wasting my time with such a long story!"

Here is another real example, even simpler:

Collectivist Joe: "Hey Steve, we missed you last night at Mark's party..."
Individualist Steve: "Yeah, sorry, I couldn't come."
To an individualist, this reply is sufficient: direct and objective. There are also privacy issues considered. If this is what Steve has to say, it's nobody's business to expect more than what he said. There is no need to add anything else, as additional information is probably of a private nature. Since privacy is highly valued in individualist societies, people tend to talk less about their private life, except with very close friends. The expectation of other individualists is also to get a short reply, like the one Steve provided. However, Collectivist Joe had a different expectation...

2. INDIVIDUALISM VERSUS COLLECTIVISM (IDV)

>   *Collectivist Joe:* "Steve didn't share the reason why he couldn't come to the party... I wonder if he had a family problem? He might be suffering in silence, embarrassed to share his problems... I'd like to help him, but how can I help him if he doesn't tell me what his problems are? I wonder if he trusts me... Or is it that he doesn't like Mark, and that's why he didn't want to go to the party? Is Steve hiding something from me?"

When the roles are reversed in the example, we would have the following situation:

>   *Individualist Steve:* "Hey, Joe, we missed you at the party last night, at Mark's place..."
>
>   *Collectivist Joe:* "Yeah, sorry, I couldn't come... Can you imagine? When I went home to change, my wife was having a big argument with our daughter, she had asked for money to go to this rock concert. My wife wanted us to have this serious conversation with our daughter, because she's going out with this guy who we think is not the right kind of guy for her... She is just 16 and the guy is much older, he dropped out of college and doesn't have a job, he's hanging around with these heavy metal types who look just plain bad... We think she might get involved with drugs, crime, you know how it is... And if we tell her she can't go out with him, then she turns against us and she will end up sneaking behind our backs... This rock concert she wanted to go to, she said she was going with a bunch of her girl friends, but I think she was going to meet the guy there, you know, I could bet on it... So we argued a bit, my wife and I, but then we sat with our daughter and we had this really long talk with her... In the end it was a good thing, but it was a tough talk, you know? I'm not sure if it'll have the effect we're hoping for... Finally, when the whole thing was over, I realized it was already past ten, and I didn't feel like going to no party... It was too late, by the time I got to Mark's it would have been past eleven. So I decided not to go. Do you think Mark is sore?"

> *Joe has no problem in telling a long story to justify his absence; by sharing details about his private life, he is showing that he has nothing to hide and that he wants to develop a friendship with a work colleague. Maybe the work colleague has a helpful opinion to share about his personal issues in dealing with his teen-age daughter. To Steve, however, it is clear that he got much more information than he expected!*
>
> *Individualist Steve (thinking): "Wow! Where did all that come from? I did not want to hear all about his personal life! It was so awkward! This is not the kind of thing you talk about at work. What does Joe want from me in exchange for all this unwarranted intimacy? I certainly don't want to share with him anything about my own private life, we're just co-workers! I'd better keep away..."*

So, when communicating with someone from a different culture, bear in mind what is the other person's expectation: does the receiver expect to get more context, or less context? If the receiver is an individualist, be objective and direct. If the receiver is a collectivist, add more information about the context.

If you're coming from a collectivist culture, accept as normal the short responses you get from individualists. They are not deliberately hiding anything from you and it's not that they don't trust you; they are simply respecting the limits of privacy that they see for themselves and for the people around them. Try to be aware, as well, that when you are sharing your whole life story with someone else, that person might be feeling embarrassed by the situation. Try to find out what is the other person's expectation regarding how much should be shared among you.

If you're coming from an individualist culture, bear in mind that collectivists expect to get to know more context about your private life; they enjoy talking about these things and to share a bit more about themselves. It's just a way of establishing relationships and developing mutual trust, something they consider important in the work environment and also in any social situation.

2. INDIVIDUALISM VERSUS COLLECTIVISM (IDV)

International political negotiations

It is already fairly evident that differences in styles of communication employed by individualist and collectivist cultures may help to explain many of the frustrations observed in political negotiations among nations.

In the numerous meetings organized between the Israeli and the Palestine, for instance, one can see that the difference in communication styles probably is not helping mutual understanding.

When we look at the scores for Israel (PDI 13 and IDV 54), we can see that the culture is egalitarian and moderately individualist; comparing it to the Arab World score (a composite of six countries, the scores are PDI 80 and IDV 38), we can see that the Arab culture is more hierarchical and collectivist than Israel.

To complicate matters a bit more, we must take into consideration the fact that the mediators between Israel and Palestine are usually Americans, sometimes joined by British or French nationals as well. The Americans are also egalitarian and individualist, while the French are hierarchical and individualist.

The expectations from Americans an British (not only the mediators themselves, but also the media covering these events) is that the Palestinians and Israeli will sit down to have an objective and focused discussion in order to rapidly reach some sort of conclusion (peace treaty or continuation of hostility).

Actually, the expectation of both parties (who are both more collectivist than the Americans, although Israel is more individualist than the Arabs) is more to the collectivist side of the spectrum. Both are likely to be more comfortable with indirect communication, rich in context, and prefer to let the core points for later, following the spiral from the outside to the center. They need much more time (specially the Palestinians) to gradually build a relationship of mutual trust, and only after that get to the issues on the agenda. This could take months, rather than hours…

The Americans probably put pressure on both sides to be objective and stay on topic. This kind of pressure doesn't go down well with them, so you can see that it's going to take a long time to get to any kind of agreement. The more the pressure, the more suspicious both sides become.

Now think about how these aspects affect multilateral meetings, like the European Union or the G-20, when you can have 30 different cultures in one room. You can imagine how frustrated these people might be sometimes. The potential for misunderstandings is quite significant, unless the people involved are keenly aware of the differences in cultural values at play and its influence on communication styles.

Collectivists are frustrated because the meeting was too short and there was not enough time to explore the many relevant aspects deserving to be discussed. Individualists are frustrated because the meeting was too long, dispersive and came to no conclusion.

How each side perceives the other side

Collectivists and individualists, of course, have very different perceptions of themselves and of others, based on the different culture values and their influence on communication styles.

As we have seen, individualist cultures value direct communication, focus on the task, content being more important than format, and explicit messages. In these cultures communication is centered on the sender and on the content, and it follows a more linear and direct logical path, with less importance given to the context. Individual opinions are considered more important than group opinion.

Individualists tend to see themselves as being frank and open, honest and true. Their definition of "integrity" is that you should always say what you are actually thinking. "We are what we appear to be, we hide nothing. If there is an issue, the best thing to do is to talk openly about. There should be no 'gilding the lily' or 'sugar-coating the pill.'" If the problem is there, let's face it once and for all and recognize that there is a problem to begin with."

However, research carried out with collectivists shows that their perception of individualists is different. They see individualists as being rude and insensitive. They describe individualists as noisy and disturbing. "They're always disturbing people around them, without even noticing. They talk too much and too loudly. They're not aware of the impact they are having on others. It's like they don't care, or they just don't notice it. They're annoying everyone around them, and they don't have a clue!"

"They're a bit slow, you know? They take some time to realize what is going on. You have to explain everything and draw them a picture, otherwise they're completely lost."

"They can't read between the lines and they don't realize that sometimes the best thing to say is to say nothing at all… If you don't have anything positive to say, then it's best to shut up, just remain silent. These people don't get that!"

"Sometimes it seems as if they can't control themselves… You know when you're about to say something, but you hold back? You refrain from saying something that might hurt the other person? Well, they don't. We can hold back, but individualists just blurt out all sorts of stuff, regardless of the impact on others. They just say things without thinking, and when people have a problem with that, they can't understand why."

On the other hand, collectivist's perception of themselves tends to be more positive than the way that they are perceived by individualists.

Objectively speaking, we know that in collectivist cultures communication is more oriented towards relationships rather than tasks. Context is considered to be very important and is frequently described in great detail. Therefore, messages may include extensive references to the background or to the past that may be more or less relevant to the topic. It is common also to refer to other broader related subjects, such as political, social, or economic aspects. Everything that somehow is part of the context should be mentioned in some shape or form.

Communication logic is more indirect and works more like a spiral, it is less linear. The message sender may touch upon several peripheral aspects, which may seem disconnected among them and in no apparent order, making connections to the main topic only at the very end of the message.

Messages often remain implicit, rather than being made explicit.

Here is another example:

John – He didn't even have to say anything… I could tell what he was going to say, just by looking at the way he walked into the room.

Pete – But, then, did he confirm that the company is moving to a different city?

> *John – He just didn't say it in all these words, right? He only said that "we are considering options for the plant's location." That means it's obvious that we'll have to move!*

Communication tends to focus on the receivers and on their possible reaction. It is more commonly seen that a message is designed with different versions, to be used according to different intended receiving audiences.

In collectivist cultures many times verbal interaction is indirect; that is, people may speak to a third party so that this person then addresses the one that the first person wishes to communicate with. The purpose of these indirect processes is to avoid "losing face", something that might occur when communicating directly.

When Paul asks Peter to ask John his opinion about a certain matter, John can express himself freely with no embarrassment regarding Paul, since he is not present. This saves them both, Paul and John, from any embarrassment. At the same time, Peter does not suffer or cause embarrassment by being "the go-between", even though he might be interested in the matter himself. In an individualist society, Paul would speak directly to John, with no "go-between." Actually, in individualist societies, "go-betweens" tend to be frowned upon, when not despised and scorned. In collectivist societies, "go-betweens" are necessary and useful, in order to avoid any embarrassment between Paul and John.

> *Tancredo Neves, a Brazilian politician who was elected President, but died before being inaugurated, was famous for his diplomatic skills; he was a master in the art of saving others from embarrassment.*
>
> *They say that once, when he had just been elected State Governor of Minas Gerais, newspapers began publishing all sorts of speculations about different politicians that might be called upon to be part of his team of State Secretaries, in charge of certain functions. Speculation grew involving a particular politician, someone who Neves had not really any intention of inviting to be part of his team.*

Neves then called the politician for a private meeting and told him: "You must be aware of the news circulating in the papers, saying that I am about to invite you to be one of my State Secretaries…"

The politician nodded affirmatively: "Yes, I'm aware of those publications."

"Well," Neves continued, "There are a number of journalists standing outside, as we speak. They are waiting to interview yourself when you leave our meeting. You will tell them that, indeed, I had called you here to invite you to become a State Secretary, but that you declined my invitation…"

By acting in this way, Neves saved the other party from the embarrassment of not actually being invited, after all that expectation had been raised in the news. He probably earned the politician's gratitude from doing things this way. One might say that Neves did the other politician a favor, and got himself a potential ally in the future.

However, please not an important aspect in all this: collectivists constantly exchange favors of this sort, but they do it with the primary intention of maintaining group harmony and avoiding conflict. They are not doing it with the intention of getting something specific in return. This is a bit hard to understand, from an individualist perspective. Since individualists are brought up to look at issues in individual terms, they tend to look at these interactions as "transactions", an exchange of favors with an ulterior motive of gaining some sort of individual advantage. Actually, the "ulterior motive" of collectivists is simply to avoid confrontation and maintain group harmony.

Collectivists see themselves as being nice and polite: they are merely avoiding unpleasant situations and embarrassment. They see themselves as being mindful and cautious, avoiding risks that might damage relationships or harm other people's feelings.

From their own perspective, their behavior is a way of showing respect to other people, to their feelings and to the personal image people must care for. They consider that their behavior is a form of offering support to others.

To a collectivist, "integrity" means expressing only whatever promotes group harmony. Anything that might cause conflict is better left unsaid. Keeping your mouth shut, in certain situations, in order to maintain group harmony, is the best way of showing integrity.

However, the impression that individualists have, regarding collectivist cultures, is quite different…

Individualists tend to perceive collectivists as being "tricky" and "scheming…" They question collectivists' integrity, for it seems that they are always "over-explaining" things, offering long-winded and elaborate justifications.

"They are not trustworthy. They are secretive and make gossip, all the time. They are also suspicious of everybody else! They are always supporting 'conspiracy theories' and assuming evil intentions where there are none. They think that everybody has got to have some ulterior motive for whatever they are doing; they never trust anybody."

"Besides, they never say what they're really thinking, not to the other person's face. They only speak behind their backs, in covert conversations, never out in the open. You can never tell what their real opinion is."

"They waste a lot of time, with this excuse about relationships! They keep running around in circles, avoiding going straight to the point. They avoid facing issues; they hide things from each other and from themselves, rather than confronting issues that need to be tackled. They worry too much about what others will think, instead of focusing on what needs to be done."

Come to think of it, when individualists and collectivists sit down to negotiate with each other, it's a real miracle that they might ever come to any kind of agreement, considering the amount of prejudice that they have against each other, and how easily they might frustrate their own expectations.

Body language

In collectivist cultures (low IDV) people learn very early how to read body language. This is a way of getting to know how the members of a group feel about any topic, so this skill is crucial to maintaining effective relationships in a collectivist society. In an individualist society, confrontation skills are more important to survive. If you are not good at confronting, asserting yourself, expressing your opinions openly, you will never earn respect from your fellow individualists.

In a collectivist society, confrontation is avoided. Group harmony is more important, so your ability to "feel" the climate in a group, by reading the non-verbal messages broadcast by its members, is what you need to develop.

In individualist cultures communication tends to be more focused on the sender and less on the intended audience. Expressing the message content clearly is considered more important than the reaction of whoever is receiving and interpreting that message.

In collectivist cultures communication tends to be more focused on the message's receiver(s). Since group harmony is more important than expressing individual opinions, in collectivist societies communicators must try to anticipate the intended audience's reaction. The message format is more important than its content, because the language style, the tone of voice, the climate of the meeting, whether there is background music or not, the attire of the message "sender", all these things will influence the communication outcome.

These differences lead to interesting consequences for the use of modern communication technologies, such as electronic mail, social networks and teleconferencing.

In individualist cultures (high IDV), e-mail is used more frequently and easily (in all its forms), as a phone-call substitute. Electronic mail and text messaging (whatever the application or social network being used) are perfect for cultures that value message content more than its format. They allow the sender to express quickly their intention, without worrying about the receiver's immediate reaction, different from a phone call or instant video. In a text exchange, the receiver might only read the message hours (or days) later.

In collectivist cultures (low IDV) people are more reluctant to use e-mail and text as a replacement for direct contact (through phone or instant video). It's not that they don't do it, but they are less at ease doing it, and they will readily switch to direct contact if they have the choice (unless the purpose is to avoid losing face; in this case, then, texting is more acceptable).

The problem is that text does not allow you to express non-verbal aspects (emoticons are not enough for collectivists) and it does not allow the sender to instantly "read" the receiver's reaction. This leaves the sender with a feeling that "there's something missing" in the relationship. Calling the other person on the phone, then, is preferred, since it at least allows you to interpret each other's tone of voice, instantly. This is why in collectivist cultures people call more often and phone calls last longer, on average, than what you see in individualist cultures (where calls are more objective, direct, and focused on content).

People from individualist cultures often complain that they send e-mail to their collectivist counterparts and they fail to get a response, or the response is only obtained much later. One of the reasons for that is certainly that collectivists value personal contact and phone calls, which both allow for non-verbal interaction.

When collectivists get a text or e-mail message, they try to "interpret" the non-verbal content of the message, and often reach conclusions that are very different from the sender's intention. They wonder what the sender was feeling when he/she wrote the message? Was he/she irritated? Worried? In pain? Or just indifferent? How important is this message, really?

To collectivists, really important topics demand personal contact (or at least via telephone), in order to convey emotions and to reinforce relationship ties. According to such criteria, any text or e-mail message is already considered to be of less importance.

Similarly, collectivists feel less at ease with group meetings using teleconferencing and videoconferencing, when compared to their individualist counterparts. For high IDV cultures, videoconferencing has great advantages over meeting in person, for it costs much less and allows greater objectivity.

Being there in person demands much more time, since that includes travel time to the meeting site. Once you get there, you certainly "lose time" with introductions and pleasantries until you can finally get to the point on the agenda. And once the meeting is over, participants spend more time and money getting back to where they came from.

A videoconference allows you to see and hear all participants, and to focus directly and objectively on the agenda. Interaction among participants is restricted; it tends to occur mostly between the meeting coordinator and each of the participants in turn, following a spike pattern. This allows you to avoid any parallel conversations that might deviate from focusing on the topic to be discussed. It is quite clear why videoconferences enjoy preferential status in individualist societies.

On the other side of the spectrum, you can also understand why collectivists do not enjoy videoconferencing and tend to use it less frequently. If, on one hand, it is true that they allow you to see and hear all the participants, they do not allow you to interact informally with the group, before and after the meting, plus during coffee breaks. It is often at these occasions that collectivists determine the group's climate, how people really feel about the topics discussed. Interacting with others at a live, physical presence meeting is much richer in subtleties and nuances that allow collectivists to "feel" what's going on. During a videoconference these subtleties are lost and the parallel conversations (that are so important in collectivist cultures) are not possible.

In an individualistic culture videoconferencing is considered a step in the right direction, it represents progress and enhances efficiency; it allows for better and faster decisions.

In a collectivistic culture, videoconferencing is regarded as a step in the wrong direction: it represents making discussions poor and restricted. It leads to making wrong decisions more quickly.

In terms of social networks (such as Facebook, Twitter, LinkedIn and many others), their adoption and use might be greater (compared to e-mailing) in collectivistic cultures, due to their emphasis on relationships. Social networks are used more frequently to interact socially, rather than to discuss work-related issues such as projects and tasks. This is also true for mobile texting applications such as Whats App and simply exchanging SMS messages.

In individualistic societies these networks tend to be used more frequently with the purpose of addressing work-related issues, such as getting a job, recommending an ex-colleague, or discussing assignments. Social networks are used as a means of achieving individual goals. By contrast, in collectivistic cultures social networks are used simply as a way of maintaining the sensation of belonging to a social network.

In summary, what we see is that the use of communication technology is influenced by the underlying values of each culture. The same technology is used in different ways in different cultures. This does not happen under the sole influence of the Individualism dimension, but rather due to the influence of all six dimensions. Power Distance, Performance Orientation and Uncertainty Avoidance, for instance, all influence the way technologies are used in different cultures. The technology may be the same, but the way it is used is different.

The notion of family

In individualistic cultures the notion of what exactly constitutes "your family" is more restricted: it includes your parents, your siblings and your children. Other relatives such as uncles, nephews and nieces, cousins, for instance, are regarded as more distant entities. You must consider yourself responsible for your own actions and for your immediate family. Therefore, if a cousin of yours gets involved with some reproachable activity, this has little or no impact on yourself, since this cousin is regarded simply as "a distant relative."

In collectivistic cultures the concept of family is broader. It includes all your aunts and uncles, nephews and nieces, cousins, grandparents, grandchildren, in-laws, etc.

As long as any family member remains loyal to the family, all its members have a duty to look after everyone else. If anyone gets involved in reproachable activities, this brings shame to the whole family, even to those distant relatives.

In individualistic cultures, due to the value placed on individual expression of opinions, conflict is more frequent and more explicit; discussions and disagreements are often observed. In collectivistic cultures open conflict is avoided; the expression of dissenting opinions within the family is suppressed. If relatives hold dissenting political opinions, politics are avoided as a conversation topic. If they support different teams in competitive sports, talking about those sports is avoided, and so forth.

In collectivistic societies conflicts are easily turned into personal issues and people easily feel offended, leading to conflicts escalating and getting out of hand and having long-term repercussions. Due to all this, conflict is systematically avoided within the family. In individualistic societies conflict in general is more accepted as a part of daily life, so it is also more accepted within the family.

Education

In collectivistic cultures, peer pressure at school has a stronger role. Children tend to express themselves when they feel that they are sanctioned by their peer group; otherwise, they tend to remain silent. One of the most important things to learn at school is how to behave in order to be accepted within the peer group.

In individualistic cultures children soon learn to speak up in class. They do not need the approval of their peer group to express themselves. One of the most important things to learn at school is "learning how to learn"; so that one is able to face any kind of situation independently.

Feedback at work

Giving and receiving feedback is something that has quite different connotations in individualistic and collectivistic cultures.

All over the world, feedback is known as an American management concept (America is a highly individualistic culture). Giving feedback to others is taught all over the world as something that should be done "in the American way," that is: it should be direct and offered immediately after the fact has occurred, and it should be based on the observation of concrete behavior. There is no doubt that all this works perfectly fine in an individualistic culture.

One must remember, however, that "feedback" means literally feeding back information about something that has happened. The classic illustration of that process is the situation in which someone uses a light switch with a dimmer to gradually turn on (or turn off) a light: you turn the dial and the light goes on. You verify, with your own eyes, the intensity of the light in the room; you turn the dial to the right or to the left and that motion intensifies or dims the intensity of the light, until you reach the desired level of illumination. Your hand's action turning the dial to the left or to the right varies according to the perceived intensity of the light in the room (the perceived intensity of light is the feedback that tells you which way to move your hand).

In a collectivistic society, an employee perceives many indirect signals about his performance: he/she sees whether customers are satisfied, if colleagues enjoy being in his/her company, if the boss praises what he/she is doing or ignores what he/she does. All of that constitutes indirect feedback. In these cultures, direct feedback is avoided, since it might lead to an undesirable confrontation between boss and subordinate. This is undesirable both by the boss and the subordinate because it entails the risk that one of them, or perhaps both, "lose face" if the confrontation results in someone feeling "wrong."

It is safer, in these cultures, to use indirect forms of communication. Instead of calling an employee over to talk in private and tell him/her that the slides she/he used in the presentation he/she made were unclear and that the figures were so small on the screen that it was difficult to read them from the back of the room (an individualistic approach to feedback), the collectivistic boss might choose to make a comment at a staff meeting about how important it is to design clear slides and to use large fonts, so that figures may be read more easily.

This boss is not being direct and also he/she is not being concrete, but the employee in question knows what the boss is talking about, and so will make the necessary corrections to improve the next presentation. In an individualistic culture, such a behavior from the part of the boss would be harshly criticized, but it is possible that this approach actually works better in a collectivistic culture, while the direct approach, in such a culture, would cause a lot of anxiety on both the person providing feedback and the one receiving it.

Contracts

In collectivistic cultures, "psychological contracts" are more important than formal ones. There is even an expression saying that "contracts are legal instruments signed between friends to be used between enemies." This means that the quality of the relationship is more important than the commitment made in writing. As long as the relationship is going well, the contract is not even referred to, it may be completely forgotten. If the relationship turns sour, that's when people look at the contract, in order to use it as a weapon against the other party.

This applies both to commercial contracts and to employment contracts.

In a collectivistic culture employment contracts are a mere formality. The implicit psychological contract establishes that an employee will be loyal to the organization and that the organization, in turn, will take care of the employee. The employee is expected to do whatever he or she will be told by the boss. The relationship is one of mutual trust, while this is usually not explicit in the formal contract.

When a breach of trust occurs by any of the involved parties, the contract's actual written content will then be subject to examination.

In individualistic societies formal contracts are more important. Generally speaking, employment contracts are more extensive and detailed, spelling out the duties and obligations of both the employee and of the employer. It is common for an employee to refer to his or her contract during a discussion with the boss, saying that "this was not in my contract", "I did not sign up for this," or "if you want me to do that, then let's re-discuss my contract."

In these societies, in many organizations it is customary to actually draw up a new contract every time an employee is asked to change jobs, due to a transfer or a promotion.

Nepotism

This exists in every culture, (President Kennedy once joked about it when questioned about appointing Bobby Kennedy to his cabinet as US Attorney General, saying that "nepotism is all right, as long as it stays within the family") but it is more frequently seen and less often criticized in collectivistic cultures. In such cultures it is often totally accepted without criticism. It is considered natural for someone in a powerful position to assign his or her relatives to key positions. On one hand, relatives are seen as people that can be trusted, and one needs to be surrounded by trusted people at work. On the other hand, people are perceived to have the moral duty to help his or her relatives, and giving them a job is part of that.

Therefore, in collectivistic cultures there are at least two arguments often used to defend nepotism.

Beer

Culture differences between individualists and collectivists are visible even in the way they drink beer...

In Brazil (and in many other collectivistic societies) the common habit among friends is to open a large bottle of beer (bottles usually hold 0.66 l, but there are also one liter beer bottles in many countries) and share its contents, pouring many glasses among people sitting around a table, whether at a bar or in someone's home.

> *This is what I did, once I invited my work colleagues for a house-warming party soon after moving to The Netherlands. There were no large bottles of beer to be had, but rather small 0.35 l cans, the common size found all over the world today. As guests started arriving, I asked them if they would like to have a beer and, as they accepted my offer, I proceeded to open a can and pour beer into glasses that I had handed out to three or four people.*
>
> *I noticed that everybody was staring at me with a funny look on their faces... so I asked: "What's the matter? Am I doing something wrong?" My colleagues smiled and explained:*
>
> *"That's not how we do it here... You're supposed to give each person their own can and they will take care of that until it is finished."*

This is clearly an individualistic habit that is adopted in these cultures without a second thought. Likewise, in collectivistic cultures beer is shared among friends from a single bottle, without thinking. In all societies, people learn these habits in childhood, observing how adults do it and imitating them.

We never think about the underlying values that drive these behaviors, we simply adopt that way of doing things as "the way to do it."

2. INDIVIDUALISM VERSUS COLLECTIVISM (IDV)

Is the world becoming more individualistic?

This question is often posed in workshops about cross-cultural management. In fact, there are some research studies pointing in that direction.

However, these studies must always be considered with great caution, and there are a couple of crucial comments that must be made. In the first place, it must be said that the differences observed have been very small. We are looking at score variations around one or two points, which is not much. When speaking of culture, a variation of one or two percentage points over a period of twenty years might be entirely attributable to statistical variance, rather than to a verifiable long-term trend. We would need to conduct several studies over many decades before we can assert that we are looking at a real trend and not at something transitory that might be reversed in a decade or two.

The second comment refers to the fact that variations in Individualism scores have been seen both in individualistic cultures and in collectivistic ones. This means that, if all cultures are slowly becoming more individualistic, the relative differences among them are remaining more or less the same. Collectivists are becoming more individualistic, but individualists are becoming even more so. The most important aspect of this, then, is that the differences are not shrinking, but rather they remain the same.

3. Performance Orientation (PER)

The third dimension identified by Hofstede is what I call Performance Orientation (PER). This dimension refers to the archetypal dilemma between putting performance as a priority, awarding status and social recognition to those who stand out for their performance, or prioritizing quality of life and caring for others, rather than performance.

All cultures dedicate their attention to both sides of this dilemma; however, the dilemma becomes visible when there are situations in which someone is forced to choose between the two sides of this dimension. When we are forced to choose, what do we consider more important, work or leisure? To show that we can perform or to enjoy life? Different cultures have different resolutions to this dilemma, and this is what defines this dimension.

In cultures that score high in PER, performance is more valued. People receive social rewards, financial and non-financial, linked to their performance. Whoever performs well, gets praise, prestige and recognition. People identify themselves with those who are perceived as "winners", with those who are outstanding performers, and they aspire to achieve the same high performance levels. Good performance is a goal to be achieved and people are motivated to reach that goal.

In those cultures that score low in this dimension, quality of life is more valued. Good performance is not rewarded in such a clear and evident fashion. Recognition and prestige linked to performance are less visible; they are subtler. People tend to identify themselves with the underdogs, with those that try hard but do not win, rather than with the winners. They avoid standing out; they prefer to be regarded as being on the same level as others. Those who do stand out are criticized, in order to "cut them down in size".

3. PERFORMANCE ORIENTATION (PER)

When he identified this dimension in the 1970's, Hofstede called it "Masculinity" (MAS) and considered that those cultures that scored low on this dimension were to be named "Feminine" cultures. His choice of labels for this dimension turned out to be most unfortunate, in practice. People reacted to these terms according to their previous experiences with notions of feminism and *macho* behavior; they deviate from Hofstede's definition of the dimension and focus their discussion in very different political and social issues.

Because of all that, I prefer to use the term "Performance Orientation" as a label; I consider this a more accurate name for this dimension, considering the essence of its definition.

The choice of label to denominate a culture dimension is, in itself, influenced by a person's cultural bias. When I discussed with my Dutch colleagues what might be a better label for this dimension, we faced our respective cultural biases.

They accused me of being under the influence of a collectivistic bias: my choice represented an attempt to avoid confrontation and conflict in order to maintain group harmony. The Dutch considered this an undesirable attempt to hide the naked truth, a truth that should be told directly, with no detours. They are not aware of the fact that, in preferring this approach, they are under the influence of an individualistic bias.

In a very Dutch way, we agreed to disagree. Most Dutch interculturalists continue to use the term Masculinity, despite criticism stemming from American and British scholars, who reject the term as sexist. In my own opinion, the most important thing to do is to understand the dimension and the behaviors associated to it. Let's just leave the discussion about the label to another moment.

In high Performance Orientation cultures, people tend to feel a sort of "white envy" towards winners. They are admired; they are what everybody wants to be. Men and women alike prioritize performance and this prioritization has important implications for life at work and at home, in family issues and in individual matters too.

Even the focus of the feminist movement is affected by the values represented by this dimension.

In high Performance Orientation countries, feminist movements tend to direct their attention to the lack of equality in reward and recognition for women who perform just as well as men do. Since society in general awards prestige and status to those who perform well, women fight for getting the same level of rewards for their performance that men get, whether at work or in other situations, such as in sports.

In low Performance Orientation countries, feminist movements have a different emphasis: they concentrate on getting men to give more attention to quality of life, leisure and family issues. Work itself is criticized, and a greater balance between "work" and "life" is sought. In these cultures, many times women choose to work fewer hours per week. It's not a matter of capability; it is a matter of choice.

In high Performance Orientation countries, a lot of value is placed on being successful at work. Therefore, if you do not concentrate on performance, you tend to feel frustrated and diminished in society. In low PER cultures, however, people from all genders do not need work as their main source of self esteem. Both men and women often choose roles that are less demanding in terms of work and career, since they feel that their main priority is to lead a lifestyle that allows them a good quality of life. In these cultures, many times people will reject promotions, if they feel that they would not enjoy the additional responsibilities and stress-related demands. In high PER cultures, by contrast, declining a promotion would be unacceptable, so people see themselves as being forced to follow a career that is not necessarily their preference. They do it for the status and prestige that are associated to that, they do it because it is what society expects from them, but not necessarily because it is what they really want. Please refer to Laurence J. Peter's brilliant book "The Peter Principle" for many examples of this.

Live to work or work to live?

The central dilemma in this dimension is often summarized with these words. In high PER societies work is seen as the very moral purpose of human beings. Only through work can people achieve their purpose in life.

In low PER countries, work is nothing more than a means to an end; it is the way to attain a good comfort level in order to better enjoy life at leisure. It is a necessary evil, which allows you to enjoy the good things in life, between periods of hard work. In these societies, work is often described as hard and tenuous; in high PER cultures, work is described as challenging and stimulating.

Competing to win

In high PER societies competition is taken very seriously in every aspect of people's lives. It is important to be " a winner" and many consider that the world consists of "winners" and "losers". The latter are openly basted in public, with no mercy, while winners are idolized.

Winners are admired and become the target of so-called "white envy": people admire them and wish to be like them. Competition must be clean and on a "level playing field", allowing equal opportunities for all to win. This is especially true in egalitarian societies, such as the US, and UK, where high PER exists in combination with low Power Distance. However, there are societies such as China, India and Japan, where high PER exists in combination with hierarchy. In such cultures competition is important, but there is added complexity due to stronger class distinctions. Competition occurs mostly among people of the same class.

In low PDI cultures with a high Performance Orientation, meritocracy is a clearly predominant value: winning should depend on performance alone and not be influenced by relationships or any other criteria other than pure performance.

When candidates compete for the same job, it is clear to all that the job should go to the best performing candidate and never to the person who needs it the most, or to the most loyal, or to the one who possesses any other attribute.

The emphasis on competition also means that, especially in sports, while winners are idolized, the person coming in second place is as despised as the one finishing last. There is little sympathy for the underdogs and the "also ran's"; the most important thing is to "be number one"; everybody else is a "loser."

It is no wonder, then, that the best sports people from all over the world usually come from high PER cultures: the US, UK, Germany, China and Japan. These countries produce great athletes and also support their performance with large sponsorships and commercial interest.

One of the ways of measuring a sports person's success is through assessing how much they earn in prizes and sponsorships. This goes beyond winning a tournament or a championship. There is a cultural necessity to determine who is the overall winner, who is the *uber* number one, across all sports. This elicits the "biggest earnings" lists, published in popular magazines: it allows people to say that a certain basketball star is "better" than another baseball star, because he made more money in the past year. Earnings lists are just a way to measure success; it's not the money in itself, but it's a way to keep score.

Winning is not everything

In low PER societies there is a different emphasis. Quality of life and simple forms of entertainment are more important than performing to your utmost. There is also competition in these cultures, there is no doubt about that, but it has a different overtone. It's important to be "among the top", but not necessarily to be "number one". There is some sympathy for those who manage to finish the race, even for those who finish last. People feel sorry for those who failed and they do not admire the winners so much more than the other competitors. Winners tend to be a bit more modest in their celebrations, because standing out as a winner does not always go down so well in societies that praise caring for others more than they praise competitions. They often appear modest and play down their victories; attributing them to luck or to the great support they have had from other people.

I worked a lot with American banks (high PER) and with Dutch banks (low PER). My American colleagues frequently discussed what our competitors were doing and how the best performers differentiated themselves from others in the market. We talked about how we could be different and better than our competitors. My Dutch colleagues, by contrast, used to say that "all banks are essentially the same" and "don't make the mistake of thinking that you can be smarter than your competitors." They considered that it was more important to foster long-term reliability and trust. Doing things better and faster was not an objective.

In these low PER cultures there is less emphasis on quantification and statistics in sports; rather, there is more talk about the way athletes play the sport, their personal style and the beauty of their movements, instead of how many aces they scored in a tennis match or what is their batting average.

Competitive spirit

The interest in competing is something that exists in every culture. What happens in practice is simply that in high PER societies this interest is expressed more intensely, more frequently and more explicitly. In cultures with a low PER, we see the opposite: competition exists, but it is subtler, it is visible less often and with less intensity.

In high PER cultures there is greater emphasis on objective measurement and the supremacy of reason over values and emotional aspects. This stems from the fact that objective measurement makes it easier to determine the results of any competition.

Who won? There is nothing better than a set of clear rules and criteria to determine the winner of any competition. Even in beauty contests, high Performance Oriented cultures are subject to the influence of this attempt to measure beauty by using an objective and quantitative approach.

In low PER cultures beauty is considered to be a matter of aesthetic values and, by definition, a necessarily subjective issue. Subjectivity is mitigated by assembling a group of judges (a jury), in which the experience of the jurors, in addition to the debate among them should come to a verdict that is accepted as fair and just.

In high PER cultures the idea is to mitigate subjectivity by adopting quantitative measurement criteria. Minimum and maximum threshold measurements for the female body are established as a norm: numbers for waist, bust, hips, height, thighs, calves, ankles, weight-to-height ratio, etc. It's no wonder that such contests are lambasted for turning women into pieces of flesh… The obsession with objective measurements leads to affecting male-female relations in all aspects. It all becomes a numbers game, devoid of emotion or ethics, reduced to the tyranny of rationality.

Fast food and slow food

Performance Orientation as a cultural dimension does not manifest itself only through situations at work or in interpersonal relations between men and women. This culture dimension may be observed in many other situations and behaviors.

The form by which a culture approaches food and eating showcases whether a culture's values are more oriented towards performance or towards quality of life and caring for others.

As an example, let's take the concept of "fast-food": nourishment that is quickly prepared and even more quickly consumed. Such a concept could only have been born in cultures like America and the UK. In both these cultures the act of eating meals is considered to be almost a necessary evil, something that interferes with the values of productivity and performance.

In Anglo-American cultures there is a notion that the first meal of the day should be quite plentiful, "the most important meal of the day" according to almost all the literature published on nutrition in those countries. Breakfast, when one "breaks the fasting", is treated with great importance and consists of a complete meal: sausages, eggs, fruit, bread, pancakes, vegetables, and sweets. Other meals in the day are usually smaller and less varied.

Publications in these cultures justify these habits using health arguments. Their authors fail to understand that their analyses and conclusions are not really that objective, they are not universal, and they are fully biased by culture values. In other cultures different eating habits are equally defended as being "healthy", contradicting what American and English people advocate. Scientific and medical expertise are not immune to culture bias; these experts often believe that they are expressing universal truths, but more often then not, their assertions are valid only within their respective cultures, but not elsewhere.

The notion of a "full breakfast" is linked to emphasizing performance as taking priority over quality of life and caring. Eating a lot in the early morning and less during the day is something that is not, in itself, an issue of better health, but rather the best choice if you want to prioritize performance throughout the day.

3. PERFORMANCE ORIENTATION (PER)

The mid-day meal should be light, and most of all, short in duration. The shorter it lasts, the less it will interfere with your work, and with your performance in the work that you are doing. Therefore, in the UK and US, lunch breaks at work are usually 30 minutes or less. When companies allow a longer period (45 minutes or even an hour), people use 15 minutes of that time to eat (a necessary "evil") and they use the rest of the time to do other things. Lunch has a different meaning in other cultures, which are more quality of life oriented, such as France, Spain, Italy and Portugal.

Lunch is not just a "lunch": it is a complete meal, much larger than the early morning breakfast. As such, it requires more time, from one hour as a minimum, to two hours or more. In some cultures, it is followed by a rest period (a *siesta*) to allow for digestion. This is very different from performance-oriented cultures, in which a short and light lunch can be eaten fast and digested quickly.

This has elicited the birth of "fast-food" networks, very popular in the UK and US, which have spread globally from their Anglo-American origins. Today one can find fast food all over the world, but it is still quite evident that these chains are much more popular in high PER cultures.

America stood out initially with McDonald's, but today there are dozens of different chains, all competing among themselves and based on the same assumptions:

1. food must be prepared and consumed quickly;
2. taste is secondary;
3. most important is to allow the customer to remain focused on performance.

In London and all over the UK fast-food chains have sprung like mushrooms, promoting themselves based on functionality and speed, rather than on leisurely appreciating how a meal tastes. One such food chain is called simply "eat." Its logo emphasizes simplicity and directness: just the word "eat" followed by a deliberate "period" mark, so that it reads: "eat, period." Nothing else, just eat! No frills, no distractions; don't be foolish, just eat and get out of here. Marks & Spencer, the famous chain of department stores, decided to get on the bandwagon and offer their own mid-day lunch outlets and called it "M&S Simply Food." These are examples of the kind of objectivity that makes the British proud (though this is criticized by other cultures).

British food enjoys a worldwide reputation for being absolutely tasteless. Why? Because taste is not important, it is performance that is important. Do you want taste? Then add mustard or ketchup; this you can do quickly, without wasting time.

A Frenchman would argue that taste is of utmost importance, as the subtle flavors of different spices will add enjoyment and pleasure to your meal. He would also say that preparing a steak with mustard sauce is something that requires some time and dedication during the cooking process. Simply adding salt or mustard after the steak is grilled is not the same thing, you get less taste as a result.

An Englishman might agree, but he would add to that his own conclusion: "why waste all that time preparing and eating such a meal, if this distracts you from your primary concern which is to perform effectively and efficiently?" It is quite obvious that these two cultures treat meals very differently, because the underlying values of performance versus quality of life are very different. It's not just the food, there is a whole cultural dimension driving these different approaches.

The cook as a hero

In France, where PER is lower, the way food is approached is, indeed, quite different. The enjoyment of eating is taken to the extreme opposite: preparing food is considered to be something very important, because the enjoyment of food is also considered very important.

Performance at work is less valued than quality of life. Lunch breaks are sometimes taking two hours or more. Why? Because you need time to prepare food properly and time to enjoy it as it deserves.

In the UK restaurant users expressing opinions on the web frequently mention such things as "nice place for a quick lunch", service was "swift and efficient". In France one can read posts where people say that "service was too quick and inconvenient; we barely had time to finish our appetizer and the waiter was already disturbing us by bringing the main dish." Lunch, in France, is an important meal and should be enjoyed with a certain ritual ceremony. At dinner, this is even more so!

What is the first meal of the day like? It is light because "it is healthier to eat just a little, early in the morning". It is called *petit-dejeuner*, which means literally "small break-fast". Even the term describes a small meal. It consists of bread, perhaps just a pastry (maybe a *croissant*) and coffee. Vegetables? Meat? Sweets? All that will come later, at lunch and dinner. Lunch, by the way, is called *dejeuner*, which literally means break-fast.

Since the culture values quality of life and the quality of food, preparing food is something that acquires a degree of importance seldom seen in high performance-orientation cultures. French cooks are greatly valued and many become the equivalent of national heroes. Outside of France perhaps only Paul Bocuse became an internationally well-known celebrity, but all it takes is for one to spend a week in Paris in order to see that Bocuse was not the first and certainly not the last *chef de cuisine* to acquire "super-star" status in the country. Thousands of French cooks, as early as in the 16th Century, became nationally famous and were admired as heroes. Many young people aspire to a culinary career and take great pride in their skills. It's all linked to the valuing of quality of life rather than performance. Work is a "necessary evil", so that one can enjoy life.

Are the French better off than the English? They are both wrong and they are both right. In culture terms there is no right or wrong, only "different". I am merely pointing out that different cultures may value almost the exact opposite of another, and no one can say which is right or which is wrong, without indulging in some kind of culture bias.

4. Uncertainty Avoidance (UAI)

This is a somewhat more complex dimension, often misunderstood. It was identified in the final stages of his original research study and it has been the subject of many discussions in academia. Many subsequent research studies confirmed the initial results found by Hofstede, but it is still widely discussed; this is mostly due to the fact that it is not so easily understood.

The three dimensions initially identified by Hofstede are readily comprehended; they are more intuitive. People immediately identify what is meant by Power Distance, Individualism, or Performance Orientation. Uncertainty Avoidance, however, contains aspects that appear at times to be contradictory and more difficult to connect to our pre-existing frames of reference.

Hofstede's definition for this dimension is that it is the extent to which certain societies create, unconsciously, mechanisms to avoid uncertainty or ambiguity. Cultures that score high on this dimension as a result of research show abundant use of these unconscious mechanisms. The most notable examples of said mechanisms are:

Planning and/or organizing

Societies with high UAI typically place great value in planning and organizing as ways to avoid ambiguity. Detailed planning, carried out with care and attention, has the purpose of avoiding unforeseen or undesired occurrences. If the plans are well made, forecasting every foreseeable circumstance, uncertainty and ambiguity will be significantly reduced.

Clear examples of this are provided by the Germanic cultures, notably Germany and Switzerland. Both these countries are widely known for greatly valuing planning, organizing and structuring their formal and informal processes and procedures.

These aspects are clearly visible at work, in private companies and in government agencies, where planning and structured processes are easy to observe. However, UAI is also shown in family life and in education, from kindergarten and primary schools to the highest levels of post-graduate studies.

In family life, children learn from an early age to expect precise and specific answers to their questions, so that no doubts are left remaining. Responses to children's questions are direct and clear, rather than vague or uncertain. On the other hand, adults often express that they feel concerned or stressed.

At school, being personally organized is something highly valued in the way children study and present their homework and school projects. The structure of homework is highly valued by teachers; the teachers themselves are considered to be experts in their subject matter. Teachers are expected to have a precise response at the tip of their lips to whatever questions may be asked by their pupils; and it is the teacher's responsibility to inform the parents about their children's performance at school.

By contrast, in low UAI cultures, people complain less often of feeling stressed or concerned. At school, children are used to discussing issues for which there are no clear conclusions; and it is acceptable that the teachers may say, "I don't know" in response to certain questions. Usually the teacher discusses a pupil's performance with the parents, but without assuming the role of expert on their subject.

At work, there is less emphasis on planning and on following structured processes and procedures. Decisions are made even when there is little information available. There is a tendency to develop more "generalist" types of managers, capable of working effectively in a wide range of different departments, rather than "specialists" who follow a narrow career path along a specific function or area of expertise.

Religiousness and/or superstition

Another aspect connected to Uncertainty Avoidance refers to religiousness and superstition. While planning and organizing deal with eminently rational elements, religion and superstition deal with subjective aspects and faith. They are both mechanisms that aim to avoid uncertainty.

Religions, whichever religions they are, address the concern with issues common to all humankind: our origins, our purpose and our future. Where do we come from? Why do we exist? What happens after we die? These questions have been with us for thousands of years in every culture, since the beginning of the human species. In cultures that score high in UAI, the answers to such questions tend to be provided by religion; in cultures that score low on UAI, people in general are satisfied with somewhat vague answers to the same questions.

The social purpose of superstition is also to avoid uncertainty and ambiguity. When I "knock on wood," I'm avoiding bad luck. Wearing good luck charms and amulets is also a way of "attracting good luck" or avoiding "the evil eye." Wearing an item of clothing that "brings good luck" in important occasions or when watching your favorite sport is another example of a habit that can be seen more frequently in high UAI cultures.

In many such cultures, religion and superstition overlap and blend. For instance, a religious symbol such as a crucifix might be used as a good luck charm, or the printed image of a Catholic saint might serve a similar purpose.

In sports it is especially easy to observe these aspects, both among the athletes and the public cheering for them. In high UAI cultures one can see more players making gestures pointing to the skies (thanking God) every time they score; one can also see in these cultures, more frequently, for instance, soccer players who stick to certain "lucky habits" like touching the ground with their right hand as they step onto the playing field, always starting with their right foot, etc.

Low UAI cultures also have their share of religiousness and superstition. What we can see is that difference is a matter of degree, frequency and intensity of the behaviors that are observed.

4. UNCERTAINTY AVOIDANCE (UAI)

Expressing emotions

High UAI cultures value the expression of emotions more than low UAI cultures do. The expression of emotions is linked to Uncertainty Avoidance because if you can clearly see how the other person feels about a situation, you reduce the uncertainty about engaging in dialogue with this other person. In high UAI cultures it is easier to "read" people's feelings, because they express them quite openly; conversely, in low UAI cultures people keep their feelings to themselves.

In high UAI cultures, children learn very early that they are allowed to express their emotions. They can see, in their environment, that adults also do that, and they learn by imitation. In such cultures it is plain to see that people cry, laugh, scream, talk loudly and use abundant facial expressions and hand gestures.

In low UAI cultures children learn to suppress the expression of their emotions. They hear more often expressions such as "big boys don't cry," and they see that indeed, their parents are more restrained in expressing how they feel. Sometimes, people from a different culture might perceive these cultures as "cold" or "insensitive"; what actually happens is not they do not feel, it is that they have learned not to express how they feel. They have been brought up with the notion that expressing your feelings is immature or unprofessional.

The English are often mentioned as an example of emotional suppression. It is part of English culture, especially among the ruling class of "ladies" and "gentlemen", to make a point of not expressing your feelings. The Finns are similarly cited as typically maintaining a "stone face", a neutral expression that does not reveal joy or sadness.

For people brought up in Latin cultures (high UAI) in which emotions are freely expressed, it may seem that "Scandinavians never laugh." The Spanish even have a popular expression that goes *"no te haigas al sueco,"* meaning, "don't pretend you're a Swede!" In other words: "stop looking at me with no visible reaction to what I am saying!" To a Spaniard, this lack of emotional expression can be very disturbing, as it increases uncertainty in the situation. By contrast, to most Scandinavians, the Spanish are "drama queens" who "make a huge row over everything, with no real reason."

In Germany there is seemingly a contradiction: the Germans are often perceived as not expressing their emotions, or being insensitive. What happens in the German culture is that the need for self-discipline (a dimension we will see next) and maintaining order (a different way of avoiding uncertainty) are stronger influences than the free expression of emotions. The result is that Germans do express anger, joy and sadness… but at the proper time and place. This might happen only away from the formal work environment, in private, or in public situations that have been sanctioned for emotional expression, like sports events, festivals and popular festivities.

It's always worth noting that people in high UAI cultures do not INTENTIONALLY express their emotions with the purpose of avoiding uncertainty… These mechanisms are unconscious; they are not consciously designed with a deliberate end in mind.

Extensive, detailed and abundant legislation

In high UAI countries there are laws, rules and regulations for everything. The Constitution is typically extensive and detailed. There are a series of norms stemming from legislation, making it even more detailed and extensive. The judiciary system is based on the interpretation of the law and on its application to specific, practical cases. Typical examples of this are France, Italy and Brazil.

The existence of extensive legislation has no link to actually complying with the law. Having long laws does not mean you go along with the laws; these are two different things. Compliance is something that is related to other culture dimensions, as we will see. In terms of Uncertainty Avoidance, it is almost the opposite: in most countries with high UAI, one can see that people tend to abide by the existing laws much less, although this is due to other culture factors such as Power Distance, Individualism and Long Term Orientation, which we will see next.

In low UAI cultures, legislation tends to be more succinct and based on general principles (examples: the Magna Carta in the UK, the Bill of Rights in the US). The role of the judiciary system is to pass judgment based on jurisprudence; that is: based on preceding cases, more than based on the interpretation of the law, since these are not so detailed.

4. UNCERTAINTY AVOIDANCE (UAI)

Contradicting Indicators

Some of the confusion arising about this dimension stems from discussing the scores of certain cultures. The problem is that a given culture might have a high incidence of some of the mentioned mechanisms to avoid uncertainty, while showing a low incidence of some of the other mechanisms. The fact that a culture scores high in UAI does not mean that all mechanisms are present in that culture; the high score might be driven by just a few of the mechanisms, but with strong intensity.

For instance, Brazil has a relatively high UAI score (65) though it does not enjoy a reputation for planning and organizing (as Germany does, with an equal score of 65). What drives the Brazilian score are different aspects: religiousness and superstition, expression of emotions, extensive legislation. The German score is driven mostly by the value put on planning, structuring and organizing.

Similarly, stoking the fire of controversy, the UK has a lower score in UAI, though the culture values planning and structuring. The lower UK score is driven by lower valuation of religion, aversion to superstition, suppressing of emotions and succinct legislation.

In practice, what you can see when looking at UAI is that it must be considered in each culture in combination with the other dimensions. The coexistence of all dimensions in any given culture is a fact; no dimension exists in isolation. Thinking of dimensions is merely an analytical tool, to facilitate the understanding of cultures. As such, dimensions are artificial. Any kind of analysis implies in "deconstructing" reality in order to better understand it. We must never forget that reality, in itself, does not exist in a deconstructed form.

Cultures are what they are. Looking at them through the prism of a model is a way of artificially reducing their inherent complexity, in order to comprehend and compare them. This way of looking them is like taking a snapshot that might be useful for us, but the snapshot must not be confused with reality in itself.

For the time being, it is important to stress that UAI must be considered in combination with the scores in PDI, IDV, PER and LTO. We will later look at many practical applications of the model and how it can be used to guide one's behavior and interventions across cultures.

Curious correlations

In carrying out subsequent research with the purpose of better understanding this rather "difficult" dimension, Hofstede and other researchers found some interesting correlations between Uncertainty Avoidance and other aspects of the societies they examined.

It was found, for instance, that high UAI cultures have a greater number of pharmacies and drugstores, compared to low UAI cultures. In these high UAI cultures it is also customary to advertise the location of pharmacies quite visibly: there are laws that require such establishments to, for example, post a green neon sign on their façade (you can see that in France, Italy, Spain and Germany). If you're looking for a pharmacy on the street, in these countries you can easily spot one a block away, much more easily than, for instance, in the US, UK or in the Netherlands.

Another peculiar correlation is that, among countries with similar GDP per capita scores, people use cleaning products in greater quantity in high UAI cultures.

Still another curious correlation found is that wherever UAI is higher, people tend to be more in a hurry; traffic tends to move at a higher average speed and the expression "urgent" is used more often. However, this is also correlated to a higher score in Performance Orientation. Once again, UAI must be considered in combination with the scores in other dimensions.

Other ways of expressing UAI

One can also see that in high UAI cultures people have the habit of re-confirming appointments more often. In low UAI cultures, people make an appointment (whether it is a business-related one, or personal) weeks in advance, and at the agreed date and time they just show up at the agreed location. In high UAI cultures there is a habit of calling to re-confirm the appointment the day before, or sometimes on the same day. It's a way of avoiding the uncertainty of showing up to find that there was some unforeseen circumstance that has stopped the other person from coming, or has caused a last-minute cancellation. In low UAI cultures, people rarely worry about this.

5. Long-Term Orientation

This dimension was identified some years after Hofstede's initial research studies, when more research began to be done about Asian cultures and especially about the Chinese culture, which until then was practically closed to external scrutiny. Michael Harris Bond, an English professor living for many years in China, led a research study using questions developed in China, and discussed his findings with Hofstede.

This was a very interesting development. Some critics had questioned whether Hofstede's initial research was too Euro-centric, since it had been developed in Europe and found greater differentiation among European cultures, in comparison to the differences found among Asian and Latin American cultures, for instance. Well, now the Harris Bond offered an opportunity to add research with a tool developed in China, with the participation of Chinese research associates, and assessing data collected in many other countries throughout the world (initially 23 countries).

The results were added as a fifth dimension to Hofstede's model, and this dimension revealed something interesting: it differentiated significantly among Asian cultures, but the differences were much smaller among the European ones, where all countries scored quite low.

Initially Hofstede named this dimension "Confucian Dynamism," referring to the work of the great Chinese philosopher Confucius, whose ideas have had a great influence on the Chinese culture for many centuries and are still very relevant today. However, this term is rather meaningless to anyone unfamiliar with Confucius' body of thought, which is the case for most people in the Western part of the world.

Therefore, Hofstede decided to change the dimension's label to Long-Term Orientation (LTO). In fact, one of the aspects of this dimension is, indeed, the greater concern with long-term issues rather than with what happens in the short term. However, this dimension is much more complex than just this aspect related to time… There are many situations in which this time aspect is relative: it has to do with eventually reaching an ultimate objective, and considering this to be more important than an immediate objective. Yet this ultimate objective might be something that will be achieved in a week, and not necessarily in a decade.

Some associates of the Dutch professor suggested the term "Long Term Pragmatic Orientation". This label was also not very helpful, for there are many cultures that are seen as quite pragmatic, such as the Dutch, the Americans, and others; yet they tend to think in shorter terms and scored much lower in this dimension than most Asian cultures.

A few authors have used "Flexibility versus Normativity/Discipline" as a label. In a way, these terms convey the essence of what the dimension is about, quite accurately. However, the label is not exactly self-explanatory. It seems that all labels tried so far continue to demand an additional explanation, without which they may be confusing or misleading. Some people might also say that this is true of all the labels used for the five dimensions: each of them might be misinterpreted if it were not for subsequent clarifications.

The bottom line is that this dimension still requires a better label. No one questions the dimension's identification as such, nor its importance to understand culture. Yet there is a need for a more intuitive denomination, one that would better convey its meaning in a clear and simple way. For practical purposes, in this book, we've chosen to use the label "Long-Term Orientation" (LTO), but with the important disclaimer that the dimension deals with much more complex than just the matters of time and duration.

What is it all about, after all?

LTO is about the extent to which eventual, ulterior, "long-term" objectives are considered to be more important than immediate, "short-term" objectives. One way of illustrating this notion is to imagine a person traveling on foot towards a distant mountain peak. LTO pertains to the degree in which this hiker considers that there are many possible paths that might be taken to reach his intended destination, and that all these different paths are equally possible, feasible, and relatively equally important options. It doesn't really matter which of the paths is taken, as long as it takes the hiker to the desired destination. There is no rush in getting there; none of the roads is necessarily better than the other.

Therefore, our hiker has the FLEXIBILITY to choose any of the roads over another, and to change roads along the way, walking a bit on one and then on another. Since the hiker's primary concern is simply to eventually reach his/her eventual destination, many paths are valid.

On the opposite end of the spectrum, a culture in which people consider that one must always choose "the right way" or "the best way" over all others, according to certain criteria that restrict flexibility (such as "this is the best path because it is the quickest", or "this is best because it is the safest"), this culture is considered to be more NORMATIVE, disciplined, less flexible and one in which immediate goals are often more valued than long-term or ulterior goals.

Practical Implications

There are a number of practical implications of perceiving the world around us in this way, and many of these implications are very different from typically "European" values.

The main aspect refers to the rigidity or flexibility of norms, rules and regulations, and to the very way of looking at "the truth." In low LTO cultures, the assumption is that there is something considered to be "the truth", a concept that is in itself more absolute. A person might be telling the truth or might be lying, but a person cannot usually be doing these two things at the same time.

In high LTO cultures, truth is always relative. There is no such thing as "the absolute truth." It all depends. Truth depends on the situation, on the people involved, it depends on the moment, and it depends on the times. Something might be true in a certain situation, but not in another. It might be true today, but not tomorrow. It might be true for one person, but not for another; and so on.

In low LTO cultures, people accept that some things might be relative, but it is believed that there are some other things that are absolute truths. In high LTO cultures, everything is relative, always.

Opposites may coexist

One of these aspects is the coexistence of opposites. I must concede that, so far, we are dealing still with philosophical and abstract concepts. Bear with me; we shall soon look at how these values affect the behavior of people at work in day-to-day situations.

In low LTO societies, two opposites cannot co-exist. If one solution is "the best solution", then there cannot be another, different, "best solution." Only one solution is "the best," by definition. In high LTO cultures it is considered that there are always many solutions and none of them is "better" than the others. It all depends.

For the Chinese (LTO = 118!), a person may be "truthful" and also "a liar" at the same time, why not? They have difficulty in understanding what is this difficulty that Westerners have in reconciling such opposites.

The concept of "Yin" and "Yang" is related to this: things are not just "black" or "white"; black contains white in itself, while white contains black in itself. Everything is in perpetual motion, nothing is fixed.

In low LTO cultures consultants speak about "unfreezing" certain notions, changing the situation and then "freezing again" afterwards. In high LTO cultures, there is no need to "unfreeze" and then "freeze again", because nothing is "frozen" to begin with… Everything is always fluid, anyway.

Analysis and synthesis

In low LTO cultures people value the ability to break down the whole into parts, and to analyze the different relations of cause and effect among these parts, in order to be able to reproduce the whole starting from its parts, in a different situation. In high LTO cultures, what is valued is the ability to synthesize, to perceive the whole without breaking it down into parts. For people from a low LTO culture, this does not seem useful, or even possible, since we are so accustomed to analyze and decompose everything we see.

5. LONG-TERM ORIENTATION

How and why

A few years ago, a Dutch medical doctor enrolled in a week-long intensive course about Chinese acupuncture, to be held in Hong Kong. Since this would be her first visit to China, she sought some assistance from a friend of mine, a consultant on cross-culture issues, and asked him some advice on how to deal with people in China. My colleague gave her several tips, trying to make a summary, in their hour-long encounter, of the most important aspects of Chinese culture that she should take into account during her trip, how to behave, etc. He put special emphasis on Power Distance, on respecting the elder, and the importance of relationships. He concluded their meeting telling her that she could call him at any time during her week in Hong Kong, if necessary.

> *At the end of the first day, the doctor was already on the phone with my friend, asking for help.*
>
> *"I don't know what it is, but I must be doing something wrong... I notice that the Professor is irritated with me, but I don't know why..."*
>
> *My colleague asked her to describe, as calmly as possible, how she had behaved in the classroom, since she arrived at the session, throughout the day, and until she left in the evening. She described everything and added:*
>
> *"I did everything just like you told me: I was extremely respectful of the Professor, I went up front to greet him in person before the session began, and I always excused myself for interrupting and asked for permission before asking any question. During our lunch break, we all went down to the university's cafeteria and I tried to sit at the same table with so that we could start a conversation and develop a relationship, but I felt that he was avoiding me as we searched for a table and he ended up sitting with other pupils, there was no other seat available for me at the table he chose."*
>
> *"In the afternoon, it was the same thing, even worse. I asked several questions, to demonstrate how interested I was, and he got increasingly irritated with me..."*

> At this point, my colleague already had an idea about what might be going on. In China, teachers do not like to be interrupted with a lot of questions and most students avoid asking them, especially if the questions might put the teacher in an embarrassing position in front of the class. So my colleague asked her:
>
> "What kind of questions did you ask?"
>
> She promptly replied: "Such as: why does this happen? Why does this needle have this effect? Come to think of it, most of my questions were 'why?' questions. And he simply ignored my questions, he did not address them at all and just continued the lesson, visibly irritated!"
>
> "Exactly," my colleague explained. "To the Chinese, an acceptable question is "how?" and not "why?"...

A Chinese student would have asked "how does this happen?" "In what situations?" "Show me, please, how should I place the needle on the exact spot, in order to get the desired effect." And the Professor will respond and demonstrate the "how" with the utmost pleasure.

The question "why?" is extremely embarrassing. Basically, because the teacher does not know the answer! He does not know why a needle placed on the right ear lobe has an effect on the pancreas, etc. He simply knows that this is what happens when he places needles in a certain way. In China people are less concerned with the "why" of things, they are more concerned with the "how."

The professor in this story felt extremely embarrassed in front of his class for not knowing the answers to this annoying Dutch lady's questions, and very irritated because she took every opportunity to embarrass him further in front of his students. During their lunch break, the poor professor must have avoided her like she had the plague... Surely she was out to continue embarrassing him in front of others, even during lunchtime!

In low LTO cultures, the "why" is important in order to be able to use cause and effect relations in similar situations. If I know what is the cause "A" of effect "B", I am probably able to reproduce cause "A" in another situation, when I want to produce a desired effect "B".

In high LTO cultures, there is less emphasis on "changing" situations: rather, the emphasis is on accepting the world as it is and understanding

HOW things are, instead of WHY they are that way. This is true not only for China, but also for other cultures with high LTO scores. This can be seen, for instance, also in the Brazilian culture, which has a LTO score of 65. This is roughly half the score of China, but twice higher than Germany.

As always, the most important aspect is comparing cultures: to the Chinese, Brazilians may seem quite disciplined, and not flexible enough; but to Germans, they may seem to be "too flexible, not disciplined enough!"

Relationships

In low LTO cultures, relationships are more often linked to work. When work changes, relationships also change. During the period in which a person is performing a certain job or function, that person will maintain relationships with the people that she/he interacts with as a consequence of doing that job: the colleagues at work, team members, the direct boss, clients and providers, government officials and regulators linked to that activity.

As such a person moves to a different job, or to a different organization, the people he/she interacts with tend to be other people. In low-LTO cultures the relationships that were linked to the previous job role tend to quickly be left behind, they cease to exist. The person concentrates energy on the new relationships that are key demands on the new job.

In high-LTO cultures, relationships tend to last longer, independently from work roles. Often one can see relationships that last a whole lifetime. There are friendships formed in childhood or in adolescence that may continue into old age. There are relationships established during a first job that continue even after a person has changed jobs and companies many times.

These long-lasting relationships may eventually provide valuable help in the future, in unforeseen circumstances. It is important to note, however, that they are not maintained due to a "transactional" reason. In these cultures nobody consciously thinks that "I'd better help other people around me on my way up, because I may need their help on my way down." This popular saying is more typical of low-LTO cultures, usually also individualistic cultures (high IDV), in which relationships have more of a transactional connotation: "I will help you and I expect that in return you will help me, since each one of us is responsible for himself/herself."

In high-LTO cultures relationships are maintained for a long time because people have been taught to value serving others and preserving the harmony of the universe, regardless of obtaining any personal gains. In collectivist cultures relationships are maintained in order to show loyalty to the in-groups, once again without consciously thinking of obtaining personal gains.

Relationships in low-LTO cultures are more geared towards immediate situations and towards whatever is considered to be "right." They do have a more transactional nature because of that, but this is by no means because of what others might regard as "selfishness." In a similar way, in individualist cultures relationships also have a more transactional nature, not because of selfishness, but because of the need to preserve each person's individuality, respect each individual's privacy and their ability to take accountability for what they do as individuals.

Special Chapter on Traffic

The traffic of vehicles on streets and roads is heavily regulated all over the world. These regulations are actually quite similar from one country to another. There are even international conventions regulating traffic laws, and specialists from different nations meet from time to time in order to discuss and align each country's local norms to the international regulatory guidelines.

However, what is different from country to country, is culture. This affects how people deal with the same norms. In different cultures, there are very different driving habits and different ways of dealing with the same traffic regulations.

In low-LTO cultures there is more respect for norms in general, traffic and otherwise. We say that these cultures are more "normative."

In high-LTO cultures respecting norms is something that is not particularly valued. We say that these cultures are more flexible, or relativistic. Everything is relative; everything depends on each situation.

5. LONG-TERM ORIENTATION

They way people behave in traffic offers many examples of culture differences, since behavior in traffic is easy to observe and easy to compare, since we can all see it when we travel from one country to another.

Figure 7: The Egyptian shortcut

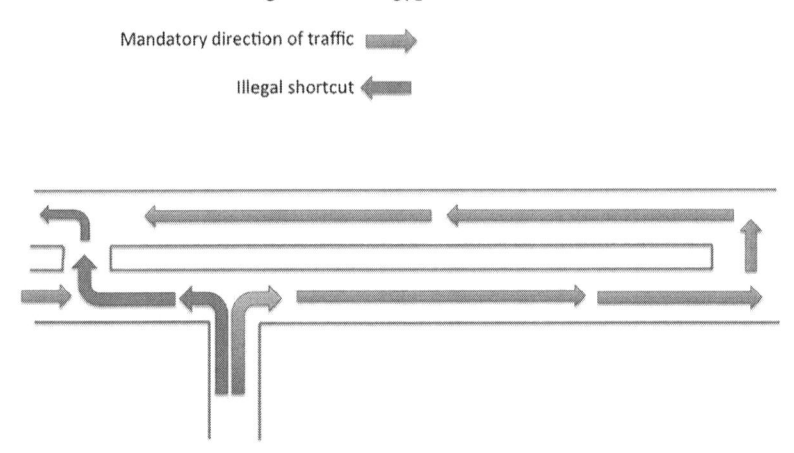

In Egypt, the driver who took me every day from my hotel to my client's office, frequently took a "shortcut" that violated traffic regulations: we came from a small side street onto a six-lane avenue and we wanted to turn left on that avenue. This was forbidden; there was even a central dividing median, built as a barrier to divide the lanes going in opposite directions. This median had been built exactly in front of our side street, clearly with the purpose of stopping people from crossing the avenue and making a left turn. However, there was a small opening in the median, about 30 meters (100 feet) to our left (Figure 7).

What did my driver do, every morning? He drove the wrong way on the avenue, against the oncoming cars, for 30 meters until he reached the opening in the median; he then crossed the avenue and made the left turn that took us in the desired direction. Of course, he only did that early in the morning, when there was less traffic on the avenue, so the risk of causing an accident was relatively low. However, he was violating traffic regulations by driving the wrong way. The drivers of a few cars on the avenue would honk their horns and yell at him in protest; that did not stop him from repeating the manoeuver next day.

From a high-LTO point of view, the ultimate objective (getting quickly to the office) was more important than the means employed (violating traffic rules). There were other ways we might have taken, but they involved driving to the right on the avenue to the next roundabout, about 300 meters away, circling it and then taking the fourth exit to drive on the same avenue in the desired direction. We always had plenty of time that would have allowed us to do that; there was no rush.

This was not an isolated incident. In high-LTO cultures, millions of people do similar things, every day. They violate traffic rules to get faster to where they want.

Physics Lesson

When I was a student in High School, in Brazil, I had a great teacher who taught us Physics, called Alfredo Steinbruch. On his first lesson, he asked our class something about the traffic in my hometown of Porto Alegre.

> "Tell me, do you know the 'Ladeira' Street downtown? (We all knew the street he was referring to and we knew that it was a one-way street, going up the hill towards the city's Main Square.)
>
> "If someone is driving a car on the Main Square, can the person drive the car down the 'Ladeira' Street, going down hill?"
>
> "No!" we all replied as one. This would be "driving on the wrong way", you can't do that.
>
> "Very well," he said. "But every morning I see cars going down the hill on that street, driving the wrong way, for about 50 meters, until they reach the entrance of a parking garage building that is located in the middle of the first block…"
>
> I knew that garage building and, indeed, I had also seen that often some drivers would do that, because otherwise they would need to take a much longer route around most of downtown Porto Alegre, in order to reach "Ladeira" Street at its bottom, and then go up the hill to the garage parking.
>
> "Therefore, you can! It's not that you can't, it's that you SHOULD NOT take that street downhill, because it means driving the wrong way on a one-way street…"

5. LONG-TERM ORIENTATION

> "That is the difference between the laws of men and the laws of Physics," he continued. "When it is said in Physics that something cannot happen, that is because that something really does not ever happen. The laws of human beings tell us what we SHOULD not do, even if it is possible to do it."

In low-LTO societies, the laws of society are considered to be as if they were actual "Laws of Physics," they are respected as if they were absolute truths. In high-LTO cultures, norms are relative. It all depends. Are there cars coming against me in traffic? Is there a policeman standing on the corner who might give me a ticket? Depending on the circumstances, I decide to obey the norm, or not.

Driving Lesson

People's behavior in traffic is also influenced by other culture dimensions, besides the discipline (or lack of it) in relation to following norms. A major influence is Power Distance (PDI).

In egalitarian cultures (low PDI) there is more respect towards pedestrians. The underlying value is that we are all equivalent; in a way, we are all pedestrians, a motorist is just a pedestrian in a car. If a pedestrian is crossing the street at a crosswalk and the culture is low-PDI and low-LTO (equality and self-discipline towards norms), the driver will slow down or even stop the vehicle, waiting for the pedestrian to cross the road. This happens automatically, unconsciously, without thinking, influenced by two factors: respect for others (we are all equivalent – low PDI) and respect for the crosswalk (obeying the rules – low LTO).

In hierarchical cultures (high PDI), whoever has more power exercises this power over those who have less of it. In practice, drivers have the right of way over pedestrians (even at a crosswalk). Buses, because they are bigger, exercise their power over cars, and so on.

In low-PDI cultures it is more commonly seen that a driver on a larger avenue will allow another driver, coming from a side street, to merge into traffic in front of him. This happens because "we are all equal" and respecting your fellow drivers is something valued as part of that broader concept.

In high-PDI cultures we see the opposite happening: drivers on a large avenue have "the right of way" and see no reason to allow other drivers coming from side streets to merge in front of them into the traffic stream. "We are not equal," life is a matter of exercising your power, if you have it, or allow yourself to be overpowered by someone else who has more power than you.

On a different topic: Honking your horn is a behavior linked to Uncertainty Avoidance; it is linked to expressing emotions and to feeling a sense of urgency. Both of these things are associated to higher scores in UAI. In high-UAI cultures you hear more honking in traffic, often to express impatience. In lower-UAI cultures one hears honking less often on the streets.

What is "a Good Driver" like?

The answer to that question, of course, depends on culture. The criteria for describing "good driving" will be different, from culture to culture.

In "normative" cultures (low LTO) the response will describe prudent drivers, those who obey traffic regulations, who respect other vehicles, who drive carefully and cautiously. "Drive carefully!" is a common goodbye phrase in such cultures.

In "flexible" cultures (high LTO) the response will describe agile drivers, capable of reacting quickly, skillful in avoiding obstacles and driving swiftly among many other vehicles, able to arrive quickly at their destination without ever obstructing traffic on their journey.

Think London or Frankfurt as examples of the first kind of "ideal driver"; think New Delhi or Cairo as examples of the latter.

Long Term

Although I have stressed that this dimension is far more complex than simply being about long-term thinking, the fact is that, indeed, time perspective is still an important aspect of LTO.

In countries that score high on LTO there is a greater emphasis on long term goals for companies, a greater focus on positioning for the long term, rather than worrying about quarterly targets or even annual objectives. In practice, what you see is that in these cultures quarterly targets are less important. Commercial enterprises (and also non-profit organizations and government agencies) speak of broader objectives, in the long term, often not very clearly defined, such as, for instance: "gain market share", "increase profitability", "eradicate poverty", "strengthen the middle class", "redistribute income", "increase return on capital." These objectives do not have a defined deadline, or sometimes they have a deadline expressed in decades or "in the next five years." There are countries in Asia that express objectives and strategic planning "for the next 25 years."

In low-LTO cultures there is greater concern over setting clear goals, measurable, with a well-defined short-term deadline. When someone speaks of a long-term objective, such as "gaining market share," they immediately get questions such as: "very well, our long-term objective is to gain market share; how much do we intend to gain in the short term? Next year? On each quarter?" The focus is on knowing, in shorter periods of time, how much progress is being made towards the long-term objective. For that purpose, it is necessary to measure, with clear criteria and at shorter intervals, how much progress is being made.

In these cultures, "SMART objectives" programs are highly successful. The acronym SMART refers to objectives that must be Specific, Measurable, Achievable (yet challenging enough to be motivating), Relevant (to the job that a person is performing) and Time-bound (have a deadline expressed as a target date). This makes perfect sense in low-LTO cultures.

In high-LTO cultures it is also possible to implement SMART objectives. However, it is likely that people will have more difficulty in defining measurement criteria, simply because they are less accustomed to doing so. When the first short-term SMART goals, eventually, are not met, people will naturally tend to understate their importance and refer to the longer-term goals, or to positioning the company in the market (something that is not measurable and has no time perspective) as being more important aspects to consider.

One can often observe disagreements among managers coming from one kind of culture and those coming from a different type, because of the clear divergence in terms of the value assigned to short-term goals. For Anglo-Saxons, measurable short-term objectives are extremely important. For the Indians, the Chinese and most Latin-American cultures, short-term measurement is not so important as positioning yourself for the longer term. Many arguments and attrition ensue, consuming great amounts of energy.

Virtue may very well lie in balance, in this case. Both sides have something to learn from each other. Anglo Saxons might become more effective if they reduced their emphasis on the short term and added a more strategic, long-term view. On the other hand, managers from high-LTO cultures may become more efficient if they learn to follow up their progress by measuring progress at shorter intervals and using objective measurement criteria.

6. Indulgence versus Restraint (IVR)

The sixth dimension in the Hofstede model was not identified by him, but by Michael Minkov, through research published in 2010. Minkov discussed his results extensively with Hofstede, who recognized their validity and accepted to include this sixth dimension in the model.

The definition of this dimension is: "the degree to which people feel in control of their lives and allow themselves to enjoy the simple pleasures of life."

In spite of Professor Hofstede's acceptance of Minkov's research studies, ever since their initial presentation to intercultural communities, this dimension was the object of much discussion.

The definition of the dimension clearly encompasses two inter-related, yet different, aspects. This is the central issue about it: we are talking about two things, and not just one.

"Feeling in control of your life" is one aspect in itself; "allowing yourself to enjoy the simple pleasures of life" is in turn a different aspect.

The first is a culture aspect strongly influenced by the dimensions Power Distance and Individualism. We know that in cultures that score low on PDI and high in IDV people feel "more in charge of their own lives;" individual responsibility is valued in these cultures and people actually seek to "be in control of their lives."

In high-PDI and low-IDV cultures we see practically the opposite: people do not feel as much in control of their own lives, for due to high PDI they consider that power holders actually control everybody else's lives; and in collectivistic societies individual responsibility is less valued. People feel that it is more important to be loyal to a group and allow groups to take care of them, rather than individuals looking after themselves.

This means that the scores found in IVR are strongly influenced by these other two dimensions. One might even question whether this sixth dimension should be a dimension in itself, considering how much it is influenced by the other two. This is one of the reasons why the subject has been the object of much discussion, and consensus has not been reached yet.

Minkov, on one hand, defends the robustness of his statistical calculations. His critics do not challenge the numbers, but they challenge the interpretation of the numbers. A surreal "dialogue of the deaf" has been going on, in which one side proposes to discuss the figures and the other side insists on discussing the psychological meaning of the dimension. The two sides are not listening to each other. They are not really interacting; they are talking over each other, rather than to each other; they are using different radio frequencies, there is no real dialogue.

A different aspect of the discussion regards the practical implication of the sixth dimension. Apparently, it reflects aspects that have little or no influence in ordinary work situations. So, is it really worth having the discussion, beyond academia?

The other five dimensions have shown to be quite useful in practice: they make it easier to understand what happens at work and what must be done to improve the effectiveness of teams and individuals. The usefulness of the sixth dimension has been somewhat restricted to Eastern Europe: practitioners from that area have said that it is often a way to explain differences between American businessmen, who have a more optimistic attitude and readily use jokes as ice-breakers, versus business people from Estonia, Latvia, Ukraine and Bulgaria (for instance), who behave in a more restrained fashion at work.

Possibly there will be more research done about this dimension and that may bring new light into its validity and practical utility. Outside Eastern Europe, it has not been very much used, so far.

Because of all this, I have continued to use Professor Hofstede's framework, as one consisting of five dimensions, as the "5D Model", until the issues about the sixth dimension are resolved. In most work-related situations, the sixth dimension is less relevant than the other five; therefore, the framework is useful to manage people and business with five dimensions already, and this will not change much when we add another dimension eventually.

Part III – A Few Countries

The interaction among different dimensions: a practical analysis of a few relevant cultures.

1. United States of America

Overview

The scores for the USA on the five dimensions are:

- PDI – 40
- IDV – 91
- PER – 62
- UAI – 46
- LTO – 29

In summary, the American culture is more egalitarian than hierarchical, in comparison with other cultures. The score on Power Distance is on the lower side of the scale. Although there are some countries that are even more egalitarian than the US (notably the Scandinavian, the Dutch and the Germanic cultures), America has a culture that is more egalitarian than most of the other cultures researched so far, located in Latin America, Africa, Asia and in Southern and Eastern Europe.

The US is more individualistic than collectivistic; actually, their score of 91 is the highest in the world in this dimension. Clearly, the American culture is more individualistic than any other culture that has been researched.

America's culture is quite geared towards performance. However, its score of 62 does not identify the US as being defined primarily by this aspect. Many other cultures have higher scores than the US in terms of Performance Orientation.

If we wish to summarize what defines American culture as distinctive from others, we need to look at the **combination** of scores rather than at a single dimension in isolation.

What defines American culture in its essence is this combination of egalitarianism, Individualism and Performance Orientation, also in combination with low Uncertainty Avoidance (compared to other cultures) and the fact that the US culture is more normative (low LTO), rather than flexible or relativistic.

When we look at scores from other cultures and compare them to those of the US, we can immediately notice that there are a few other cultures with similar value characteristics: they are all high on Individualism (IDV), low on Power Distance (PDI), high on Performance Orientation (PER) and low on Uncertainty Avoidance (UAI). These countries are the United Kingdom, Canada and Australia; basically, Anglo-Saxon cultures. They all share a similar profile in terms of their underlying core value dimensions.

Of course, there are very relevant culture differences among these countries; however, the differences appear in the more superficial layers of culture, in terms of rituals, symbols and heroes. In the deepest levels, where we find the core underlying values, we can see the similarities. This is the level that most influences people's behavior in terms of work, communication and interpersonal relations.

If you tell an Englishman that his culture is very similar to that of America, most probably the first reaction you will witness will be one of disbelief and plain disagreement. The reason for this is simply because most people are most impressed by what is most visible: the outer layers of culture that can be easily observed.

A superficial comparison portrays these readily apparent differences: the English are more traditional and conservative, overall; they treasure a history that spans over 1,000 years. The Americans, by comparison, are a young nation, who emphasizes the present and the future. The English have a government system based on a parliamentary monarchy; they have institutional nobility with a clear class distinction between "the ruling class" and "the working class." On the other side of the Atlantic, the Americans have a presidential republic with no class distinction. The

"American Dream" is that anyone could become President, since all have equal opportunity.

The British love football, rugby and cricket, sports that they invented; the Americans prefer their own sports: basketball, baseball (inspired by cricket) and American football (inspired by rugby). A recent development is the growing popularity of football, which Americans prefer to call "soccer."

These aspects, however, all refer to the outer layers of culture. When we look at the core values of the US and the UK, and when we observe people's behavior at work and in social situations, we see basic similarities that lead to very similar styles of managing people and businesses.

In this chapter we will focus on the American culture. In a different, much smaller chapter, we will look at the UK culture and what differentiates it from the US in terms of underlying value dimensions.

The land of the free

The US enjoys describing themselves as "the land of the free." This vision of their own culture is directly linked to Individualism (IDV), to the freedom of the individual, to freedom of individual expression. This value manifests itself in many ways, many of them widely spread through American films and television. It is also expressed through popular sayings such as "it's a free country", which reinforce each person's right to say and do what they want.

One can soon observe that freedom is also linked to egalitarianism: no one has the authority to tell me what to do or what to say, because we are all equal. Individual freedom, of course, is something that exists in every culture, to a lesser or greater degree. What is different from one culture to another is exactly the degree by which individual freedom is valued in comparison to the need to respect "the common good."

In all cultures an individual person's freedom is limited by another person's rights. Cultures differ as to what they employ as a practical definition of these limits between "saying and doing whatever I want" and "saying and doing whatever is best for all and is not offensive to others."

Since the American score for Individualism is the highest in the world, we know that in American culture individual freedom is extremely important, perhaps more important than in any other culture. Freedom as a concept is something taken to the extreme: it is the object of huge discussions that galvanize public opinion.

The political movement known as "Tea Party" in the US was created from a feeling of rebellion against the Federal Government, perceived to be interfering with the individual freedom of citizens.

The original "tea party" was a patriotic movement of the American colonists against the despotic power of the King of England, who had just created a tax on tea imports. In protest, a group of colonists boarded a cargo ship docked on Boston harbor and threw all their tea bundles into the water. This incident became known as "the Boston Tea Party" and is considered the first manifestation of American patriotism, to sever ties with England and become an independent nation.

The 21st Century Tea Party Movement was born as a political movement against the interference of Federal Government on individual issues, notably the proposal to adopt a compulsory universal health assistance plan, to be funded through mandatory contributions from all citizens. Although such universal health care systems are quite common in most countries throughout the world, in America it was perceived as a blow to the values of individual freedom, and became hugely controversial. Citizens rose against what they saw as a burdensome tax on the population, imposed by a despotic government; they compared this to the tea tax created in the 18th Century. This conflict between individual interests and the common good is present in many social, political and economic aspects of the American way of life. It also shows in American management techniques and leadership styles.

Freedom to be exploited?

Defending individual liberties goes to the extreme of denying Government the right to intervene even to protect individuals. The Republican Party has been the primary representative of this ideal, even though the party has shown a record of hits and misses, like any political party in any culture.

The core concept behind this is that everyone is responsible for him/herself and there is no need for Government to protect him/her. As

Margaret Thatcher, "the Iron Lady" once said: "there is no such thing as 'society', everyone should look after themselves!" At the most, the State might occasionally protect individuals against crime, by enforcing a few broad and basic general laws (the less rules and regulations, the better). Government should never perform the role of protecting individuals from themselves, from their own decisions.

The opposing view is that this leaves a lot of room for scoundrels and business people with no scruples, who might take advantage of the naïve and foolish individuals in society. However, the doctrine of free markets preaches that government intervention can easily be overdone and end up interfering with individual liberty; therefore, it must be always kept at the minimum possibly necessary.

Even when prominent business leaders proclaim openly that "there's a sucker born every minute!" the idea is that suckers are responsible individuals. As such, they need to know better than to be fooled by a smart person. People should be allowed to freely exploit each other when doing business, as long as they are not breaking the law. The law, by the way, should be very basic and general: there is no need for excessive detail, since that would only complicate things and increase bureaucracy, limiting individual freedom unduly. Beyond the respect for basic laws, anything goes. Excessive government control leads to socialism or communism, systems that have been historically demonized in American culture because they place common interest above individual interests.

From a political point of view, all this leads to some peculiar alliances, between business tycoons interested in exploiting the suckers that are born every minute, and the paladins of individual freedom, who fight against totalitarian regimes that deny the basic human right to liberty.

A culture of competition

The American culture values equal opportunities for all to seek success. Success is obtained by performing well and winning the competition that is life. This concept is based on low Power Distance (all people are equal), on Individualism (everyone has the opportunity to express themselves) and in Performance Orientation (success is obtained through performance).

1. UNITED STATES OF AMERICA

The most important thing is to win (in the contest of life). For the competition to be fair, so that all involved have an equal possibility of winning, it is important to have equality and individual freedom. It is also important to have very clear and simple basic rules. The fewer the rules, the better, since this simplifies the competition. However, the most important rule of all, which must also be extremely clear, is the criterion for deciding the winner. It must be perfectly clear who will be the winner and this usually happens through objective and quantitative measuring.

The objectivity of quantitative measurements increases the clarity and acceptance of the winners in any competition. It should not be about accepting anybody's opinion to declare a winner; there should be "undisputable" criteria.

This may be clearly seen in the practice of competitive sports, where the rules establish a format for accruing points (or goals, or any form of scoring) that define who shall be the winner. The winner is not the one who plays a beautiful game; it is whoever scores the most points or crosses de finish line first.

This clarity of measuring in sports is taken to all aspects of the American way of life.

A nice example of this is regarding beauty contests. The notion of beauty is a subjective one, difficult to measure. A woman might appear beautiful to some and not so beautiful to others. Beauty depends on many subjective factors that affect the perception of the beholder.

Then we have the American approach, brought into force by the culture of competition under objective measurement criteria. In beauty contests, the winner is decided by a panel of judges, a jury assembled for the occasion. If all of them agree on who is the most beautiful among the different candidates, then that person should be declared the winner. However, what should be done when there is disagreement within the jury (something that happens in 99% of cases)? Measurement criteria need to be adopted. Therefore, standard measurements were implemented in inches and their fractions (since the Americans have not adopted the metric system yet) to stipulate that the height of the candidates should never be less than "x" nor greater than "y", that the waist measurement should not exceed "z", that the proportion between hips and waist should be "such", the difference between the measurements of breasts and hips should be no more than "this", and so on.

It's not surprising that soon this approach was criticized for treating women as "pieces of meat." Regardless of "feminist" or "macho" considerations about treating women solely as sex objects (nowadays we can also see some male beauty contests becoming popular), it's important to understand that this all stems from the valuation of competitions and the need to determine a winner objectively.

Crazy for money?

Another way of quantifying things that are difficult to measure is by monetization, or converting their value into financial value. In the US it is common practice to compare the success of professional golf players by adding up the prize money earned during a season, or during their whole career.

This happens because players participate in very different tournaments throughout the year, and some of these contests are more important than others. There are so many golf tournaments, that the players have to make choices and participate in some, but not in others. How do you compare two different players (because you need to have a winner!) who have played in different tournaments during the year? By looking at the accumulated money prizes they have won. This way, you can say that "Leopard Forest" was the best player of 2016 because he accumulated US$ 12,599,641.52 in prize money, while the second best on that year had only US$ 11,781,607.93.

The issue is that money is simply a form of measurement, a way of quantifying success. People from other cultures sometimes criticize the Americans for being "mad about money", but the real issue is not money in itself. The issue is how do you determine who is the winner in the competition of life.

As a consequence you also see lists of "the richest people in the world" published in business magazines. No magazine has ever published a list of "the 50 happiest people in the world"… That would be considered ridiculous. And why would it be ridiculous? Because (American) people's goal in life is not simply to "find happiness", but rather "to be a winner."

And how do you determine who are "the winners?" Through objective quantitative measurement, preferably linked to performance.

Another consequence of this passion for competition is the widespread practice of "pay for performance" as a management tool. If performance is of utmost importance, then (financial) reward must be linked to it, rather than to other factors such as hierarchy, seniority, tenure, etc. In this context, bonus plans linked to performance acquire a significant role.

The US has developed a practice of paying out significant performance bonus amounts, which often exceed the annual fixed salary of corporate executives and can reach figures in the millions. The main thing, once again, is not the money in itself, but rather what those figures represent on the score-sheet of the competition of life. An executive might be quite pleased when he gets a 5 million-dollar bonus for his performance at the end of the year. This joyful feeling might quickly fade as he learns that a colleague is getting a 6 million dollar bonus. This means that he has "lost" the competition… The 5 million are worth much less, if they are not a symbol of victory.

Only what can be measured has value

This emphasis on measurement is very useful in the business world, where performance is essential to an organization's fulfillment of its purpose. However, there are other aspects in life that involve interpersonal relations, friendship, love, enjoying the company of other people at work or in social situations. These aspects may be distorted or become dysfunctional due to an exaggerated emphasis on measuring performance.

It's easy to measure the performance of a salesperson, tallying his/her sales volume in money terms. Ii is much more difficult to evaluate a salesperson's performance if "Jack Salesman" sells a lot but his peers hate working with him, his clients complain and switch to a competing company because they feel cheated by Jack in negotiating prices and deliveries. Meanwhile, "Joe" does not sell as much, but his clients are satisfied and he always gets a lot of repeat business, year after year. At the company, everybody enjoys working with Joe, because he's such a nice guy, always willing to give a hand.

The challenging issue here is how to measure the differences in performance, going beyond simply looking at sales volume. In a different culture, perhaps more hierarchical and collectivistic, the Team Head, who supervises both Jack and Joe, will usually have absolute authority to pass judgment subjectively and decide. He might fire Jack and promote Joe, for instance, and nobody would challenge his authority as boss (if indeed they are part of a hierarchical and collectivistic culture).

Since the American culture is egalitarian and individualistic, the boss's decision needs to be justified as being right. Any decision might be challenged (since all are equal and all have a right to express their opinions) and it will only be accepted if it is consistent with other values within the same culture. In this case, consistency is required in relation to the performance, as objectively measured. The boss's decision is accepted when it is supported by measurement.

This is also the reason why many organizations adopt a "balanced scorecard" (for individuals, teams, departments and whole companies). In these scorecards there are measurements relating to various aspects of the business: finance (sales, revenue, profit, return on investment, etc.), relationships with clients (client satisfaction surveys, number of complaints filed, etc.), managing people (employee turnover, time to fill vacancies with new hires, internal promotions, etc.) and also aspects linked to internal process efficiency (time to market, production schedules, quality standards, etc.).

All these management practices and forms of measurement originated in the US and UK, including "Management by Objectives". They are all ways of making it easier to determine who are the winners in the competition of life.

The bigger, the better

Competitions based on sheer size are the easiest to judge, since size is something not only easy to measure, but often clearly visible to all involved. It is only when two competing entities are similar in size that it will effectively be necessary to actually measure it. Therefore, American culture values size in many things, because subjectively it is the easiest way to verify who is winning the competition of life.

All this, of course, is subconscious; but it is not difficult to observe the manifest expressions of this phenomenon.

American cars are bigger, more powerful; they have bigger motors, that consume more fuel, but the fact is that American consumers prefer big and powerful cars. While German cars prioritize reliability and resistance, French cars try to innovate in appearance and elegant design, and the Japanese seek innovation in electronic components, American carmakers continue to emphasize size and power above all else.

In American society an expression was coined referring to "living large," a way of summarizing a lifestyle. This means having a big house with big rooms, a big car, a large-screen TV set, large-sized furniture and so on. The whole idea is that bigger is better.

In large corporations, good performance is rewarded with things that are visibly bigger: the more important the job, the bigger the office, the bigger the company car.

The corporation itself should be located in a large (and tall) building. The building entrance should be large and sumptuous, to impress visitors since the very first contact with the company. Similarly, hotels are valued for their size, for the number of rooms, the amount of swimming pools and restaurants (even if the quality of the latter might be debatable).

In interpersonal relations size is again important: a man should have a large penis, a woman should have large breasts. A fiancée should get a wedding ring with a large diamond. Design of the ring is secondary; it is valued for the size of the precious stone, above all.

Neighbors compete among each other with status symbols based on size: a big house, a big car, also a big lawn in front of the house, a big swimming pool in the back yard. A garden is not valued so much for its design or the quality of its maintenance, but mostly for its size.

The cult of heroes

No other culture expresses so intensely its admiration for the role of the hero as a "winner." American heroes are those who won because they performed better than their peers or their enemies.

The American hero is the one who does more or better than others. It is true that every culture has its heroes; it is also true that each culture values as heroes those characters who reflect the values of that culture. Therefore, American heroes are those who perform better and especially those who came from a humble background (egalitarianism) and who achieved their victory single-handed (Individualism), with no help from others. They became heroes not by luck or for being favored by others, but due to their performance. After all, the US is also the culture that most favors meritocracy as a management style.

Heroes in America are admired with a sort of "white envy": people want to be like them. In other cultures there might be "green envy" towards "winners," that is: people might bear ill wishes towards those who beat everyone else, or resent those who have the prestige you would like to have yourself. In such other cultures, winners can easily acquire enemies simply because others envy (in a bad way) what they have achieved.

In the American culture heroes have as enemies only their direct competitors, or those who aim to beat them in the next round of competition. Those who do not compete with them directly, tend to become admirers.

It is no wonder that a society that admires its heroes so much and where equality creates opportunities for many heroes to sprout has also been the birthplace of "superheroes", the ultimate super-winners.

The first superhero was Superman. To this day, he is the most famous, worldwide. He was "super" not because he was the most virtuous, or the most handsome or the most pure; he was super because of his performance, because of what he could do. In the original version, created in 1939, he did not have "supernatural" powers": he could not fly, but he was able to leap high and far, even jumping over tall buildings.

In other words, he could do the same things other men could do, only more and better. He was stronger, he could run faster, jump higher, and his skin was harder.

As years went by, other competing superheroes appeared in comic books and the authors gave the original Superman some additional superpowers so that he could remain competitive: x-ray vision, telescopic vision, heat vision, super-hearing, and the ability to fly.

The most revered heroes, however, are those who are just like anybody else and who managed to win on their own. They reinforce the idea that "anyone can be a winner."

Rocky, the character created by Sylvester Stallone in the movies, is the prime example. The film won the Best Picture Award from the Hollywood Academy of Motion Picture Arts and Sciences, became a box-office hit and generated six sequels (so far). The public already knows the plot, which is basically the same one, repeated in every sequel, and everyone knows how each film is going to end (with a happy ending), but they never tire of watching the same story over and over again, like a child who asks her father to read her favorite bedtime story once again before she goes to sleep.

Stories that reinforce a culture's values are the ones that become part of national folklore and continue from generation to generation, contributing to the perennial aspect of a culture's essence.

Employee of the month

The appreciation of performance in American organizations is focused on individual performance, rather than team achievements. It's due to the combination of high Performance Orientation and the world's highest score in Individualism; this explains the emphasis on the individual who performs better than his peers. This is also the foundation of meritocracy.

Years ago, I was the HR Director for Banco Iochpe in Brazil and we formed a joint venture with Bankers Trust New York. I traveled to the American bank's Head Office and proposed the implementation, in Brazil, of a bonus scheme that would reward not only individual performance, but also team performance. My argument was that we should reward both teamwork and outstanding individuals.

My boss in New York did not even want to talk about it. "We are committed to rewarding individual excellence, it's simple," he told me flatly. "Anything different from that will distract attention from what we want to focus on: individual excellence. There's nothing to discuss."

Throughout the years, many individual performance reward and recognition schemes were created in the US, beyond cash bonuses. There are many incentives and rewards, financial and non-financial, such as medals, trophies, travel, household appliances, homes and automobiles, all of them offered to staff who perform in an outstanding way.

One of these typically American schemes is the "employee of the month" award. Years ago many companies chose an "employee of the year" to serve as an example for all others; other organizations gave out a "President's award" to outstanding individuals, usually also once a year. These practices were born in the USA, but they were used by American companies all over the world, wherever they had branches and subsidiaries.

Then someone had the idea of increasing the frequency of these awards and created the "employee of the month" concept, one that has become well known all over the world through the McDonald's chain of fast-food restaurants. Clients can see the name and picture of the employee of the month hanging on the wall just behind the counter.

Other companies followed suit and the concept spread all over the world.

However, one has to be careful when using such incentive schemes; they will work very well in individualistic cultures with a high Performance Orientation, but not necessarily elsewhere. In other cultures, where one finds a tendency towards Collectivism, or with a lower Performance Orientation, the ultimate effect might be the opposite of the initial intention.

In the Netherlands, giving an award to the "employee of the month" is something that backfired; instead of motivating people, it made staff members upset. This is because in the Netherlands someone who is picked out to stand out above his or her peers becomes the target of "green envy," rather than "white envy." Standing out is considered inappropriate in that culture; it is tantamount to showing off and bragging, and all of that is frowned upon. Rather, the Dutch culture values equality, leveling, and considers performance less important than quality of life and caring for others.

The "employee of the month" scheme is regarded in the Netherlands as a form of undue favoring of one employee in detriment of others. People consider that no individual team member will perform well without support from all other colleagues, each doing his or her part to make the whole work right. It is actually de-motivating for the team to see that one person only gets picked to stand out among the rest; and it is demotivating for the chosen individual, who feels uncomfortable from being singled out and becomes the target of "green envy."

Another example of how this practice may be rejected comes from China, due to Collectivism. In spite of the fact that the Chinese culture is quite performance-oriented, it puts greater value on the collective efforts of a team, rather than on one person standing out among all others. Unless, of course, that person is the formal team leader: the boss is allowed to stand out, because of the position of authority enjoyed by a boss in the hierarchy. The team, however, is more important than any of its members.

This is a problem often faced by American managers of multinational companies: the organization was successful in its home market and begins to grow beyond borders, opening branches in different parts of the world. What made it successful in the US, however, will not necessarily make it equally successful elsewhere, depending on local culture.

I once met an American entrepreneur who boasted about leading "a very international business, quite successful in different cultures." Our conversation revealed that the company had branches in Canada, the UK, Australia and New Zealand. It just so happens that all these countries share a very similar set of core values, besides also sharing a common language.

This business leader confessed that they were in the process of opening their first branch in the Middle East, but they were facing a number of difficulties that they had never encountered before. That is because they were, for the first time, dealing with a culture that had core values completely different from their own.

The American Challenge

The US, the UK and Canada publish two thirds of the management literature on the planet. The management principles described in this literature are the foundation for most graduate business courses, not only in those countries, but also in many universities and business schools almost all over the world. What few people realize, both in America and in other countries as well, is that these management principles and practices carry within them a cultural Anglo-Saxon bias. This means that all of this is very valid in an Anglo-Saxon culture, but doing the same things in another context might lead to disastrous results.

Think of it: you're a young Business School graduate in the UK and you've done very well in your studies; you get your first job in London and you do equally well. After three years or so, because of your very good performance, the company moves you to an overseas operation that needs boosting: not to some far-flung branch on the other side of the planet, but simply across the English Channel to the Netherlands, a country with a reach history of partnering with American and British companies. You get there and your first impression is that the Dutch look pretty much the same as your colleagues back home (except that there are more bikes). People dress in a similar way at the office, they all speak English fluently and you see familiar brands on outdoor advertisements.

As you start working with your Dutch colleagues you can get quite a shock: they behave quite differently regarding a number of issues. Meetings are run differently, targets are set in a different way, the attitude and communication style is different. Things that you learned in college and applied successfully at home are handled very differently here, such as performance appraisals, reporting, delegating, and negotiating running projects.

British managers who insist in doing things abroad exactly in the same way as they did at home, show a lack of sensitivity, to say the least. Companies in other cultures who blindly adopt Anglo-Saxon practices without making the necessary adjustments, show a lack of intelligence, to say the least.

The free market culture

When Adam Smith, a Scotsman (Anglo-Saxon culture), published his ideas in the 18th Century, he established the principles of what is now known as "the free market economy," which remain valid for many conservative economists to this very day.

Smith is misquoted as saying that "people behave rationally according to their own self-interests and the economy maintains its balance as if guided by an invisible hand." The truth is that Smith never said that in so many words; this is rather a summary of some of his ideas, gathered from three different books and pieced together by 20th Century economists to form the concept of a "market economy" devoid of government intervention.

They forgot to tell these economists that Adam Smith's ideas were the product of a certain era and of a certain culture. The principles may still be valid for an individualistic and egalitarian culture oriented towards performance. In a hierarchical and collectivistic culture with low Performance Orientation, the market works differently. This happens not because these markets are underdeveloped, but because they are driven by different underlying values.

In a global economy, where many different cultures are in constant interaction, the market is much more complex and is no longer consistent with Mr. Smith's principles, which were valid for 18th Century England (and also for America in those days). The situation in the 21st Century is quite different and Smith's principles no longer apply to a globalized world.

The contract culture

In a culture where people act according to their own self-interests, the celebration of formal contracts is important and necessary. Such written documents establish clearly, explicitly and in detailed form, the obligations and rights of all parties involved in a commercial relationship. This is needed do define the limits among the individual rights of each party and the rights of the remaining parties.

In collectivist cultures such as most found in Asia, Africa and Latin America, a contract is considered to be "an instrument signed between friends to be used between enemies." That is to say: a contract is signed to formalize a business relationship, but it is only used when there is disagreement between the parties involved. Only then do people refer to the contract's clauses to support their arguments in discussions or in a legal dispute.

In the American culture contracts are references used frequently during their duration. They are used not only to confront the other party in case of disagreement or conflict. Contracts are consulted to clarify whether we are all doing what we effectively agreed to do. "This issue here:

is it our responsibility or is it the other party's? Can we do this? Should we do this? What does it say in the contract?"

Contracts are usually long and detailed, since one of their purposes is to reflect the totality of the business relationship among the involved parties.

Whenever something pops up that had not been foreseen in the contract, what do you do? A meeting between the relevant parties to agree on how to proceed in face of the unforeseen circumstances; followed by the joint writing of an additional clause to the contract, describing what has just been agreed, for future reference.

People used to say that banking loan contracts were quite extensive for a reason: they included an additional clause for every single case in which a client had refused to pay a loan. Each time someone refused to pay a bank and took the case to court, a new clause was added to the standard contract, in order to strengthen the bank's legal position if ever the same situation were to occur in the future.

The advantage of using contracts in this way is that it provides clear references. The disadvantages include the fact that by doing so the business relationship is restricted to the terms of the contract. This prevents the mutual commitment to become broader or deeper, going beyond what was originally foreseen and put in writing.

Employment contracts are a good example of this. In collectivist and hierarchical cultures, such as my native Brazil, labor contracts are short and very broad. They are usually one or two pages long, contain a dozen clauses or so and basically state that an employee must do whatever his/her boss tells him/her to do, throughout their whole employment career with the company, as long as it does not go against the law. In such cultures, staff members never refuse to do something and say that "it's not in my contract!"

In America the typical employment contract is a bit longer and more detailed. It does not cover the whole employment relationship throughout a person's career within the same organization. Usually, it refers solely to a certain job or function; and when the person is promoted to a different job or transferred to another location, this requires negotiating a new contract outlining new responsibilities, or at least adding some clauses to the original contract.

In this kind of contract environment, it is fairly common for a staff member to refuse doing a certain task, saying: "this is not in my contract," or: "I did not sign up for this!" If this happened in a hierarchical culture, a refusal like this would cause immediate firing of the employee. In America, the employee is merely exercising his right as an individual, restricting his/her duties to whatever is described in the contract. The employee takes responsibility for whatever is in the contract; whatever is not there, is not the staff member's responsibility.

Years ago, as Chief HR Officer in a multinational organization, I discussed with an executive from Head Office the issue of a stressed Country Manager in Latin America.

The executive I was talking to came from an egalitarian and individualistic culture. His comment was: "the problem with this Country Manager is that he thinks he is responsible for everything, that is why he is so stressed!"

In a hierarchical and collectivist culture, such as most cultures in Latin America, Africa and Asia, bosses consider themselves to really be "responsible for everything." In the US culture, individualist and egalitarian, each individual has a clearly limited responsibility, pertaining to his/her own actions in performing a job described in a contract. This holds true even for Country Managers and CEO's.

Litigation culture

In a "Contest Culture" such as the United States (and also in other Anglo-Saxon cultures) litigation is a way of determining whether the rules of the competition were followed, if the competition was indeed fair, and if the pertinent parties have complied with whatever was agreed in a contract.

In other cultures one can often see people joking about what is perceived as "the American obsession with suing everybody, no matter how silly the issue." Many anecdotes circulate on the internet about so-called absurd court cases, such as the woman who sued McDonald's for spilling hot coffee on her own lap while leaving a Drive-Thru, and many other similar cases.

In American TV and movies there are numerous plots that reach their climax in a court scene. This happens in all kinds of stories: action, thrillers, crime, politics, romantic comedies… It is remarkable how often these stories are constructed to have their peak at a court scene, in which the audience will see the final outcome of the whole plot.

This happens because the court is the ultimate instance to decide who will be the winner in the competition of life. For this reason, a judgment in court has a much stronger emotional impact in the American culture.

Black and white

This is also connected to Hofstede's fifth dimension: Long Term Orientation (LTO). As we've seen earlier, this dimension reflects not only a time perspective, but also most of all issues pertaining do normativity and relativism (see Part II, Chapter 5).

In the American culture, which is normative, it is important to know "who is right," since there is always "a right way to do things, and a wrong way."

Issues tend to be perceived in extremes: either clearly "black" or clearly "white." There is little room for different shades of grey. This way of thinking is rather the opposite of the "Tao" symbol in the Zen culture, and the concept of "yin" and "yang." In Zen culture "black" contains a bit of white in its own composition; and "white" contains a bit of black. Therefore, everything is relative, and in real life there is no pure white nor pure black: everything is a variation of grey. Zen culture is the epitome of relativism, the opposite of normativity.

There is a tendency towards polarizing and taking issues to an impasse, when one side does not win against the other. None of the parties is willing to concede and both have equivalent force. This is normativity combined with Individualism and egalitarianism.

Facing a deadlock, it is necessary to resort to a tribunal court, in order to resolve the issue and decide on a winner and a loser. Once this is done, a new contest may begin. The match is over, but the championship tournament continues. Tournaments may end, but the competition of life continues always, until its ultimate end in death.

Conflict culture

In many cultures conflicts are avoided. Conflicts always imply in a certain degree of risk, and at work they may have a number of negative effects on team spirit and organizational climate, distracting people's attention from performing their tasks.

In the American culture, conflicts are regarded as a part of life and as something that needs to be accepted, instead of avoided. They should be faced head on, as a challenge, and managed. This values message is present in all American films, in fiction writings and also in technical management literature, in Business Schools and MBA courses.

I once discussed with an Anglo Saxon and a Spanish manager what was the best way to manage a conflict between two members of the same team. The Anglo-Saxon said: "I would call them both to my office and tell them that they should resolve the issue right there and then in front of me, and that would only be allowed to leave the room after they had resolved it, one way or another!"

The Spaniard said: "I would never do that! I would talk to each of them separately, in private, asking them to resolve the issue between them, but I would never bring them together into my office for a confrontation!"

Once again: there is no single right way to do things, when we compare cultures; each has its own preferred way, consistent with its own values-system.

In the American culture confrontation is preferred. It is a direct approach, with no beating around the bush, no dissimulation. Speaking separately with each employee is considered "office politics," fostering gossip, fear of facing the situation, etc.

The American way of embracing conflict and treating things as either "black" or "white" can be seen every day on the news.

When positioning himself for the invasion of Iraq, President George W. Bush simplified the issue in his address to the international community: "you are either with us, or against us; you need to take a position." He left no room for neutrality.

When many European countries (except the Anglo-Saxons) hesitated, attempting to resolve the issue with Iraq through diplomacy and taking a neutral stand in the impending conflict, American public opinion immediately interpreted that as "they are against us."

Even French fries suffered from this. Many Americans began a boycott of French products; but to stop eating fried potatoes, an American staple food for decades, would be asking a bit too much… A politician began a campaign to call potato chips "Freedom Fries," a way to make a patriotic statement every time you had a meal, opposing anything French. Perhaps without realizing it, he was proposing something consistent with the very core of the American culture: Individualism and freedom.

My favorite enemy

This aspect also manifests itself in the need to "have an enemy" against whom it is necessary to fight. Without an enemy, there is no competition and life has no purpose.

For many years the enemies were the English, against whom it was necessary to fight the Independence War in order to become an autonomous country in 1776. The animosity persisted for many years and spanned generations, fed by the need to remain independent.

In the 20th Century the enemy was Communism, demonized by the US media as "an enemy of individual freedom." During World War II the enemy was Nazi Germany, equally demonized by the media. Once again, this demonization persisted for generations, long after the war was over. Nowadays, in the 21st Century, American books and films clearly depict "the good guys" and "the bad guys," polarizing situations as always reflecting "the eternal fight between Good and Evil." The "bad guys" have German or Russian accents, even a century after WWII was over and half a century after the fall of Russian Communism.

The ascension of China as an economic world power brought with it the consequence of becoming "the next enemy." Actually, in real life, two big economic powers do not necessarily have to be enemies. They do not need to march towards confrontation and war. In the American collective unconscious, however, this confrontation is something permanent and unavoidable.

This also explains the attitude of most American politicians and diplomats to reject the idea of "multilateralism." In the American mindset, there is always polarization and conflict. This is seen as an essential part of life, and as something that will eventually result in positive things. According to this mindset, conflicts are the foundation of creativity and of dynamic balance. They should be accepted rather than be avoided, both at a "micro" level (among individuals and teams at work) and at a "macro" level (in international relations).

The Brazilian author Luis Fernando Veríssimo once said that "Americans are simple minds." The statement is consistent with the issue of polarization, which is a way of simplifying complex interaction among multiple conflicting forces.

In the 1991 movie "City Slickers" the character played by Jack Palance was an old cowboy who gave life lessons to the "city slicker" coming from New York City, played by Billy Cristal.

Looking at the sunset, he said: "In life, you have to find that 'one thing' that gives meaning to all other things…"

"And what is that?" asked the New Yorker.

"That's what you have to find out: what is that 'one thing,'" said the cowboy.

This scene summarizes this American cultural value: life can be reduced to one single thing that gives meaning to everything else. To a Frenchman, whose culture treasures conceptual complexity, this American notion might seem "ridiculously simple-minded," an unacceptable and misleading form of reductionism. To an American, the French conceptual complexity is a misleading distraction, because life is essentially simple.

Both these cultures have nurtured a love-hate relationship for centuries: the Americans (and also the British) despise the intellectual complexity of the French; at the same time, they have a certain admiration for this ability to deal with complex issues and for the French approach to discussing concepts passionately. On their part, the French criticize the British and the Americans for their oversimplification of issues, while at the same time nurturing admiration for their ability to focus on a simplified way of looking at reality.

When President Obama was awarded the Nobel Peace Prize barely a year after being in office, most Americans were taken by surprise. This award went against some of their collective Superego assumptions: Obama had not **done** anything spectacular to deserve the award, and awards are supposed to be given to people who **do** something, who perform in an outstanding way. Besides, his statements supporting diplomacy were perceived as a **lack** of decisive action and a sign of weakness. How can someone get an award for showing weakness and not doing things?

President Obama faced a curious issue in terms of his popularity: he was much more popular outside the United States of America than within his own country. That is because his diplomatic stance was well received abroad, but regarded in the US as a sign of weakness.

Hillary Clinton was more popular than Obama, because her personal style was more confrontational, and, as such, much closer to the American ideal of embracing conflict and winning competitions.

Who is "number one?"

Life is a competition in which it is important to win and be admired as a winner. This is tantamount to being "number one," the best of all. Whoever finishes in second place (according to the American mentality) is already "a loser." In doesn't matter if the second place has beaten 56 other contenders: even so, he is regarded as "a loser."

The American culture has incorporated these terms into daily use: people regularly refer to others as winners or losers. This is emphasized by the normative aspect of culture: there is no middle ground. A person is either a winner or a loser. There can only be one winner. Everybody else is a loser.

This aspect is also connected to the short-term mentality, and it allows a winner, admired by many, to be rapidly converted into a loser. All it takes is to lose one competition, to miss expectations in a certain situation, to fail to resolve a challenge with the expected speed and accuracy, and the hero falls in disgrace; his previous victories disappear from collective memory at an amazing speed.

A President who has been elected by a landslide can quickly become unpopular; a sports idol can be publicly thrashed. The expectations thrust upon a winner are quite high and difficult to be continuously satisfied. The people, unconsciously, want new winners, because this frequent rotation at the podium reinforces the notion that "anyone can make it to the top." If the winner is always the same person, that diminishes the chances of others who want their turn at winning.

Equal opportunity of winning must prevail, so that everyone may get another chance, yet another opportunity. Whoever lost needs to get back in the game and seek victory in the next round. This way, the competition remains interesting and everyone can nurture the hope of one day becoming "number one," becoming famous and admired.

Andy Warhol said that "in the future, everybody will be famous for 15 minutes." His comment was an acid criticism towards the fact that there were more and more people becoming famous, promoted by the American media, hungry for new winners to adore. Yet, this fame was increasingly shorter, because the media needed to constantly make room for new winners to take their turn at the top.

Optimism and arrogance

In order to maintain momentum and keep the competition constantly alive and interesting for participants and onlookers, people should express optimism in every situation. Pessimism is rejected; optimism and the expression of self-confidence are greatly valued.

To other cultures this may seem like arrogance and cockiness. In the American culture, it's a matter of survival.

> *A Dutch Country Manager from a multinational corporation told me that years ago he was assigned to his company's branch in Australia.*
>
> *He was welcomed by the Administration Manager, un American expat, who told him: "We were waiting for your arrival in order to make the final decision about three candidates that we have for a single vacancy as management trainee. The three are the finalists after a long selection process. We had about 50 candidates for the job and we narrowed it down to these three. We'd like you to meet each of them for an interview and to make the final choice."*
>
> *The Country Manager interviewed the three candidates and met with the Administration Manager at the end of the day.*

> "Actually," he started, "I didn't like any of them… They are all very arrogant and conceited! They spent the whole time talking about themselves and how talented they were! I would not hire any of them!"
>
> The discussion that followed between them revealed that both had a very different idea about what constituted "a good candidate" for the job. The Administration Manager valued self-confidence and a "can do" attitude, while the Country Manager saw those traits as negative aspects.

Eventually a fourth candidate was hired, someone they both could agree on. It was only a few years later, when the Country Manager followed a Cross-culture Management course, that he realized that their difference of opinion about the candidates was based on culture differences.

When individuals express self-confidence, they are not only "talking about themselves." In the American culture, people interacting with them see in their behavior also the reinforcement of that cultural value. Self-confidence is important and everyone should express it. This reinforces the notions of equality and equal opportunity for all and it endorses how important it is to compete to win.

If you ever watch football (soccer for American readers) in British television, it is striking how the narrators and commentators attribute a player's success to his degree of self-confidence. Whoever shows self-confidence and commitment is playing well; whoever plays badly, does so because they are lacking confidence. As you listen to them, it appears that talent has got nothing to do with a player's performance in the game.

Similarly, in professional tennis, two players have amazed American and British commentators because of their casual style of playing: Nicholas Kyrgios and Dustin Brown. When you watch them play, it is striking that they play in a way that appears to be very relaxed, but they both regularly score some incredible points in very unusual ways. They have talent in abundance, but the fact that they seem so relaxed is actually disturbing to American (and British) commentators, because it goes against the culture value of commitment being more important than talent.

Instead of praising the players' great talent, commentators often criticize them for not appearing to be as committed as they should.

The reason for this is that these kinds of comments, unconsciously, serve to feed the notion that commitment is central to success. Everyone has equal opportunities, anyone can play well and become winners, if only they can believe in themselves and try hard. If sports commentators focused their observations on talent, they would be emphasizing the differences among players and not their equality; and this goes against the basic values of the Anglo-Saxon culture.

Lay an egg and sing like a rooster

Some people have said that Americans "lay an egg and sing like a rooster;" that is to say: they do something ordinary, that any chicken can do, but they sing as loud as a rooster, calling attention and advertising what they have done.

Indeed, this behavior can readily be observed and it is linked directly to Individualism (treasuring self-expression) and Performance Orientation (boasting about your performance).

It is important to advertise your own performance, this is valued and is not perceived as undue bragging. In a culture where everyone speaks out about what they have done well, if you do not do the same, then you will fall back in the competition, you will go by unnoticed.

Because of all this, the advertising industry is highly developed in the USA and in all Anglo-Saxon cultures.

Also connected to these two dimensions is the proliferation of self-help literature, emphasizing self-confidence as the most important attribute to become personally and professionally successful. In recent years there has also been an increase in the concepts of personal marketing and self-branding: how to advertise yourself as if you were a product. To Americans, doing personal marketing is easier; it comes naturally, reinforced by culture. In other societies it is much more difficult, notably in those cultures that frown upon standing out as an individual (for instance: the Scandinavians and the Dutch).

Privacy

In individualist societies privacy is very important and the US is no exception. If, on one hand, Americans like to boast about their performance to one and all, the fact is that each individual is the sole judge about what should be made public about his or her personal life. Plus, in many cases, other people do not like to hear about anyone's private life.

Invasion of privacy goes against the value of individual freedom. If such an invasion happens through the actions of Government or of any authority figure, this is even worse: it also goes against the value of equality (low Power Distance), which stipulates that "no one has authority over myself regarding my own life."

In the USA invasion of privacy cases have a big impact on public opinion. They are more important than many other crimes and misdemeanors.

The Watergate scandal that led to the ousting from office of President Nixon started with the issue that people who were part of his campaign for re-election were eavesdropping on phone conversations carried out by his political opponents. This wire-tapping of private conversations gave relevance to the whole case, which snowballed and culminated with his resignation to avoid the formal impeachment procedure approved by a committee in the House of Representatives.

By contrast, the faults committed by President Clinton, accused of having sex with a White House intern and later lying about it to Congress, were not sufficient to remove him from office. You might say that American public opinion put more weight on Nixon's invasion of privacy than on Clinton's adultery and lying.

Short Term

The typical American mindset is more geared towards short-term perspectives, both at work and in interpersonal relationships. Factory workers refer to their wages per week (compared to per month in other cultures). Companies listed on the stock exchange must report their financial situation every quarter (compared to once a year in other cultures). Stock prices fluctuate significantly on the same day, immediately after certain bits of news are made public: the market does not wait for an analysis of longer term trends, but rather reacts on the spot to any variation of company performance in the short term.

This is all linked to the contest mentality. In any competition it is important to gauge your progress during its course and not only after it is finished, so that you may correct your performance. The shorter the time frame by which you have information about how well you are doing in comparison to your competitors, the better your ability to adjust your own performance accordingly, by increasing or decreasing your pace, improving your aim, etc.

This focus on the short term has advantages and disadvantages. It allows organizations to adapt rapidly to changes in their market; on the other hand, it may lead to hasty decisions when it would be wiser to wait a bit longer and confirm if those market changes are indeed part of a consistent longer term trend, or just a hiccup with temporary impact.

In the 90's I watched an interview on TV with the CEO of Merryl Linch, one of the leading stockbrokers in the New York Stock Exchange. He was being interviewed to explain why they had just announced earlier in the day that they were firing 3,600 staff. He stated that the decision was another demonstration of the company's competence, because they knew the market better than anybody.

The Dow-Jones Stock Index had fallen from 6,000 to 5,800 points in the previous week. He explained that this fall was the beginning of a downward trend; the whole American economy was beginning to slow down. Merryl Linch was showing that they were not afraid of facing the difficult days that were about to come; they decided to act quickly and reduce the size of their workforce. Sooner or later other Wall Street firms would need to do the same, due to market circumstances. Once again, his company was demonstrating their effectiveness by taking action more quickly than their competitors.

But he was wrong… A week later, stocks went back up. In another week, the index went over 6,000 points and continued to climb steadily until it reached 7,500 points, three months later. Merryl Linch had spent a fortune in severance pay, and then had to hire new staff to replace the people they had fired. Today, that firm no longer exists: it was one of the first "victims" of the financial meltdown of 2008, taken over by Bank of

America before it was declared bankrupt. Its brand name has been assigned to the Wealth Management division of the bank.

When norms are taken literally

In 2012 The Pentagon made a small change in the form that was sent to Americans living overseas (both civilians and military) and who intended to vote in the November elections.

A field was added in which a person had to choose between two options:

1. I intend to return to live in the United States as a resident.
2. I do not intend to return to the US as a resident.

This small item caused a widespread discussion and was the object of a half-page article on The New York Times. Let it be noted that the Pentagon's intention was simply to determine what type of ballot should be sent for those expatriates who were voting abroad. Whoever ticked the box "I intend to return" would get a ballot that included state and county elections, in addition to the presidential one. Whoever did not intend to return would get a ballot for the presidential election only.

People were at a loss about how they should respond to that item. They took the question literally and considered that their response implicated them in a life-long commitment (a typical reaction in a normative culture).

If they ticked the box "I intend to reside in the US again," they felt that this meant that they would have to necessarily return, some day. Not returning would be somehow considered a breach of their promise to do so, and they might be accused of lying to the government, or something similar.

On the other hand, if they ticked the box "I do not intend to return…" it seemed to mean that they might never be allowed to return, that this option of returning might be denied to them in the future, if they ever changed their minds.

Apparently, many people considered that "changing their minds" would be severely frowned upon; it might be considered a crime or a misdemeanor. In other cultures people might tick any of the two boxes without a second thought; they would consider that it was merely an expression of their intention at present, but anyone is allowed to have a change of heart at any other time, without suffering negative consequences as a result of that.

Cultures such as Brazil and The Netherlands have a higher score in LTO and deal more easily with flexibility. In the American culture, which is much more normative, expressing an intention implies (in people's minds) a legally bonding commitment (even if it is not so, in practice).

Crime, punishment and revenge

In the American culture many drivers lead to a certain difficulty in forgiving and forgetting. Crimes and misdemeanors carry heavy sentences, often exaggerated. Public opinion rejects crime and any offence towards cultural norms and laws, going beyond that: it demands that the offender be severely punished and that there must be some form of retribution to the victim and to society, to compensate for the offense. These aspects may be taken to extremes seldom seen in so-called "civilized" societies.

Criminals and legal offenders in general are punished so harshly that it becomes quite difficult to rehabilitate them. Actually, the whole concept of rehabilitation is challenged, since the penal system emphasizes punishment and retribution, rather than rehabilitation. When someone breaks a rule in American culture (whether it is a legal issue, or not), strong desire for vengeance is unleashed, to an extent that goes far beyond correction of behavior or punishment.

This is evident in the proliferation of films in which killing criminals and taking justice into your own hands is a behavior presented as plainly justified. The ultimate message is: killing other people is allowed, as long as they deserved to die. The fact that when you kill a criminal you are also committing a crime is presented as being beside the point. The issue is supported by the cultural values of treasuring competition, tolerating violence, and by normativism, which leads to being intolerant towards those who infringe norms.

On TV, there is less tolerance towards nudity and sex, and more tolerance in relation to violence (as long as it is presented as "morally justified," that is: in defense of the culture's values).

When transgressors are caught, they need to be severely punished and also are required to pay compensation to the victims of their wrongdoing and to society in general. These principles are taken for granted in the US (and in the UK), but in many cultures they do not exist: punishment is less severe and compensation is not always part of the process.

The most extreme cases stand out and reach the media headlines. They are cases of legal suits in which the Court awards huge punitive fines to a corporation, an amount that is much larger that the damage suffered by the victim. This happens because the fine is calculated in proportion to what the company is capable of paying, not in proportion to the damage infringed. The motivation of the legal system is based on the emotions linked to culture values, more than on a legal principle.

The most famous example is that of the fast-food company that was condemned to pay thousands of dollars to a client who spilled hot coffee on her own lap. Another notorious example of exaggeration regards the man in California who received a life sentence for stealing a pair of socks. It was his third offense, and the state law stipulated that sentences were cumulative and increased threefold for repeat offenders. Still, the punishment seems disproportional to the offense. There is even a website on the Internet dedicated to collecting these extremes of the American justice system.

It is perhaps ironic that the population often criticizes "the system" for being too lenient; and this is why films often depict individuals taking justice into their own hands. Then they can be as severe as the culture demands.

A management Guru in the States, but not elsewhere?

The author and consultant Tom Peters made millions running workshops and making lectures about the key characteristics of excellent organizations. His presentations had a strong American culture bias (not recognized by the audiences, who were equally American). They praised organizational characteristics that were very consistent with the American culture, such as: a bias for action; focus on measurable results; setting ambitious targets; etc.

However, these characteristics were not always a sign of success in other cultures, different from America and the UK.

In his book "In Search of Excellence" (1982), Peters studied in depth ten organizations that showed outstanding performance according to a set of criteria he developed.

Ten years after the book was published, nine of the companies had run into serious financial trouble. Some of them had even disappeared, taken over by larger organizations or going bankrupt. Over time, they proved to be incapable of adapting to a global market, in which success became dependent of performing equally well in many different cultures outside the US.

The American's challenge

When I was a Human Resources executive at the ABN AMRO corporate Head Office in The Netherlands, an American expatriate who had moved there six months ago came into my office asking for help. He was in charge of a global corporate clients segment, in which our biggest clients were in the US, but there were also large companies from the same sector based in Europe. He had been assigned to his position because he new the industry and especially the American portion of it. It made sense for him to be based at the Head Office in Amsterdam to better liaise with other important clients based in Europe who were exporting to the US.

He expressed a series of complaints about his direct boss, a Dutch executive. According to the American, his boss showed no real interest for the segment he was responsible for. He did not follow up on his performance and up to that moment had not even established targets for him to achieve, although he had already been on the job for six months.

I heard his complaints and I went to talk with the Dutch boss to hear the other side of the story. The Dutch executive told me that he was quite pleased with the American's performance, but it was still early to discuss performance issues, since he was "barely just six months on the job... we need to wait until he completes his first year in this role, he is still adjusting to it."

The first culture difference I noticed, therefore, was the disparity in terms of time perspective. The American (bent towards a short-term perspective, eager to show how well he could do) was already impatient after six months. The Dutchman (low sense of urgency, valuing quality of life over performance) thought that it was too early to discuss performance.

"What about the American's targets for the year, how is that coming along?" I asked. He replied: "In this first year, since he is still adapting himself to a new role in a new country, he will not be appraised against targets, it would not be fair. For the next year, I will ask him to propose his targets."

"The American has the expectation that you would set targets for him... And you should show more interest in what he is doing, follow his progress more closely," I suggested.

"How can I set targets for him? He knows his role's market much better than me... He needs to propose targets and then we can have a discussion about it. I should not supervise him too closely, that might interfere with the way he does business with his clients. I hate it when my boss meddles with the way I do my work; and I don't want to do the same with my direct reports!"

We can see other culture differences in this dialogue. The Dutchman was giving the American more autonomy than he wanted. Without realizing it, the Dutchman was keeping the American from showing just how good he could perform.

When I met the American again and suggested that he should propose his targets to his boss, his reaction was: "ME propose my own targets? But then there's no challenge in achieving them! My targets should be set by my boss, and they should be ambitious, they should be challenging! Then I can show him that I can step up to the challenge and achieve the difficult targets he has set. If I'm the one setting my own targets, there is no motivation in achieving them..."

Eventually I got them together in the same room and they managed to reach an agreement regarding the whole process. I share this case as an example of how different expectations, driven by culture differences, can lead people to reach misguided conclusions about each other's behavior.

The Dutchman wanted to give more autonomy to the American. In turn, he saw this as a lack of interest and perceived the absence of targets as a demotivating factor. The Dutchman thought he was motivating the American; but the effect was actually the opposite.

Running away from the lion

Two guys were on a photo safari (no guns) in Africa, and they found themselves split from the main group. After a couple of hours walking in circles in the jungle, trying to find their bearings, they came to a clearing. They could see their camp in the distance, at the opposite side of the clearing, about half a mile away.

As they started walking towards the camp, they suddenly realized that they had been spotted by a lion coming from behind them. The beast was walking towards them with a fixed gaze, preparing to run and charge upon them.

"What now, Joe? We have no weapons to confront this lion. We'll have to run for it, but the camp is so far that we'll never make it there before the lion catches us!…"

Joe wasn't paying attention to what his colleague was saying; he stopped walking and reached in his backpack for a pair of running shoes. He proceeded to remove his hunting boots and put on the shoes.

"What are you doing? Putting on those running shoes won't be enough for you to run faster than a lion!"

"I don't need to run faster than the lion," Joe replied. "I just need to run faster than you!"

The ideal leader

During the American presidential election campaign of 2008, a voter created a parable that summarizes well what American culture considers an ideal leader to be like.

During a "Town Hall meeting," a woman took the microphone and said: "I want to vote for a candidate that, when the phone rings at 3:00 in the morning, and it's some White House aide telling of a sudden international crisis, the President will know what to do!"

The expectation is that the President will decide on the spot, even half-asleep at 3 AM, and will tell people what needs to be done immediately, to address the international crisis (see also the next topic: "hero dependence").

This is the American ideal: to decide quickly, in any circumstance, solve the problem and spring into action.

The hypothetical situation raised by that person became a campaign theme and went far beyond the campaign itself, it lasted a few years.

In 2012, four years after the fact, Hillary Clinton spoke in interviews as Secretary of State and referred to that situation. She said: "I am that kind of leader. I will be there to take that 3 AM phone call, and I will know what to do!"

Whenever a leader shows signs of hesitation, of not knowing immediately what to do, this ideal of decisiveness crumbles and disappoints expectations (realistic or not) about how that leader should behave. It is then rather easy to turn "from hero to zero," in the perception of other people. An admired leader may very quickly be rejected and harshly criticized if showing hesitation.

Hero dependency

This cultivation of leaders as heroes sometimes reaches the point of dependency towards individuals. At first this might be mistaken as the kind of dependence observed in societies with high Power Distance towards authority figures, but that is not the case.

A closer look reveals important differences between hero-dependency seen in the US culture, and authority figure dependency, observed in many high Power Distance cultures in Latin America, Africa and Asia.

1. The hero needs to perform in order to be respected and admired; if not, (s)he will be harshly criticized. Authority figures (in high PDI cultures) do not need to perform: they are respected for their position, not

for their performance. They have what is called "ascribed" power, while the power enjoyed by American leaders is "achieved" power, obtained through their deeds.

2. American leaders/heroes are accessible, as shown by the expression of having "an open door policy." Anyone can seek to make contact with leaders; their doors are always open so that people may come in to talk. In high PDI cultures, leaders are "not supposed to be bothered" with less important issues, they are most often not accessible.

3. American leaders often "manage by walking around" (MBWA), that is: they walk around the company, talking to people informally. It's a way of showing that they are accessible and checking how things are going. If leaders try to do the same in high PDI cultures, people tend to respond in a different manner: they are afraid of the leader's authority and might perceive the leader's visit as threatening.

American leaders are often challenged by their subordinates, from time to time, by circumstances, and need to prove, through their actions, that they still deserve respect from their subordinates. If they fail, they might lose their position relatively easily. The leader must accept the challenge and demonstrate performance. In high PDI cultures, challenging the boss is unthinkable, because there is a lot of fear linked to the boss' perceived power. Whoever challenges the boss gets fired. Challenges are rejected by bosses, who impose their authority by fear.

Work-life balance

As in most egalitarian and individualistic cultures, there is in the US a clear separation between work and leisure time. American often mention "work and life balance" as an important issue: the need to keep a certain balance between the amount of time and energy that you dedicate to work and how much do you allow yourself time for leisure activities.

In other cultures this expression does not initially make much sense: how can you separate your life from your work, if work is a part of your life?

What happens is that in the American culture work is seen as something separate from your "life," which is synonymous to leisure, or to doing what you want to do, rather than doing what you have to do as a work obligation.

In work situations, the focus is aimed at completing the necessary tasks. People should rarely speak about their personal life or their leisure activities during their work periods. If you want to do that, you should do it during breaks. When you're having a break, you should not talk about work, but rather about other matters and you should enjoy playing and joking.

If someone calls an American to talk about work during the evening or on a weekend, that is perceived as an intrusion on their leisure time. If you really need to do that, you should begin by excusing yourself, asking for permission and, if permission is granted, then address the work issue after normal working hours.

In Brazil and in most collectivist cultures it is common practice to mix work and fun at the same time. Telling jokes and playing around is often seen during work meetings; and it is also common to see people engaged in discussions about their work in the evenings or on weekends. This is more rarely observed in the US, where it is thought that these things should occur in different moments. When it's time to work, you should do your job. When it's time to have fun, forget about work.

Men at work (and women too)

The American culture is quite demanding towards both men and women regarding what is expected of them at work. These demands are linked to a high Performance Orientation and amplified by the normative dimension. It is important in America to behave according to social norms. There is not much tolerance towards behaviors deviating from these norms.

According to these unwritten norms, in modern America women should have a job and work outside the home; otherwise, they should not feel that they are accomplishing something. Women who do not work are seen as "inferior," because "they are not fulfilling their potential." Those who do work must dress and behave like men; otherwise, their appearance and behavior will be considered "unprofessional."

Some fashion stylist from other cultures have gone as far as saying that the typical American female executive dresses like "a stylized nun…" The culture's Normativism combined with the emphasis on performance results in rejecting any kind of behavior or appearance that might suggest sensuality. The puritans arrived in New York in the 17th Century, but their mindset endures.

These demands of the American culture also apply to men. On one side, many American women complain that American men should be more sensitive and romantic. However, the Puritan culture asks them to be bold, aggressive, ambitious and competitive. There is not much room for being romantic when you are supposed to be focusing on performance all the time.

When an American male announces that he quit his job because he wanted to "spend more time with his family," his colleagues immediately interpret that this is a poor attempt to mask what has most probably really happened: "he was fired for poor performance."

American feminism

In the United States, the feminist movement is actually quite masculine.

Feminism as a social movement promoting the liberation of women is, on one hand, universal: it is seen in many cultures throughout the world. On the other hand, it is also very particular, in the sense that it expresses itself differently in each culture. Feminism is influenced by the underlying values of each culture.

In the USA, feminism stresses equal job opportunities to men and women, equal pay and equal career possibilities. Since the American culture itself stresses the importance of performance on the job and competing to win, feminist movements also focus on similar aspects.

By contrast, in countries where culture emphasizes the importance of quality of life and caring (such as The Netherlands and in Scandinavian countries), feminist movements demand that men should be more involved in caring for their children and their homes. In these cultures, you can see men engaged in such activities much more often than in America.

American culture norms demand that men and women should emphasize their jobs and careers. Therefore, this is also the emphasis of feminist movements in America: women should have the same job opportunities as men and they should earn the same financial rewards for their performance.

A common mistake is to consider that feminist movements fight the same battles all over the world. It is more correct to say that the overall war is the same (equality between men and women), but the battles are actually different in each culture, depending on the underlying values of said cultures and the different demands that each culture places on men and women.

Gender wars

The American culture's emphasis on life as a contest, and on confrontation, has lead to coining the expression: "gender wars." That is: men and women fighting against each other in the quest for determining "who wins" that conflict.

In essence, without taking into consideration the influence of culture, male and female roles are complementary. As in any complementary relationship, there is a certain amount of conflict or antagonism between parties who complement each other. Depending on underlying culture values, this antagonism may be amplified or minimized. In the case of America, it is amplified.

American films, as a reflection of culture values, are constantly exploring this angle, about the competition between a man and a woman. The interactions as a couple goes out "dating," as they become "boyfriend" and "girlfriend," as they become engaged and eventually marry, the so-called "mating rituals," are characterized as being more about conflict and competition, rather than by complementarity.

In contrast to this Anglo-Saxon approach, one can observe how the French deal with gender relations (the hopelessly romantic French, as the stereotype goes): "vive la difference!" (Hooray for the difference!). Instead of arguing about equality between men and women, the French propose the acceptance of important differences between them. They suggest that people should live in such a way as to appreciate the differences instead of fighting against them.

Perhaps the most important aspect is that accepting the difference between men and women does not mean that one gender is better than the other. In fact, they are not equal; but they are equivalent. They have the same value.

Dealing with sex

The interaction among genders, in terms of flirting, infatuation, falling in love, and other rituals, is a topic worthy of a fully dedicated book. We will touch on the subject rather superficially here and leave the deeper aspects for another opportunity.

Anglo-Saxon cultures have a certain difficulty in dealing with sexuality, compared to other cultures. The combination of different culture dimensions helps to explain the dynamics, in terms of underlying values.

High Individualism combined with high Performance Orientation means that caring for others and quality of life are not as important as performing at work. In practical terms, this value goes against flirting on the job, since this is seen as totally unacceptable and unprofessional. At work, men and women should dress in a way that minimizes their attractiveness to the opposite sex.

By contrast, in Latin cultures one can see a somewhat different situation. In all situations (including at work) people dress and behave in ways that aim to appear attractive to the opposite sex. Flirting is common. Men and women learn to deal with this since puberty. They become used to "hitting on someone," to "scoring" or "failing" in such interactions. However, in the American culture, people do not have that kind of exposure and these situations are very awkward and embarrassing, even leading to lawsuits for sexual harassment.

The Collectivism in Latin and Asian cultures leads people to learn, since childhood, how to read and interpret non verbal body language: different ways of looking at each other, tones of voice, gestures, body posture; and also "reading between the lines" and using "double entendre." All this is important in flirting.

Anglo-Saxons don't even have a word for "double entendre:" they have, of course, the term "double meaning;" but they usually use the French expression to convey the concept when it relates to sex.

Americans (and other individualistic cultures) focus communication on explicit content. This leads the culture to put less emphasis on trying to perceive what is implicit, compared to collectivistic cultures. They seem naïve to the eyes of people coming from collectivist cultures like most Latin Americans and most Asians. This aspect highlights a comparative difficulty in dealing with very nuanced issues, such as flirting.

Language always mirrors a culture's core values; it is one of the outer layers of the culture onion. In terms of sensuality, the American difficulty in dealing with the subject is revealed in expressions that refer to sex as if it were something less nuanced, as if it were a machine. "He's a sex machine" is one such expression. "He pressed all the right buttons" is another, an expression sometimes used by women to describe someone they found attractive. They rarely are aware of the fact that they are describing themselves as if they were a machine to be operated by a masterful mechanic.

Sexual encounters in America are influenced by the culture's bias in favor of measuring results. Therefore, after having sex, it is common to refer to "how good was it?" "Was it good for you too?" There seems to be an unconscious need to evaluate and rate the intercourse: "Wow, that was great!" Or "that was amazing!" This is done without thinking, rather than simply expressing affection or just remaining together in silence.

Similarly, the expression of "scoring" on a date has been coined among the males of the species. "Did you score?" is the standard question among boys referring to how well did the other guy do on his date. It is implied among males that dating has an objective, and it is important to assess whether that objective was achieved.

Emmanuelle in New York

Many years ago the French erotic film "Emmanuelle" became the first picture of this genre to be commercially distributed in theaters to the general public, outside the seedy pornography circuit. It caused major impact because of that. In some countries it was simply banned completely as pornographic, but wherever it was tolerated, it became a box-office hit.

When it opened in the US, it was subject to a harsh review in "Time" magazine. The movie critic expressed his amazement at why the film was so successful, since it "showed less skin than any typical American X-rated movie."

This critic was assessing how erotic a film could be by using an objective and measurable criteria: the amount of skin exposed by the actors. He was unable to analyze eroticism with all its nuances, indirect and implicit characteristics. In fact, a film can be very erotic without showing anybody's "skin," while another can have lots of nudity and be not erotic at all. The American culture does not focus on dealing with less-tangible aspects such as sensuality and eroticism.

Carl Rogers versus B. F. Skinner

The polarization that is characteristic of many aspects of the American culture is also present in differing schools of thought in Psychology. It was very evident in the debates between Carl Rogers and B. F. Skinner in the 60's. They were both leaders in the field, followed by millions around the globe, and their clash of ideas represented a synthesis of the opposing forces in American Psychology.

On one side there was Carl Rogers: one of the leaders of Humanistic Psychology, a clinical psychologist, creator of the "client-centered" approach to psychotherapy, emphasizing human values, ethics, understanding and emotions.

On the opposing side there was B. F. Skinner: an experimental psychologist, creator of "behaviorism," who gained notoriety for having raised his own daughter, since she was a baby, in a laboratory crib, as a real-life practical experiment to test and demonstrate the validity of his ideas about operational conditioning and reinforcement of human behavior.

Rogers represented a counter-culture movement within the predominant American culture. He valued intangible aspects of the human condition.

Skinner represented the dominant values of the US culture. His emphasis was on observable and measurable behavior. He despised considerations about feelings and values as being "figments of imagination," impossible to observe and measure, and therefore not worthy of receiving attention from true scientists, who should dedicate themselves only to what could be seen and measured.

They both passed away towards the end of the 20th Century, leaving behind them extensive works that influenced millions all over the world. Seventy years after their ideas were published, what we can see is that in the US Skinner's ideas flourished and were widely adopted, influencing management practices and Business Schools. Rogers' ideas had their climax in the 1970's and then became restricted to sphere of clinical psychology and to a few scattered nostalgic fans of the hippie movement.

It is much more difficult, in the American culture, to deal with intangibles, with anything that cannot be observed and measured, anything that lacks a clear cause and effect relation to results (to be tallied in the competition of life). Freud's ideas and psychoanalysis in general, European philosophers, all of that draws a certain interest (but not much more than that), as if they were peculiar aberrations. The fleeting interest of some is followed by the contempt of many, since these peculiar aberrations seem to bear no visible and undeniable link to practical results.

However, one of the most interesting aspects of the American culture is its ability to foster debate and the coexistence of opposing ideas. Therefore, contrarian ideas are stimulated, confronted and discussed. Over time, those ideas that are too much against the culture's predominant values tend to be shunned and eventually abandoned, while those that are consistent with the underlying values of the culture, tend to remain accepted and be reinforced. This phenomenon can be observed in many other cultures, as well. The American culture, at least, allows that contrarian ideas be brought to the surface and be debated in confrontation, until one eventually predominates over the other. In many other cultures, such confrontation of ideals is often avoided by suppressing anything that challenges predominant values.

What irritates most Americans?

Every culture values and treasures certain things, usually detesting the opposite of what they appreciate.

The American culture treasures equality, individual freedom and performance. Therefore, it is no surprise to find that most Americans are very upset with situations in which they observe the existence of high

Power Distance, restrictions on the freedom of expression, or putting quality of life ahead of performance.

This accounts for the outrage expressed in American media about military governments in the Middle East or in Latin America. American values are totally against Power Distance and steep hierarchies. Even if the people of a country are quite pleased with a leader who is strong, powerful and authoritarian (it sometimes happens), to an American it is hard to understand that attitude. Because of this, Americans tend to exaggerate their perception of the opposition against these all-powerful leaders. Actually, they are projecting their own feelings and values, thinking that surely the people of that country must hate that leader, and they must be suffering terrible oppression. In fact, in most cases, these leaders are supported by the majority of the people, who feel that such an authoritarian leader is necessary to bring order and stability. This is difficult for Americans to accept, because it clashes with everything they have learned since childhood.

Examples abound, the most notable being the regimes in Russia, China, Iran, North Korea and Venezuela. Americans get genuinely upset by the demonstrations of authority from the leaders of these countries and they find it difficult to understand that the issues are basically cultural. In each of these countries the authoritarian leaders remain in power precisely because they correspond to the culture's expectation of how a leader should behave. They are always supported by the majority of the population, or at least by a very large minority.

The same happens in regards to governments that restrict freedom of expression, such as in China. These restrictions upset the Americans much more than they upset the actual Chinese, who appreciate maintaining collective harmony and respecting hierarchy, more than expressing individual opinions.

Still another source of irritation comes from cultures where performance is not a priority, such as Scandinavia or in the Mediterranean. The fact that in these countries people usually enjoy long vacation periods elicits irritation in the US; to them, this seems to be immoral, somehow.

The irritation is amplified by the fact that the American culture is quite normative, rather than flexible (the fifth dimension, LTO). This aspect drives less tolerance for behaviors that are contrary to the culture norm. This explains why, in certain situations, the reaction of Americans may seem exaggerated. It is because that situation touches on a "culture nerve," a rather sensitive spot that elicits an extreme, emotional reaction, which seems exaggerated to the neutral observer.

Pro and anti-Americanism

To many people of other cultures, the American culture, with its specific combination of culture dimensions, represents an ideal that they long for. Millions of people in different parts of the world admire the American culture. At the same time, certain aspects of that culture are also hated by millions. Sometimes, the same people are the ones loving and hating different aspects of America: there are many aspects of the American culture that someone might admire; and that same "someone" might also dislike other aspects of the same culture.

The ideals of freedom and equality are almost universal. Few people anywhere in the world would actually stand up against these values as ethical principles. In a similar fashion, most people in all cultures look positively at achievement and performance. Excellent performance is an ideal consciously sought in nearly all cultures.

Also in terms of the notion of "right" and "wrong" (Hofstede's fifth dimension as identified by Harris Bond, that is linked to "normativism") practically all cultures appreciate the importance of having a clear idea of what is one and the other, what is considered appropriate or inappropriate in each situation.

However, the fact is that culture values manifest themselves unconsciously and in practical situations. Thus the complexity of culture is revealed, because people's behavior is determined by unconscious drivers (values). In practice, people act differently from the values that they consciously express. They say that they value one thing, but in a given situation they act according to something else, without even realizing the contradiction.

People from other cultures tend to admire the American style in terms of the country's economic power, the comfortable material lifestyle of its upper and middle classes. They also admire America's entrepreneurial spirit, the optimistic attitude, the self-confidence, the dedication to work, the enthusiasm and courage to face challenges.

For many Latin Americans the US culture is regarded as an ideal. A Brazilian writer once said that "Miami is Rio that works." Behind the humorous phrase, one can see that America represents an ideal: a place where everything works, there is less corruption (by comparison), your dedication to work is rewarded and people are free to express their opinions.

However, all cultures have a bright side and a dark side, and the US is no exception. The same aspects that are admired may lead to unwanted outcomes under certain circumstances. For instance: the ability to make quick decisions may lead some people to jump to conclusions that they later regret; self-confidence may be perceived as hubris; dedication to work may lead to stress; and so on.

At the same time that the American culture is seen as an ideal by millions of people all over the world, there are millions of others who actually despise it. This is often referred to as "anti-Americanism." Both stereotypes are equally wrong, the positive and the negative.

Like all cultures, America's has positive and negative aspects, "good" and "bad" characteristics. Actually, whatever is considered "good" or "bad" in the American culture is something that has to do more with the culture of the beholder and his/her cultural bias than with the American culture itself.

An American outside-in point of view

Mark Haskell Smith is an American author and screenwriter who has lived in Europe and in Brazil; among his works is the script of the Brazilian film "A Partilha," which he co-authored. In his novel "Baked" (2010) a Portuguese female character goes Los Angeles to meet her American lover and reflects upon the situation, as she is packing for the trip:

"Marianna looked at the laptop's screen. The temperature in Los Angeles was in the mid seventies. That was in Fahrenheit. She did a quick translation in her head and still decided she might want to take a sweater. It was weird that the United States didn't measure temperature in Celsius. They didn't use the metric system, either. Was it because they thought inches and miles were better units of measure? Or did they see themselves as iconoclasts? Maybe they were just stubborn. She didn't know many Americans and had never been to the States before. What kind of people don't use metric?

She took a sip of her mineral water—it was carbonated and the bubbles tickled her nose and helped settle her stomach—and thought for the thousandth time that she was making a big mistake. What if the Miro who lived in Los Angeles wasn't like the Miro she had spent a perfect weekend with? How would he react to the news that she was pregnant? Was he stubborn? Would he convert to metric for her?"

Americans may seem strange and difficult to understand, to people from other cultures. The underlying values of the American culture have their bright side and their dark side. The difference between these two sides is much more in the eye of the beholder than in the behavior of Americans themselves.

Working with Americans in America and elsewhere

At work, Americans are focused on measurable results and they have a bias for action.

Communication is direct and objective, going straight to the point and "the bottom line," because this is what you need to obtain results in the short term. Meetings are short and geared to solving problems quickly, assigning tasks and deciding who is going to do what (and by when). In the next meeting, each person's progress will be checked and further actions will be discussed as needed. Meetings are "a necessary evil;" people prefer to do things, rather than discuss what needs to be done.

The competitive spirit may bring with it internal competition, among the members of the same team or unit. This is useful to drive constant performance improvement; people are constantly trying to outperform each other and beat the competition from other companies in the market. However, internal competition can sometimes go over the top and generate conflicts that ultimately harm performance. When everybody is competing to make the best presentation to the Board, to perform the best at the team meeting, to show who is the best candidate for the next promotion opportunity, this might lead some individuals to sabotaging a colleague's performance.

It might also lead some people to leave aside certain "philosophical" issues like ethics, or long-term issues such as sustainability and avoiding harm to the environment.

Optimism and self-confidence might also go too far and turn into being insensitive to criticism, even when meant constructively. An individual who expresses a critical viewpoint regarding the risks involved in a project, or who points out the obstacles that might be found along the way, can sometimes be perceived as being too negative or pessimistic.

When there are differences of opinion, about the aforementioned issues or regarding other matters, they are usually solved by resorting to facts, concrete data, figures, dates and quantifiable information. Arguments that are not based on concrete data are seldom taken seriously.

The leader (of a team, or company, or country) should be "a decisive type." He/she should listen to people's contributions beforehand, and then decide. After all, as the expression goes: "the buck stops here."

In the American business world this expression is frequently used to convey the message that "I'm the one who decides on this issue." Managers who want to be respected for their ability to decide will sometimes put that phrase on their desk.

Once a decision is made (the quicker, the better), the necessary actions need to be assigned to different members of the team. The boss should follow up on the expected results, measuring progress against challenging (motivating) targets that he (she) has set, but there is no need to get involved in "how" the work is being carried out. The most important thing is the outcome, and the progress made against the expected result.

2. United Kingdom

Overview

The United Kingdom has scores that are very similar to those of the United States:

- PDI – 35
- IDV – 89
- PER – 66
- UAI – 35
- LTO – 25

Of course, this is no coincidence. The American culture was basically formed by the British culture. English immigrants were those who came to the American "New World" in greater numbers, followed by other nationals of the United Kingdom: the Irish and the Scots. It is true that the Dutch founded the city of New York (they called it New Amsterdam) and later exchanged the Isle of Manhattan for Curaçao and Surinam with the British in 1664. Many Dutch families remained in America and gave origin to traditional American names such as Van Dyk and Vanderbilt, but the prevailing values in the colony were Anglo-Saxon, who were the vast majority of immigrants.

After the Declaration of Independence in 1776, the Americans tried very hard to stress how different they were from the British. This was necessary in order to form the new country's identity. However, what we see 250 years later is that the American culture's underlying values are still very similar to the ones found in the UK. Culture values are very long-lasting and they change very slowly, if ever they do.

2. UNITED KINGDOM

Since the similarities between the US and UK are many, in terms of their value-dimensions, our focus in this chapter will be on a few specific aspects in which the American and British cultures are indeed different, pertaining to the angle that interests us the most: managing people at work.

Communication

The use of language has a very special connotation in the UK. Throughout the centuries a certain notion was developed by its culture, according to which speaking English correctly was a sign of nobility, or at least that you were close to the aristocrats; that you are "a gentleman" or "a lady."

If you employ language correctly, in writing or in speech, by articulating sentences correctly, enouncing proper pronunciation, expressing yourself in a somewhat sophisticated manner, by using figures of speech, employing metaphors and subtle phrases or euphemisms, then you are regarded as erudite, noble, a part of "the ruling class," even if you are, in fact, part of "the working class."

Whoever speaks poor English is not speaking "the Queen's English." These people are those who mispronounce words, use slang and express themselves directly (which is perceived as rude, blunt and lacking in sophistication).

Although British society is clearly individualistic, the people who are economically more affluent (both nobles and commoners) use a language style that is more indirect, full of subtleties and coded phrases. This is done unconsciously to imply that those who employ language in this way, and those who understand these ciphered messages, both belong to a different class, within a low Power Distance society as a whole.

This aspect of coded messages in Britain has quite a broad scope. It also affects, among many other things, the way in which the media communicates certain news items. For instance, whenever someone commits suicide, the media makes an effort to avoid mentioning that bit of information. The cause of death is simply omitted from the news. People already know that, when this happens, the deceased committed suicide, but everyone avoids saying it explicitly.

The British have a certain difficulty in discussing aspects that are regarded as "negative" (such as suicide) more even than the Americans, who are more direct. The British prefer to say that "something is not right" or "there is room for improvement," rather than say that "things are bad" or "it's all wrong."

There is even a widely known table that has gone viral on the internet, often used also in culture workshops, describing "what the English say," "what they really mean" and "what people understand." British people usually have a hearty laugh when they see this table and immediately recognize its content as valid.

What the English say	What they really mean	What people understand
With all due respect…	I think you are wrong (or an idiot)	He is listening to me
I suggest/You might consider this…	This is an order, do it now, or justify yourself	I should consider this, but do what I think is best
Interesting	Not at all interesting	He is interested
Oh, by the way…	Most important aspect of our conversation	This aspect is not important

The class system

The British culture has a distinction between what is called "the ruling class" and "the working class." The actual dividing line between these two social classes is somewhat blurred, it is not so precise, but the concept is clear enough to distinguish the people who are well above or well below this fuzzy border.

The ruling class is composed by the nobles, officially recognized by the monarchy, and also by top executives from private and publicly owned organizations. The working class is made up of everyone who works for a living, except for those who have climbed the social ladder to outstanding positions and have achieved (officially or informally) a status equivalent to nobility. They are the so-called "industry barons" and their peers.

In spite of the existence of this class distinction, the UK is still considered a low Power Distance culture, and also in spite of being a monarchy. First of all, as mentioned earlier, the political regime (monarchy or republic) bears no correlation with Power Distance: many high PDI countries are republics (ex: Brazil, Egypt, Spain), while many low PDI cultures are monarchies (ex: Netherlands, Denmark, Sweden). The main factors to drive the UK's score down to the low PDI portion of the scale are the existence of equal opportunity as a culture value and the fact that PDI is clearly lower within each of the two classes mentioned above.

In high Power Distance societies the difference in status symbols and rituals is very visible between each rung in the social ladder and the next, both in the top layers of the hierarchy and on the bottom levels. In the UK, the distinction among members of the working class is quite subtle; when it exists, it is more linked to Performance Orientation (achieved power, rather than ascribed power), that is: the status is gained by performing, rather than ascribed by others because of the position that someone occupies.

In a similar manner, the distinction among members of the ruling class (noble or not) is much more subtle than what one can observe in high PDI cultures.

At work, a Department Manager will often listen to his subordinates' opinions and engage in work-related discussions on an equal basis. Persuasion, rather than authority, is used frequently to get people to do what is required. A superior's decisions may often be challenged and frequently are. The boss needs to prove his/her competence through performance; otherwise the respect of subordinates will be lost.

Aristocrats, especially the Queen and the Royal Family, are duly respected as in any established monarchy. However, monarchy itself is openly criticized and challenged as the best political regime for the country, without such opposing voices being silenced or put in jail. Among the nobility, those who show a solid performance in their professional affairs earn the respect of their peers and of the general public. Those who restrict themselves to living off the wealth accumulated by their ancestors do not get the same attention and respect.

In addition, it must be noted that those who perform in an outstanding way in arts, business or in public affairs, may be elevated to a noble status by the Queen, by decree. Therefore, musicians, rock stars, actors and sports celebrities, as well as successful business people who were born as part of a humble family, may "become aristocrats" by the will of the Queen. Even though a certain distinction remains between the ruling and the working classes, members of the working class can ascend to the ruling class as a consequence of their performance.

Working with the British

The main challenge that people mention regarding working with the British pertains to communication. As described previously, the British put a significant emphasis on the correct usage of the English language and they employ certain subtleties that may be difficult for outsiders to understand.

This is the first barrier to be overcome by foreigners, and it is actually made of two obstacles: the first one is to pronounce the language correctly when speaking and to understand the language as pronounced by the British; the second obstacle is to understand the subtleties and the coded expressions often employed by the British.

When in doubt, ask for clarification. Apologize for your less than perfect mastery of the English language and ask for additional information or explanation. It is better to get things clear at the beginning of your interaction, rather than have to face a much bigger problem later, because of a misunderstanding.

Like the Americans, the British put a lot of emphasis on clearly measurable results. They often delegate quite easily, allowing individuals and teams a lot of liberty regarding how they do their work, as long as they obtain the expected results. On the other hand, the British tend to not provide very detailed guidance, as this is seen as an intrusion on the worker's autonomy. If you need guidance, ask for it. If you don't, the typical behavior of your British superior will be to set your target and leave you to your own devices.

If you are the one managing a British team, focus on clarifying the expected results and allow freedom for the team to tackle the task at hand. Supervise from a distance, check progress against targets, but avoid micro-managing (this can be very irritating for your subordinates). Ask if the team needs further instructions and dispense these as needed.

3. Germany

Overview

Germany's scores on the five dimensions are:

- PDI – 35
- IDV – 67
- PER – 66
- UAI – 65
- LTO – 31

The German culture has been the object of distorted perceptions because of the ascension of Nazism and World War II. The information that people received about Germany since the 1930's went through a couple of very heavy filters that distorted any kind of objective point of view: first it was Nazism itself, a strong political movement that does not represent German culture as a whole; and the second filter was the war propaganda of the Allies who fought together against Germany and which, naturally, demonized the German people as part of the war effort.

As a result of this, many generations born in the 20th Century were taught to consider the German people as being autocratic and rude, above all. The war propaganda movies showed thousands of Nazi soldiers parading in front of Hitler; this gave rise to the mistaken notion that Germany is a hierarchical, high Power Distance society.

Actually, Germany's scores in the Hofstede research studies revealed that it is an egalitarian culture, individualistic and oriented towards performance. Its underlying values are not that different from Anglo-Saxon cultures, in that respect. What really differentiates German culture is high Uncertainty Avoidance and low LTO (normativism).

German culture is highly disciplined, but not as a result of respecting hierarchy; rather, the main driver is a need for order and structure. Germans treasure individual freedom and equality, as long as these are organized according to a certain pre-determined process, as part of a clear structure, following a certain order, so as to avoid any uncertainty or ambiguity.

Each individual must be responsible for his or herself in observing these norms and structures. If anybody does not follow the norms (which are often unwritten), any other member of society has the duty to call that divergent individual to attention, so that he/she will, please, re-establish the overall order, by following the norms. This is done regardless of hierarchy.

Curtains and plants

Years ago, a German friend of mine who married a Brazilian woman, recounted an experience they had when living in a small village on the Northern part of Germany. My friend was tending to his garden, in front of their house, when one of the neighbors, very amicably, struck up a conversation. In the middle of that, the neighbor remarked:

"I noticed that on your windows you have plants, while all the houses on this block have curtains…"

"Yes," my German friend responded. "My wife is very fond of plants and we decided that they would look very nice on the window, instead of curtains."

"They are very beautiful plants, but all the houses on this block have curtains, rather than plants."

"I can see that, but we prefer plants… They are rather tall and compact, so no one can see inside the house. In that way, they serve the same function as curtains. Do you think people can see inside our house?"

"Oh no, no! That is not the problem. It just happens that all the houses on this block have curtains, and not plants!..."

The neighbor was unable to articulate a specific rational argument against the plants, but he felt annoyed by a certain rupture in the pattern. He tried to be subtle, insisting ever so politely, but he kept insisting. In this case, the neighbor was never direct or authoritarian, but the politely conveyed message was: "don't break the pattern!"

While he was very careful and tactful to respect my friend's individual freedom, he could not bear to let the fact go by that this couple was breaking the pattern and this in itself was quite annoying.

Cars made in Germany and in other places

The world market for cars became globalized at the end of the 20th Century. A handful of automobile brands became dominant in this market and began competing against each other everywhere, be it in Europe, the Americas or Asia.

It is interesting to note how the different national cultures of the main automobile producers influenced the trademark characteristics of different brands.

American cars reflect the values of the American culture: big, powerful engines, large size (the bigger, the better), standing out (being noticed and standing out from the crowd are things that are valued and praised). Americans use the expression "muscle cars" to describe their most famous "cult" models, such as the Ford Mustang, the Chevy Camaro and the Dodge Charger. There is a whole generation of "SUV's" (Sport Utility Vehicles) that are typically American: big and powerful. American vehicles are not known for being discreet, economical, functional or safe.

By contrast, cars designed in the Nordic countries, notably the Swedish Volvo brand, became known worldwide for their safety features, mainly. This aspect is clearly linked to the culture values of low Performance Orientation, placing more importance on quality of life and caring for others. Scandinavian cars are also not known for their beauty, nor for "standing out" above the crowd; rather, they tend to look like any other

European brand. The idea behind that is very Scandinavian: it is "leveling," remaining on the same level as others, rather than standing out.

The French cars made by Renault, Citroen and Peugeot reflect the values of their culture: they seek to stand out not by a bigger size or by sheer power, but rather by sleek design and a comfortable driving position. They aim for modern beauty and discreet elegance as ways of differentiating their models from those of other brands. They have also used slogans in French in their advertising, even outside of France, as a way of highlighting the "Frenchness" of their brands, such as Citroen's *creatif technologie*. Nationality is also a brand.

Japanese cars have become globally successful thanks to their high quality standards: reliability, functionality and fuel economy. The main differential driving force behind the Japanese culture is Uncertainty Avoidance and Japanese car brands reflect that culture value.

In a similar way, the German brands Audi, BMW, Mercedes Benz and Porsche (in the luxury segments) and Volkswagen (in the more popular segments) gained market shares all over the world because of German engineering and manufacturing standards. German cars are smaller than the Americans, not as beautiful as the French, not as fuel efficient as the Japanese, and usually more expensive than the competition; but they have come to dominate the higher portion of the market.

Their quality in terms of reliability, durability and resistance is still perceived all over the world as the standard of excellence that other brands (including the Japanese) must beat. It might be argued that the Japanese brands are just as good as the German ones, and offer a lower price. The fact is that the image of German brands is still superior, notably in the luxury segment; this allows them to charge a premium price and still have significant sales volumes. They have also used German-language slogans abroad, such as Audi's "*vorsprung durch Technik*", which means "leading through technology."

These distinguishing trademarks of German car brands have originated in their cultural values: high Performance Orientation, Uncertainty Avoidance and Discipline, which all drive excellence in engineering and manufacturing. Performance is defined in Germany not only by sheer size and power, as it happens in the American culture, which is less concerned with uncertainty. In Germany, performance is seen as the combination of efficiency, power and stability.

American cars aim for being big, strong, and standing out. German cars try to be smaller, stand out a bit less, but they seek to represent the best combination of high power and low weight (a Porsche trademark), coupled with reliability and endurance. The German car is an example of how much the German culture values engineering: detailed planning of an expert production process, carried out with rigorous discipline, resulting in products with excellent technical qualities. An appealing design might be important, but not that much. Many critics have labeled the BMW Series 5 downright ugly when it was redesigned in 2004; even so, it sold more than any of its predecessors: the buyers were not looking for beauty, but rather for engineering and reliability.

The expert is more important than the boss

The combination of scores in the five dimensions (low hierarchy, high Individualism, Performance Orientation, Uncertainty Avoidance, and "Normativism"/Discipline) means that, in practice, experts are more respected than people with managerial authority.

It is rather commonplace to see that the real leader of a project is not the most senior person (in terms of hierarchy), but rather an engineer (or other professional specialist) who best understands the technology involved, which is key to the said project's success. For all administrative aspects of the project, the company's hierarchical line might be followed; but in the technical discussions the opinion of the manager is ignored and people follow the expert.

In fact, if the manager is smart, (in Germany) he/she will do the same: allow the expert's natural leadership come to the surface and direct the technical discussions. Such a manager shows true management skill when endorsing the expert's proposals and suggestions. If the manager is foolish enough to make decisions that go against an expert's recommendations, he/she will soon lose the team's respect. The team will do everything they can to implement the expert's ideas, regardless of what the manager would like to see happening.

This hypothetical conflict between the team manager and the teams main expert rarely is observed in practice, for a very simple reason: they are usually the same person. Organizations tend to promote experts to management positions, even if their management skills are notably lacking. Since experts are respected so much, because their knowledge helps to avoid the uncertainty associated with complex technical issues, it is only natural that organizations prefer to have such experts leading their teams in formal management roles.

There are, mostly in other cultures, companies that adopt job rotation as a common practice, as a way of preparing people for higher positions. This practice may be quite successful in countries like the US and UK, where Uncertainty Avoidance is lower. In Germany, however, where UAI is higher, assigning someone as a manager who does not have in-depth knowledge of a unit's subject matter would be questioned. In the rare cases when this occurs, people will follow the expert, and not the manager. They may respect the manager's authority regarding purely administrative matters, but they will follow the expert on anything that has to do with the actual content subject of the unit.

Participative management

The basic principle driving management (and everything else) in Germany is order, the structuring of tasks in accordance with clear policies and procedures. How are these policies and procedures established? By making use of the expert knowledge accumulated by experts and subject matter specialists. Thus, uncertainty and ambiguity will be avoided, and task distribution will be carried out in an optimal way.

Since German society is also a low Power Distance culture, it is important that structures and procedures are set in a way as to ensure that there is no imposition of management's will based solely on hierarchy. The experts' opinions must be heard and taken into account, having a much greater weight than those of management authorities. It is in this context that the Works Councils (*Betriebsrat*) were formed.

These councils are actually committees in which representatives of the operational workers discuss plans and structures (and eventual changes to them) with the top management of organizations. The underlying values of different cultures affect even the choice of labels for these committees. There are similar structures in other cultures, but the use of different names for them shows the influence of the values.

In other cultures these committees are known as "Workers' Councils." This implies that there are two sides confronting each other: "workers" and "managers." The German values of equality and focus on discussing the work itself, rather than conflicting opinions, led them to coin a term that reflects this: they are "Works Councils," and not "Workers Councils." The difference seems subtle, but it is an important one. The focus of the councils should be the organization of work, a joint responsibility of employers and employees, of workers (including experts) and management.

In practice, these Works Councils discuss proposals to change organizational structures and plans. They then issue a formal advice to support or disagree with the proposals (that are usually originated in senior management). Thanks to the principles of equality and mutual respect that are in force in German culture, these discussions occur usually in joint meetings among managers and employees, and they are quite polite and well-mannered discussions, even when opposing arguments are debated.

Such arguments are often mediated by experts. These may be mediation experts, who in turn may invite subject-matter experts to testify about the issues at hand. Any kind of structure or policy change, such as closing down a plant, or opening a new factory, or even small changes in production procedures, all may only be implemented once the issue is examined by the Works Council and a formal advice is issued.

Since what is most important is the rational aspect of each issue, usually the Works Council will agree with the proposals, as long as they are supported by hard data and logical arguments. The formal advice may also be favorable only in part, recommending amendments to the initial proposal. However, these amendments must also be supported by reason and data.

The final outcome is the product of negotiating between parties, until all consider themselves reasonably satisfied and the solution is then implemented. These discussions are all extremely rational and objective. Any of the people involved will feel free to agree or disagree at any time, always based on well-grounded rational arguments.

All this happens in a way that is quite different from what is seen in the high Power Distance cultures found in Latin America and other parts of the world, where managers and workers (usually represented by aggressive union leaders) argue with each other as a matter of principle. Those discussions soon become emotional and they are based mostly on ideological differences, rather than on the objective analysis of information and hard data.

I once witnessed a meeting between Brazilian union leaders and the members of German Works Council. After it was finished, the Brazilians came to me and complained that "these German workers are worse than negotiating with our Brazilian bosses!" This was because the Germans demanded concrete data and fact-based arguments from the Brazilians in order to express their opinion. When the union leaders were unable to provide them, the Germans argued that perhaps the manager's point of view should be accepted as valid.

Planning and implementation

In the German culture there is more emphasis placed in planning than on execution. Correct execution is taken for granted. Therefore, if something goes wrong in execution, the assumption is that this must be due to a flaw in the planning. The plan must be re-examined and corrected, so that the execution problems are not repeated.

In a similar fashion, whenever an organization is not achieving the expected results, the first attitude is to examine its structure, its policies and procedures, looking for flaws to explain the below-par performance. It is only after making sure that the structure cannot be improved, that issues regarding the people themselves involved in work execution will be examined.

The assumption is always that if the plans are of good quality and so are the policies and procedures; the only reason for something going wrong is if the people involved have not followed the predetermined procedures, as they should have done. Only then will it be necessary to consider if people have failed due to lack of discipline (the solution will be punishing them or replacing them) or due to lack of knowledge (the solution will be more training).

In order to guarantee the quality in planning, specialists are often employed. In practice, consultants are frequently hired for that purpose, the more renown, the better, so that their capabilities as subject matter experts is not questioned.

In terms of training and development, the best way to ensure its quality is to hire experts widely recognized as such, who can also certify the pupils who attend their courses. In Germany there is a clear preference for hiring universities and business schools to run in-company executive development programs, rather than using independent consultants or utilizing experts employed directly by the company as in-house experts. A business school can issue certificates to the participants and these documents are highly valued, since they testify that the participant has also become an expert by attending the course.

Certain companies use different external entities matching their level of prestige with the seniority of the target audience: middle managers attend courses administered by the University of Berlin; senior managers attend courses run by Duke University; and top management will go to courses administered by IMD in Switzerland. The renowned expertise of these educational institutions is greatly valued and this is deemed to be more important than considerations about the practical effect of the courses on actual performance on the job.

Specialists are more valued than generalists; and certified specialists are valued even more. For this reason, academic titles are commonly used when referring to people at work. The production manager is introduced as "Mister Professor Doctor Engineer Johann Stressman," to convey his degree of expertise.

Work is more valued than quality of life

The combination of scores in Germany contributes to amplify the effects of a high score in Performance Orientation, due to high scores also in Uncertainty Avoidance and a low score in LTO (which means a high degree of "normativism", or emphasis on discipline).

In this way, it becomes clear that performance is important and that good performance is characterized by discipline and certainty.

The culture's high score also in Individualism also contributes, in addition to the dimensions just mentioned, to having a clear distinction between moments of labor and moments of leisure. Everything should be done at its proper time and place. At work, there is no joking around; at home, no work is done. From 9 to 5, focus is on work and on nothing else. After working hours and on weekends, focus is on leisure. The two are rarely mixed.

The priority is set on work, which must be carried out with discipline and order. That means beginning at the assigned time and finishing at the predetermined time as well. Working beyond office hours is a sign that one is lacking in organization. Once the assigned tasks are done, according to the assigned schedules, one may relax and enjoy leisure. However, even leisure must be carefully planned and organized.

Martin Luther and the Protestants

The birth of Protestant religions as a divergent stream of Christianity has everything to do with underlying culture values. It is no coincidence that Martin Luther and Lutheranism were born in Germany: they were products of the German culture.

Luther rebelled against the Pope's authority and the hierarchy of the Catholic Church. This rebellion was typical of a low Power Distance culture against an institution characterized by high PDI. Luther's movement was endorsed and gained traction because Germany, already 500 years ago, was a low PDI society in comparison to the hierarchical structure of the Catholics.

Soon other streams of Protestant Christians began appearing, all basically created in the low PDI cultures of Northern Europe. They all demanded more autonomy for local parishes and priests, and less subordination to a distant hierarchy. It is also no coincidence that the Catholic religion remained stronger in high PDI societies, while the Protestants thrived in lower PDI cultures.

The discussions about dogmas, such as the Holy Trinity, worshipping the Virgin Mary and worshipping saints, all these were rational arguments to justify the separation of these Churches; but the determining factors were the notion of equality against the respect for hierarchy, and power decentralization versus power centralization.

All religions are currently losing followers in Germany. Uncertainty Avoidance is emphasizing planning and order, more than religion and superstition as a way of avoiding ambiguity. This is in contrast to what we see in other countries, where religion still plays a strong role in helping to avoid uncertainty.

It is quite possible that what we see happening in Germany is, as always, due to the combination of different dimensions: the high score in Uncertainty Avoidance combined with Performance Orientation leads to valuing planning and order as mechanisms to avoid ambiguity. In other cultures, where UAI is also high, but Performance Orientation is lower, planning takes a back seat and religion is the main driver to avoid ambiguity.

Anyway, Germany's low score in LTO reveals that self-discipline is highly valued. This means that whoever embraces religion tends to really practice the religion they have espoused; and those who declare themselves "non-affiliated" or "atheist," simply do not go to church. More than 30% of Germans declare themselves as not affiliated to any religion. It's worth noting that taking individual responsibility for ones attitudes is also typical of individualistic cultures.

In Latin America, there is the well-known figure of the "non-practicing Catholic:" someone who declares himself a Catholic, but does not go to church, does not practice the religion. This is consistent with collectivist cultures, with high PDI and high LTO (everything is relative, including discipline). The acceptance of hierarchy blends well with the acceptance of hierarchy in Church.

By contrast, Lutherans allow the free interpretation of the Bible by all individuals, with no obligation to follow directions from a supreme priest. When he translated the Bible from Latin to German, Martin Luther reinforced the notion of a religion that is less hierarchical, more egalitarian and individualistic, consistent with the characteristics of the German culture.

Some authors are mistaken when they consider that religion determines culture values; actually, it is the other way around. A culture's core values determine what kind of religion will flourish in that community.

Nowadays the German population is more or less divided in three thirds of similar size: Protestants, Catholics and "non-affiliated" or atheists. Muslims represent less than 4% of the total German population. This kind of balanced pluralism is typical of individualist and low Power Distance cultures.

Stopping on the sidewalk

Valuing order and organization is something that transpires in every aspect of the German culture, from the most sophisticated and complex, to the simplest.

During my first visit to Germany in 1968, with my sister and my parents, we were sightseeing in Frankfurt. At a certain moment, we stopped on the sidewalk, the four of us, to decide where to go next: should we go to the hotel and take some rest before dinner, or should we go straight to have dinner at a restaurant and afterwards go to our hotel? In less than ten seconds a pedestrian chided us, irritated: "what are you doing? You're blocking the way!"

I was shocked. Years later, I understood that the need for order leads to feelings of irritation when you are required to deviate a few steps from your path in order to avoid a group of four people standing on the sidewalk…

To avoid uncertainty, in German society people expect that everyone must do their part, according to the normativism associated with low LTO. This includes not standing still on the sidewalks.

Children at the toy shop

A few decades later, in 1997, we were again visiting Germany and I was in Dusseldorf with my wife and two of our smaller daughters, who were then five and four years old.

Inside a toy shop, one of children grabbed a box from one of the shelves and turned to show it to me, excitedly: "Look, Daddy, they have doll clothes for going out in the snow!"

Before I could even respond, a saleslady appeared and admonished her in German: "this cannot be taken off the shelves!" And she took away the toy from my daughter's hands, putting it immediately back where it was.

In that moment, I realized that I could never live in Germany, despite my German ancestry from my mother's side. Discipline goes to the point of not being tolerant with small children in a toyshop. The kids' behavior, which might be tolerated in other cultures, had to be immediately repressed.

No, means no. Do not insist.

In many collectivist cultures people have difficulty in simply saying "no" in response to a request. People prefer to say "I'll think about it," "I will do my best," or "this is not up to me, I will see what I can do."

In the Netherlands, the most often heard response to a request is "that's not possible." However, if you insist politely, and adopt an attitude of humility, you might actually get whatever was initially denied to you, as an exception, taking into account the specific characteristics of your request.

In Germany, exceptions are very rare, not to say simply inexistent. When people respond with a "no," they will very rarely change that to "yes" or even to "maybe." Insisting with your request is likely to only strengthen the robustness of the initial denial. This happens because the low LTO indicates a strong appreciation of discipline and obedience to all norms, written and unwritten. The simple consideration of the possibility of an exception is already perceived as something threatening. It is the duty of every member of society to defend compliance with all social norms, without exception.

Double parking means jail

> *A Brazilian friend of mine who had just moved to Germany a few weeks before, agreed to pick up his wife at a shop, with his car. When he arrived, he could not find a place to park; so he left his car double-parked and went inside, asking her to hurry up and pay for her purchases, because he was double parked outside.*

As he left the shop, he found a policeman writing him a ticket and a tow-truck already maneuvering to take his car away.

He appealed to the policeman in fluent German (his grandparents were German and he had learned the language as a child), asking for mercy.

"Mr. policeman, please, I left the car here for less than two minutes, I just went inside the shop to tell my wife that I was waiting for her outside; I came out to move my car out of the way…"

"Tell that to the judge."

"OK, then. Give me the fine, I will move the car away from here."

"No. Your car is going to be taken to the car depot and you are under arrest. Please come with me."

"What? I don't believe this! You don't have to do this!"

"I am doing my job. You broke the law and I must arrest you and take you to the presence of a judge. I am not allowed to release you; only the judge can do that. That is his job. State your arguments to the judge, he will decide. Please come with me."

Indeed, my friend was unable to dissuade the policeman. He climbed into the police car and went with him to the nearest station. Once there, he had to pay a fine and listen to a severe admonishment from the judge, who then released him.

Respecting speed limits

An aspect perceived as curious by foreigners coming to Germany, regards the speed limits on roads. In many stretches of the excellent German roads, there are no speed limits. These stretches are clearly marked and drivers are allowed to travel as fast as they want, according to their individual criteria.

What happens then is that many drivers will go literally over 200 km an hour (about 120 miles an hour). I drove on these highways myself, at 180 or 200 km/h, only to see that, to my surprise, other cars were coming behind me, flashing their headlights to overtake me at over 240 km/h.

> *I once took a taxi to the Siemens corporate training center just outside Munich, after 10 pm. As soon as he was on the highway, the cab driver stepped on it and drove at over 220 km/h until we reached our destination.*
>
> *As I walked into the adjoining hotel, I met a Canadian colleague at the lobby, who greeted me: "sit down and have a Scotch with me; I'm still recovering from the scariest taxi ride I've ever had in my life!"*

What happens is that in those stretches where there is no speed limit, drivers drive as if they were in a Formula One race. They enjoy that moment of freedom that a very strict society allows them to have, and actually take a rather surprising level of risk, considering a culture that scores so high in Uncertainty Avoidance.

On the highway, as soon as drivers arrive at a stretch with a speed limit (approaching an exit, for instance), they all reduce speed to comply with the limit (130 or 100, depending on the road). Sometimes there might be construction works on the roads, and limits are signaled by a temporary sign restricting maximum speed to 50 or 70. Everyone respects these limits, without exception. And as soon as they reach a stretch with no speed limit, they go back to the standard of driving over 200 km/hour.

In this respect, Uncertainty Avoidance does not influence the drivers' behavior to avoid the risk of accidents. The will to enjoy freedom is stronger. On the other hand, truth be told, German highways are of such good quality and German cars are so safe, that these high speeds have not caused a greater incidence of traffic accidents, compared to other countries.

Merkel and the proposals for the EU

When the Euro currency had a crisis, around 2010, due to the high level of debt accumulated by Greece with international banks, all of Europe went into intense discussions, even those countries that had not adopted the Euro, such as the UK, Switzerland and Norway. This happened because the Euro would affect the whole European economy, so everyone expressed their opinions about the situation and how to solve it.

As the old joke went: "the problem is complex, and as such it may have many different solutions…" Different proposals were presented and discussed by different economists, at the time. They all reflected the culture values of their respective countries. It's a pity that most people in the international media remain ignorant of cultural aspects, since this severely restrains their comments to very superficial statements that contribute to a general feeling of confusion.

The German proposals advocated by Chancellor Angela Merkel seemed perfectly obvious to countries sharing a Germanic culture (in addition to Germany itself, Austria, the Czech Republic, Switzerland and Northern Hungary): it was necessary to create more rules forcing all members of the European Union to show greater fiscal accountability. If these additional rules would be followed with the necessary discipline, the issue would be resolved.

The Germans did not realize that the proposal they presented would only work in countries with a Germanic culture, where people value planning, setting clear and explicit rules, and where compliance with rules is a priority. If something goes wrong, all you need is to improve the plans and rules, and that will be enough to avoid the repetition of problems.

Other countries, with other values, have other priorities and prefer other solutions. They rejected the German proposal, on the grounds that, in their eyes, it would not be effective.

The British preferred immediate action, which would produce quick effects. Discussing rules and structures would be secondary. "We must act now!" shouted David Cameron. The priority for the British would be to do something that would solve the Greek crisis with the banks in a matter of hours. At the time, the BBC announced on a Thursday evening that the meeting among European leaders would happen during the weekend and the announcement of their decisions would be made only on Monday, "when it might already be too late!" NOTE: there was no conclusive outcome of that meeting and the problem dragged on for months before being eventually resolved. The sense of urgency of the British was not endorsed by other countries, to the despair of the former, but the European Union survived.

Countries like France, Italy and Spain also criticized the German proposal. To them, the most important thing was not to create more rules and structures, because they know that, in practice, such rules are never followed with the strictness intended. What they proposed was to create a series of mechanisms to handle emergencies and exceptions.

"Exceptions? What do you mean, exceptions? There cannot be any exceptions!" cried the Germans. And so, discussions ensued in Europe for months…

The Dutch and the Scandinavians have played an important role in mediating these different ideas, simply because their cultures value such a role: the most important thing is to listen to all parties involved and patiently seek consensus.

If more government leaders in Europe would learn about their own cultures and about the cultures of their neighboring countries, possibly we would have quicker and more satisfactory resolution of political and economic issues. Eventually that day will come.

Since Germany is the largest economic power in Europe, its proposals usually get accepted, even if it does take a lot of discussion. However, this does not mean that the implementation of the approved measures (whatever they are) will go according to plan, nor that they will produce the intended results. A German designed structure might work very well in Germany, but not necessarily in other places. It might fail miserably in countries with different underlying culture values.

Germans value rules and discipline, but the low PDI and high IDV mean that they dislike frequent inspections and close supervision, which are seen as interfering in people's autonomy. Besides, they don't even think these should be necessary. Rules are important and they should be complied with thanks to self-discipline and individual accountability. It should not be necessary to create an agency with the responsibility of reminding you of your responsibility.

This is also the reason why Germans react with irritation, such as in the previously mentioned examples, in the toyshop and on the sidewalk. People get irritated because everybody should be complying with the rules without someone having to be corrected by others. They feel compelled to intervene in order to defend the social system that is being threatened by the lack of discipline, but they take no pleasure in doing this: it causes them anxiety, because it means that the system might fall apart and create uncertainty.

Merkel's proposals usually mention rules and structures, but they are based on the assumption that all countries will exercise discipline and responsibility in complying with those rules, with no need for external control and frequent inspections.

In practice, it does not work like that; simply because in high PDI cultures the only control is always external control. In these cultures, people consider that if something is not inspected frequently, that means that it is not deemed to be important enough. If it were important, it would be inspected. Unless there is better understanding of these intercultural connotations, German proposals will continue to be condemned to failure.

Breath analysis at the bar's restrooms

In 1997, in Munich, I saw something I had not yet seen in other places. At the Hofbrauhaus beer garden, one of the city's main tourist attractions, there were breath analysis tools at the men's rest rooms. This was free and it allowed people to test their own degree of alcohol intoxication.

The underlying principle was a very German one. You should yourself have the discipline and responsibility to decide if you are capable of driving after drinking a few beers. To determine what exactly is your situation, you should not rely solely on how you feel; it is best to consult an expert or, in this case, a precision instrument manufactured with German technology. The tools were fixed to the wall, with instructions printed at their side in German and English. There were throwaway mouthpieces, which each user would take to blow into the device. An electronic screen would then show you the degree of alcohol in your lungs and allowed a comparison against a table beside the instructions, where the acceptable levels for driving were shown.

Why not have these devices all over the world, in every bar rest room? Wouldn't this allow people to develop a greater sense of individual responsibility? Wouldn't this lower the risk of traffic accidents due to drunk driving?

It happens that in other cultures there are different underlying values and different assumptions about how people will behave.

In a high Power Distance culture there is less individual responsibility; people tend to "delegate upwards" and consider that it is not up to them to regulate their own behavior. This should be done by a higher authority, such as the police, the government, etc. It is up to these authorities to enforce the rules, through frequent inspections and the application of penalties to those who break the norms. If there is little discipline, people think that the solution is to implement more severe penalties. In these societies, the average thinking goes something like this: "when I drink and drive, I worry about getting caught by the police; I don't worry about the risk of causing an accident."

The assumption in high LTO cultures is also that everything is relative. Complying with norms is something that depends on the circumstances of each situation and exceptions are abundant. There is always an excuse to justify non-compliance. And there is more room for corruption.

We cannot say that there is no corruption in Germany; but it certainly happens less frequently and more discreetly than in cultures with high PDI (concentrated power) and high LTO (high flexibility and tolerance).

Economic austerity

It is obvious that culture values influence economic policy in each nation. Facing the meltdown of the international financial system in 2008, different countries adopted different measures to solve their problems. It should be noted that the rational discussions that occurred about economic policies have more to do with culture values than with economic theories as such.

It should come as no surprise that Germany, when facing the global economic crisis of 2008, decided for an approach that increased the austerity of its already austere economic policies.

American economic policies are based on consumption and on spending more than you earn, by having easy access to abundant credit. German economic policies are based on practically the opposite: a high savings ratio and the export of products that are consumed abroad.

When the 2008 crisis broke out, American economists issued a prescription: we need a set of stimuli to increase spending, thus generating more demand. The whole world needs to spend more, to increase demand for American products. In turn, German economists proposed the opposite: we need to spend less and the whole world needs to spend less, to reduce debt in general.

You could argue that the American approach would also benefit Germany by increasing demand for German products; but the discussion reveals that behind rational arguments, economists tend to endorse policies that are consistent with their cultures' underlying values.

By 2009, the Americans were accusing the Germans of spending too little and thus damaging the attempted recovery of the world economy. The Germans were accusing the Americans of spending too much and blaming them for having started the crisis with the mortgage-based securities debacle in the United States. Both countries advocated opposite solutions for the world's economic woes. The reason for the difference in approaches is eminently cultural.

Germany has a much higher Uncertainty Avoidance than the United States and values austerity much more, in all aspects of life. That is also a way of avoiding uncertainty, saving today for an uncertain future. Americans value other things: "spending more here and now, enjoy while you can; we will cope with the future when we get there."

Since both these cultures are normative, they both tend to recommend the same solution regardless of the nature of the problem, without a lot of room for flexibility or adaptation depending on circumstances.

German economists find it more difficult to propose policies to stimulate growth; they were brought up in a culture of austerity and they tend to think that austerity is a remedy for everything and anything. If Greece is in a situation of excessive accumulated debt, the solution is austerity. It's no use arguing that you would first need to boost economic growth in Greece; stimulating growth is perceived as being immoral and is therefore rejected. In practice, they are not duly examining the economic issues per se. Unconsciously, economists choose the economic approach that is most consistent with their own culture bias.

In a similar way, if a company performs badly and starts losing money, the first reaction is not to increase sales and revenue. The knee-jerk reaction is to cut costs and increase austerity in management.

German original better than American remake

The German film "Bella Martha" (released as "Mostly Martha" in the United States) won many awards at European film festivals. It told the story of a female German chef who was obsessed with perfection. At the beginning of that story she has a big argument with a client who complains about his dish (a filet of salmon) being undercooked. She bursts into the restaurant's dining room screaming, arguing that it was impossible for the salmon to have been undercooked, because it had been cooked at precisely 400 ºC for exactly 15 minutes.

What is important here is that her character's focus was on the process, rather than on the result. In other words: if the process has been duly followed, it is impossible to get a wrong result. This is a typically German attitude: focus on process, planning and structure. If the result is different from what was expected, then surely there must be a problem with the planning.

The underlying cultural assumption is that it is possible and desirable to plan and control everything. One does not consider that life is, in effect, an open system; and as such, subject to innumerable uncontrollable variables that affect the desired outcomes.

In the film, the main character learns that life demands more flexibility and adaptation, because an unforeseen tragedy occurs and she is suddenly forced to do things that she had never planned for. Also, an Italian assistant chef is employed at the restaurant by the owner, and this new guy has a completely different life style, quite the opposite of Martha's. The film centers on the contrast between these two very different life styles.

Hollywood producers appreciated the success that "Bella Martha" had in Europe and decided to remake the film in the United States with Catherina Zeta-Jones cast as the main character, with the title "No Reservations." However, this version was quite poor as a film, turning a deep and moving story into a superficial romantic comedy torn apart by the critics.

The producers, however, did not complain. The American version grossed ten times more revenue than the German one had done in the US, in spite of the negative reviews. In America, people prefer movies that are spoken in English and featuring big stars in the cast. In Germany, the original was more successful because it won awards, and that served as a quality certificate, something that is more valued by German audiences.

The autonomy of the *"Lander"*

Germany is a Federal Republic and this denomination is no political fantasy. The German "states" (*Lander*) have a degree of autonomy and independence that would be the envy of any American Tea Party member. After all, Germany was only unified as a single country in the 19th Century thanks to the efforts of Bismarck, who went down in History because of that feat.

The high score in Individualism and the low Power Distance in German culture support a certain rejection of a central government with a lot of power. The German federal system determines that power lies with the provinces (*Lander*), which approve or reject federal proposals. At the apex of the Euro crisis in 2011, there were those who suggested that Germany should stop using the Euro and go back to the German Mark. Then people were reminded of the fact that such a decision could never be taken by the Federal Government, and not even by the German Parliament. The proposal would have to be submitted to different independent referendums at each German State, and only if all of those had the same outcome, it would be possible to make that decision.

By comparison, it is worth noting that if the same rules applied to the UK, the Brexit referendum would need to be split by individual countries; and since Scotland voted against it, the UK Government would not be allowed to leave the European Union. That could only happen if all independent countries approved the proposal.

Although the role of Chancellor might appear to be similar to that of a Prime Minister in other countries, from a formal point of view it is quite different. The country's most important position is that of the President, elected by Parliament. The President has the power to dissolve the government and call new elections. It is the President who appoints the Chancellor, based on a suggestion put forth by Parliament.

The second most important position in the German political system is the Head of Parliament, elected by its members and who runs the Parliament's sessions.

3. GERMANY

The Chancellor comes in as the third position in importance; the candidate is chosen by Parliament and suggested to the President of the Republic, who then appoints the person to the position.

All this means that, in practical terms, power is more distributed than concentrated. The central government is in no position to impose anything on anybody, unless they have the support of Parliament and of the Governors of the different *Lander*.

Each *Land*, in turn, has its own Constitution and government structures, sometimes quite different from each other, since they are very autonomous.

Working with Germans

In order to work effectively with the Germans, whether as colleagues in the same company or negotiating with clients or suppliers, you must respect the things that Germans value the most: order, good organization, discipline, expertise, prioritizing tasks rather than relationships.

They admire the boldness of the Americans, their objectivity and focus on results, and also how they might easily strike up a conversation, making small talk with people they have never met before. However, they might be annoyed by attitudes that, in there eyes, deserve condemnation: excessive confidence without careful analysis of the situation, lack of planning, unclear processes and structures.

To be successful at work with Germans, you must demonstrate at least some level of organization and careful consideration; you must show that you have prepared for meetings, "doing your homework" before you attend. If you have expert knowledge about something, it's OK to demonstrate it, but don't overdo it, to avoid being perceived as "showing off." And if a topic is raised about which you know very little, it's perfectly OK to be modest and confess your ignorance.

It is important to maintain your credibility. Speak sparingly and only when you can make significant contributions to the discussion. You will earn a lot of respect by doing that.

Do a lot of detailed rational analysis, whenever there are opportunities for that. If you enjoy making jokes and having fun, make sure you do that during breaks or after hours. It will be highly appreciated at the proper place and time.

4. The Netherlands

Overview

Dutch scores on the five dimensions are:

- PDI – 38
- IDV – 80
- PER – 14
- UAI – 53
- LTO – 44

Similarities and differences

The Dutch culture is egalitarian, individualistic, clearly oriented towards caring and quality of life (rather than towards performance), has a moderate concern with avoiding uncertainty and is not notably flexible (though more than most of its European neighbors). The combination of these value scores reveals that the Netherlands has a fascinating culture, with quite interesting similarities and differences when compared to neighboring countries. This mixture of similarities and differences often baffles the foreign visitors, while at the same time enhancing the fascination with the culture of "the low countries."

When we compare the Dutch culture to that of Americans and British, we can immediately see that there is a significant similarity in terms of egalitarianism and the appreciation of individual freedom. In these aspects, the Dutch, the Americans and the British all share a lot in common, and this fosters spontaneous cooperation at work among people who value similar aspects of what they do.

When it comes to looking at performance issues, however, the contrast could hardly be sharper: while Anglo-Saxons are clearly inclined to consider performance on the job a priority, to the point of generating millions of "workaholics," the Dutch fall on the opposite extreme: they prioritize caring for others and quality of life, rather than performance.

Another aspect directly connected to this dimension regards the amount of individual recognition you can get for performing in an outstanding way. In America the winners in the competition of life are rewarded with lots of prestige and they are proud to show off the status symbols that represent their good performance. In the Netherlands you see the opposite: standing out is frowned upon, it is considered a form of exhibitionism and strongly condemned as such. Society punishes those who stand out and it reinforces mechanisms that promote the leveling out of its members.

"*Doe gewoon*," the Dutch say, which means roughly "just do the ordinary, do what others would do." The aim is to lose yourself in the crowd, be like everybody else and NOT stand out. The goal is equality and not differentiation, especially if being different has the implication of being better than others. You can try to be different, as long as this difference does not mean that you think of yourself as appearing to be better than others. Equivalence is actually better than equality. People may be different from each other, but they should not attempt to have more value than others.

This, of course, leads to many arguments and debate between the Dutch and the Anglo-Saxons. It is quite a contrast, compared to how much both cultures value equality (aversion to hierarchy) and freedom. The paradox is that since both Americans and Dutch value freedom of expression, they tend to discuss quite passionately their differences regarding Performance Orientation, overlooking what they share in terms of Individualism and low Power Distance. These discussions can be quite entertaining for the neutral observer.

In practice, these confrontations generally finish in a truce. In spite of their differences, both cultures have a lot more in common. It is no wonder that some of the largest multinational corporations in the world are partnerships that have been formed between the British and the Dutch, of which Shell and Unilever are the best-known examples, leading their industries. In spite of their differences, the Dutch and the British manage to work well together, complementing each other. The Dutch help the Anglo-Saxons to be less addicted to work and the Anglo-Saxons help the Dutch to be more productive and results-oriented.

Of course, both sides tend to deny this mutual influence and insist on expressing their own different values… They emphasize their own contributions and minimize the influence that the other party has over their own behavior.

Performance, yes; but not as a priority

Recently, someone asked me: "how can you say that the Netherlands has low Performance Orientation, when it has some highly developed industries, sophisticated manufacturing plants, the largest sea port in Europe, and some world-class brands admired all over the globe?"

I started by reminding him that value-dimension scores are not absolute, they are always comparative. This means that having a score of 14 (the Dutch score) does not mean that they are close to having "zero" interest in performing. The lowest score in the world for that dimension is Sweden's (PER = 5); this just means that, compared to other countries, Sweden puts more emphasis on caring for others and on quality of life, rather than on performance. Yet, it does not mean that in Sweden most people don't care about work. A low score on a comparative scale might still be rather high if we were measuring this on an absolute scale.

In the Netherlands people do work, and they work a lot. However, when faced with a situation in which they are required to make a choice between performing at work and enjoying quality of life, most people (statistically speaking) will choose quality of life. This can be seen through different manifestations.

Many people in the Netherlands prefer to work just three or four days a week. Organizations allow them to do that (unlike in other cultures), even though this does affect their efficiency. The rational argument supporting this practice is that it is better to have an employee who is well-motivated three days a week, and another one equally motivated for two days a week, than to force someone to work five days a week with below-par motivation. Even if this does cause some issues regarding communication and workflow, when two people share the same job position, still people and organizations engage in this practice much more often than, for instance, the US or Germany.

It is also more common to see people leaving their jobs at precisely 5 PM and, on Fridays, a bit earlier.

> *Once, on a Friday afternoon, I called KLM to change a flight that I had previously booked for a few weeks later. It was 5:35 and I knew that the airline's call-in customer service center was available until 6 PM. A pleasant-sounding female attendant heard my plea and then argued, in a polite tone: "Sir, this change that you are requesting will require a bit of complex work to carry out, and in a few minutes it will be 5:45, when we need to start procedures to close down for the day. I suggest you call us again on Monday, when we will be better available to give you all the time you need."*
>
> *I was shocked by her attitude, but only for a few seconds. I knew that, faced with a dilemma between showing good performance and choosing for quality of life, the typical Dutch employee will decide for the latter.*

By the way: when shops and services advertise that they are open until 6 PM, it means that, in practice, staff will begin shutting down work stations (including cashiers) 15 minutes before that. At exactly 6 PM the lights are turned off, the doors are shut, and by 6:01 everyone is off the premises, on their way home.

Business can wait

> *Some years ago ABN AMRO was about to close a complex financial transaction with a multinational corporation involving millions of dollars financing exports from Brazil to the United States. To close the deal, the final required step was issuing a letter of guarantee by the bank's Head Office in Amsterdam. This had already been agreed to by all parties involved. All that was needed was for the administrative officer in charge to commit the standard text to paper, sign it and then send it by fax (in those days…)*

to the bank's office in São Paulo. The Brazilian office had negotiated the deal with the client and with a couple of other banks forming a syndicated loan for that specific project.

At 12 noon in São Paulo, the relationship manager leading the project called Amsterdam and spoke directly with the staff member accountable for issuing the letter. It was 5 PM in Amsterdam.

The Brazilian heard this following explanation from his Dutch colleague.

"I cannot send you the letter today, because I'm on my way out. Don't worry, I'll send it to you tomorrow, first thing in the morning."

"But this is a multimillion dollar deal! Everything is ready and done, everyone is waiting: our client, the other banks..."

"Yes, but if I don't leave now, I will lose my parking spot in front of my house; I will need to park my car two blocks away. See you tomorrow." And he hung up, leaving a furious Brazilian on the opposite end of the line...

The Dutch consider that leisure is more important than work; work is "a necessary evil" that allows you to enjoy the simple pleasures of life, such as being with family and friends. Deadlines and haste are often questioned, whenever they seem to interfere with a better quality of life style.

The secretaries and the beach

Once upon a summer day, in Amsterdam, I and some other senior executives received a circular message signed by two secretaries who were part of the pool that provided service to our floor.

"Dear Colleagues,

This Wednesday, the day after tomorrow, you will need to work for a day without the support of our secretarial pool. This is because in our team of four, one is ill and another is on vacation, so that only two of us remained at our posts this week. Since the weather is so nice, with plenty of warm sunshine, Inge has decided to move her scheduled weekly day off from Friday to Wednesday;

and I have decided to use one of my pending vacation days so that we can both go to the beach and enjoy this great weather.

We are sure that you will be able to manage things in our absence for just one day. And we hope that you will also have a chance to enjoy this beautiful summer!"

My expatriate colleagues (Americans, British, Indians, Spanish) and I had our jaws on the floor… The authors of that message were not asking for anyone's permission: they were simply informing us of a decision that they had made. In most other countries in the world, they would be simply fired on the spot… In the Netherlands, when we questioned our Dutch colleagues about the message, they simply shrugged and saw nothing extraordinary about the whole situation.

The world's most communist country

This story about the secretaries and the beach is a good illustration of how equality works in the Dutch culture. The secretaries (and all employees of an organization, regardless of their hierarchical level) have the same rights and privileges as the senior executives in the company. In the 1970's, when China and the Soviet Union were at the height of their Communist regimes, an American businessman described Holland as "the most Communist country in the world."

He was referring to the equality of duties and rights (low Power Distance), which was (and still is) much more evident in the Netherlands than in China or Russia, who were always high PDI cultures, both in the days of Emperors and Czars, as well as during the height of their Communist regimes. Culture is stronger than political regimes and the Netherlands demonstrates that in comparison to China and Russia.

Please refer also to other Dutch examples mentioned earlier in the section about Power Distance in Part 2 of this book.

The Chairman trying to leave the building

Once upon a winter's day, at ABN AMRO's recently inaugurated Head Office building in Amsterdam's Gustav Mahlerlaan,

4. THE NETHERLANDS

I witnessed a curious incident. It was almost 6 PM and I was walking on the mezzanine toward the elevators, when I saw that on the ground floor below me two people were about to leave the atrium, going through turnstiles that required each staff member to use their company ID card to check out of the building.

A few yards away to the left, a receptionist sat behind a small counter, waiting for the clock to strike six, allowing her to leave her post and go home. The first of the two people leaving was a good friend of mine, an Indian colleague. I recognized him immediately and I paused for an instant on the mezzanine to wave him goodbye. As he went through the turnstile, he looked back, glanced at the mezzanine and saw me there. We had a brief dialogue in gestures, signaling that we should call each other the next day.

At that moment, I realized that the other person about to leave was Jan Kalff, ABN AMRO's Chairman of the Managing Board. I noticed that he was having some difficulty in going through the exit turnstile: first, it took him some time to find his corporate ID card, in his pocket; then, when he slid the card in the slot provided for that purpose, the turnstile did not turn to allow him through.

My Indian friend was visibly disturbed observing the scene unfold before him, three yards away. Mr. Kalff tried flipping the card, thinking he was using the wrong side with the magnetic strip pointing up instead of down; that did not work. He tried flipping it again, and still nothing happened.

My friend and I both looked to the receptionist, who watched everything without moving a muscle. For the two of us, the situation was embarrassing: the most important person in the organization was in trouble, he could not leave the building that he had ordered to be built, due to some technical glitch in the bureaucratic access system to the premises. Something should be done to avoid causing further embarrassment to our Chairman!

Mr. Kalff, as a good Dutchman, made no mention to use his position in order to obtain any kind of privilege; he considered himself a staff member like any other and as such he should respect the building's established access procedure. He should set the example of following procedures like anybody else. The fact that he was unable to properly use his ID card to set the turnstile in motion was within the scope of his individual responsibility; it was up to him to show his individual ability to manage his own departure from the building, just as any other employee should be able to do the same.

The receptionist, in turn, as a good Dutchwoman, did not want to interfere with Mr. Kalff's privacy. It was not her role to award him the privilege to leave without going through the staff exit turnstile. There was a little door to the side, which would open if the receptionist pressed a button at her counter, to be used by people in wheelchairs; but this was not the case, since Mr. Kalff was perfectly capable of walking through, or even jumping over, the turnstile, if necessary. If the receptionist were to offer assistance without being asked to do so, she might be deemed to be inconvenient.

After yet another failed attempt by the Chairman, my friend could not bear it any longer; he went to the receptionist counter and asked her to open the little side door to allow Mr. Kalff to go through it. Since she now had an explicit request to help, she promptly acquiesced. Mr. Kalff saw the side door opening, went through it and waived to the receptionist, thanking her.

On the next day, my friend and I talked between ourselves about what had happened. He thought it was totally absurd that the receptionist did not spontaneously help the Chairman; he saw it as a lack of respect. I explained all the different cultural factors at play influencing each person's behavior during that simple situation. The whole thing had lasted less than a minute, but it showcased the PDI and IDV aspects of Dutch culture and the sharp contrast with the cultures of India and Brazil.

The only BMW on this street

In Dutch society people seek to be at the same level as all its members; standing out is frowned upon and considered to be a form of exhibitionism.

4. THE NETHERLANDS

Status symbols should be subtle and discreet; "showing off" is seen as very negative.

> *An American friend of mine living in a town just outside of The Hague told me that, after living in his home for about two years, he bought a BMW Series 3, which at the time was the most modest car on the BMW line.*
>
> *A neighbor who was also a good friend met him on the sidewalk one day as they were both heading for work:*
> *"Bob, why did you get a BMW?"*
> *"Well, it's a nice car, it drives very well, it's very reliable…"*
> *"Yes, but on this street nobody has a BMW… Now you've put us in an awkward position…"*
> *"Why? I don't see any problem at all… You could get a BMW, if you wanted one… Anybody on this street can afford a BMW; this model is not so expensive and everyone in this neighborhood as a good level of income…"*
> *"Sure, but BMW is a 'status' brand. You know that on this street everybody has modest cars… Why don't you sell it and change to another brand? Then you can avoid this awkward situation…"*

It is important to stress that, in this instance, the solution proposed by the Dutch neighbor was to lower the American's status, rather than to raise everyone else's. Leveling is pursued by taking everyone to the lowest common denominator, rather than to the highest.

One cookie, one potato

This avoidance of "showing off" goes a long way and it leads to being thrifty in every aspect of life. The Dutch culture values economy, saving, it avoids wasting anything and using more than what you need. People from other cultures might say that the Dutch are stingy or greedy.

A politically incorrect joke often told in the Netherlands itself is that a Dutchman is able to buy from a Scotsman and sell to a Jew, and still make a profit… Leaving stereotypes aside, the Dutch themselves tell these sort of jokes with a bit of pride; they treasure their skills at negotiating and their ability to save resources.

> *An anecdote regularly told by Dutch people about themselves is the one stating that the typical Dutch housewife would ask her teenage son if he intended to have dinner at home on that evening.*
> *"I think so, yes, Mom; why do you ask?"*
> *"I need to know how many potatoes I will cook for dinner!"*

The unwritten norm is that each family member is entitled to one potato at dinner and the meal should be prepared with the exact number of potatoes, in order to avoid any waste. When this anecdote is told, Dutch people will have a hearty laugh, and I've often heard someone in the group say: "you're all laughing, but in my family it was always like that!"

When coffee is served, whether at a restaurant or at a company, the custom is to add a single cookie, individually wrapped, to go with the coffee. The proportion is always the same: one coffee, one cookie. If you want more than one cookie, you are seen as being greedy; if you offer more than one cookie, you are seen as showing off.

Giving birth at home

In the Netherlands, about half of childbirth instances occur at the mother's home, assisted by a designated midwife. Only pregnancies diagnosed as being subject to risk are scheduled to occur at a hospital, or if the mother-to-be insists with her doctor (but it might not be easy to persuade the doctor…).

After childbirth, the health system assigns a nurse to spend a week with the mother at her home, helping her in learning how to care for the baby. This nurse will care for the mother, teach her how to care for the baby, care for the house so that the mother may rest, recover and dedicate her full attention to the newborn.

A friend of mine, a Brazilian woman who married a Dutchman, had their first baby following this procedure. She told me that she found everything to be fine, up until the moment when, three days after childbirth, she had her first visitors: three Brazilian friends who were also living in the

Netherlands. The nurse took care of everything: she received her guests at the door and took them to the living room, where my friend awaited them, comfortably seated with the baby on her lap.

The nurse offered coffee, which everyone promptly accepted; she served the coffee and brought a cookie jar from the kitchen; she took out one cookie for each guest and then took the jar away back to the kitchen… My friend felt like she could die of shame, because in Brazil the custom is different: cookies are served on a big dish left at the center of the table so that people may more whenever they feel like it; and the amount of cookies is plentiful, because "you can never run out of whatever you are serving!"

In Brazil (also in Italy and in many other cultures), by comparison, when you have someone visiting your home, you can never allow to run out of food or drink: this would be a terrible embarrassment for the hosts, who sometimes are known to sneak out through the back door and buy more of whatever is needed, in order to replenish what is being offered, without the guests ever noticing what happened.

In the Netherlands, if you run out of beer, the host will simply announce to all: "Hey, everybody! We ran out of beer! Would you like anything else?" This is not embarrassing for anyone.

Ambition? What for?

Since quality of life and thrift are both valued, rather than showing off your performance skills, the average Dutch worker behaves quite differently from the typical employee in other cultures. Dutch people seek simple pleasures that are not expensive, and they do not have big ambitions in terms of their careers; also because climbing the organizational hierarchy usually entails increased responsibilities, longer hours and plenty of worrying about things that are beyond your individual control, in exchange for a small difference (in the Dutch egalitarian culture) in terms of remuneration, benefits and prestige. In the American culture, top executives who perform well can become millionaires and are revered as heroes; in the Dutch culture senior executives are regarded with suspicion and they earn much less than half of their American counterparts.

In the Netherlands it is fairly common for people to decline promotions to other jobs, preferring to remain in their current positions. They often consider that higher status and a small increase in salary are not worth it. Since what is regarded as most important is to enjoy a good quality of life, it is best to keep a pleasant life style than to become a stressed- out executive.

This attitude also affects feminist issues. Many women constantly fight for equality with men at work, because indeed it does not yet exist. Although it is true that women are better off today than they were 50 years ago, they are still less recognized on the job than their male counterparts in the Netherlands.

Many Dutch women, however, simply choose for a life style that will allow them to work less hours a week and with less concerns. They have an attitude that is similar to that of many Dutch men, and that is: they do not aspire to a top management position, because that would affect their life style in a negative way.

Likewise, different top male politicians who enjoyed great prestige on a national level, leading their political parties, have announced that they were quitting politics in order to change their life style towards spending more time with their families. In the US and UK, this expression is widely known as an euphemism for failing in your career; that is not true in the Netherlands, where this is often simply a depiction of the real situation. Many people actually make a career choice for a less stressful role, for a function that will demand less emotional sacrifices.

Competition to avoid losing

Considering all that we've seen so far, it might seem that most Dutch people do not enjoy competition. Actually, they do; but competition in the Netherlands has a different connotation, most of the time. The Dutch most often do not compete to win, but rather, they compete to avoid being the last in the contest.

Competition may actually get quite tough, but the goal is leveling, so that nobody gets far behind the others. People aspire to being among the top five, that is considered enough; being "number one," standing out above all others, is something that is seen negatively.

Competition in NL is driven by Individualism, but as an expression of the individual who wants to be acknowledged as such. It does not mean that this acknowledgement should come to the point of a person being considered "better" or "more" than others.

Whenever someone stands out somewhat, the person's peers will try to criticize him/her to "put him/her back in his/her place," which is: at the same level of the peers. On the other hand, no one wants to be considered "less" or "worse" than their peers.

In companies this means that people often compare their own career to that of their college colleagues, with those of the same age and/or with people who were hired to the organization on the same year. If someone feels that their former college colleagues are being promoted more quickly than themselves, then this is reason to confront the boss and ask for a promotion, in order to keep up with the others.

Punctual from start to finish

Parties organized at home or in other places usually have a set time to begin and a set time to end. Both times are observed strictly, and they usually are clearly stipulated previously in your invitation (verbally or in writing).

"We have the pleasure of inviting you to the party celebrating our daughter Annemieke's fourth Birthday, on such and such a date, at such and such address, from 3 to 5 PM."

"Why don't you join us for dinner on the 23rd, from 7 PM till 10?"

Guests will arrive punctually on time, give or take 5 minutes. If someone will be more than 5 minutes late, it is customary to call the hosts advising them of the delay; when the late guests do arrive, they should apologize for being late, even if it was just for 15 minutes.

If it is a business meeting, rather than a social one, and something happens that causes you to be late, you should call in advance apologizing and suggesting that the meeting be rescheduled to another time and date. This is because your delay might have an impact on your host's remaining schedule for the day and this needs to be avoided.

In the case of social commitments, when the pre-set time to end them is reached, the hosts will cheerfully announce: "Well, it was great that you accepted our invitation to come! Now it's time to say goodbye, so thank you again for coming, drive safely and we hope to see you again soon!"

Sense of urgency? What do you mean?

There is no such thing in Dutch culture. That is to say: compared to the sense of urgency commonly found in the US, UK or Germany, in NL the sense of urgency is virtually non-existent.

This is basically due to the very low Performance Orientation. The Americans coined the phrase that "time is money," and money is an outcome of performance. Therefore, time is an important factor in assessing performance. In the US and UK cultures it is important to be bigger, stronger; and also to be faster. Doing things more quickly is a competitive advantage in the competition of life.

In the Dutch culture people ask: "what's the hurry?"

Being in a hurry interferes with quality of life, and therefore this attitude is rejected. Meeting deadlines is not as important as getting everybody on board. What good is making it on time if you had to leave some people behind? If meeting a deadline means increasing stress and damaging your quality of life, then you should postpone your deadline. It's not the end of the world.

The typical time frame for something to happen "immediately" is, in practice, two weeks. Invoices that are due "upon presentation" are expected to be paid two weeks after the date they are presented. If you bought goods that will be delivered immediately, that means they will be delivered in two weeks. Regular meetings at work happen every two weeks. When are you free for dinner? In two weeks.

In Dutch cities there are many narrow streets, often set for one-way traffic, wide enough for just one car at a time. It is fairly common to see that someone will stop their car in the middle of such a street, to unload passengers or merchandise. When this happens, traffic is stopped, because there is no way around the vehicle on such narrow streets.

No one complains; everybody waits, without honking their horn or shouting. There is no rush. This is basically because PER is low; therefore performance, deadlines and hurrying are not so important.

In Brazil, by comparison, everything is urgent and everything is late. In NL, nothing is urgent. You might argue that in fact, sometimes, something is referred to as "urgent" in the Netherlands. This usually means that it is due in two weeks; in the US, "urgent" means it is due today. When, in the US, someone is asked to do something "immediately," it means "do it now;" in the Netherlands, it means "do it in two weeks."

Low service quality

Practically all foreigners coming to the Netherlands, either as visitors or living there as expatriates, they all complain about the bad service they get at shops, restaurants, or when they hire domestic services such as painters, plumbers, repairmen, electricians, etc.

Curiously, most Dutch people are quite surprised when they hear such complaints; they do not recognize the problems described to them by foreigners. This is because there is a clear difference in expectation regarding service, due to the differences in cultural values. People from other cultures come to the Netherlands bringing with them certain expectations based on their home cultures. When this expectation is not met by the typical Dutch person, frustration and criticism ensue.

Usually these experiences are related to differences in Power Distance and Performance Orientation.

Many people expect that someone who is rendering service will show an attitude of mild subservience or submission. This is either because these people are coming from hierarchical cultures, such as the Latino or Asian, or they come from a culture where clients are greatly valued, such as the Anglo-Saxon cultures.

The phrase "the client is always right" has absolutely no resonance in the Dutch culture. The client is someone just like anybody else, like an acquaintance or peer, nothing special. He/she does not enjoy special status nor deserves any special attention for the fact that they are clients and are paying to get service.

Low PER means that the typical Dutch people will value their own quality of life, but not necessarily the client's. Caring for others means that you sympathize with the underdogs, but this does not apply to clients, unless they are perceived to be victims. This is especially not applicable to clients who act superior and demand better service. The louder the complaint, the worst become the attitude of whoever is rendering service, because they tend to refuse being submissive and they do not understand why this client is in such a hurry, since being in a hurry is something that is usually not important.

Most of foreign people's complaints refer to slow service and to getting a negative attitude when they express complaints. Americans are used to getting fast service in their culture, birth of "fast food" and similar concepts; in NL they get quite irritated at restaurants because service is much slower than in the US. When they complain to the waiters, they are treated rudely and things only get worse.

The ten-week sofa

When first moved to the Netherlands in 1996, my wife and I went to a well-known furniture store to buy a sofa. We drifted apart inside the store and a few moments later she came to me asking for some help: "I think I must have misunderstood this salesman's pronunciation, because I heard him say they would take ten weeks to deliver that sofa, but that cannot be, it would be far too long…"

Well, she had understood him correctly: the delivery schedule was for ten weeks later, since the item they had on display, was there for that sole purpose, and each sofa was made to order. The factory's manufacturing schedule was already taken up by previous orders, so the next available delivery could be made no sooner than after ten weeks.

We ended up agreeing to the long wait and we submitted the order. In effect, ten weeks later the delivery truck was in front of our house with the sofa. However, as they began to unload it, we noticed that they had the wrong color… It was easy to demonstrate that there had been a mistake at the factory, since we had a copy of the order with us and it clearly stated that the sofa should be blue, while the item in the truck was definitely green.

The deliverymen apologized and the next day I went to the store to complain, speaking to the same salesman who had taken our order. He apologized profusely and assured me that a new order would be placed and that this one would be for urgent delivery. In the following day he called me to confirm that the new order had been placed and that it would be delivered urgently… in ten weeks.

Treating the client badly when he is trying to pay

Once, in a well-known camera shop, I witnessed a discussion between the sales clerk and a client who was trying to pay for a purchase with his credit card.

> *The sales clerk said: "Your card does not work, the payment has been declined."*
> *"I'm sure the card is not the problem, because I just used this car in the shop next door and there was no problem there. Please try again."*
> *"I already tried two times. You will have to pay cash."*
> *"The problem must be in your card reader, or maybe it's the connection… I have just used the card in another shop. There must be some way that I can use it here."*
> *The sales clerk became visibly irritated and raised his voice: "Then go shop somewhere else! I told you that your card does not work!"*

Don't think that this instance was something exceptional… I have witnessed several similar cases myself, and I've heard countless other similar stories from many people visiting the Netherlands. I mention just two cases because I don't want to fill this whole book with instances that illustrate the same fact: clients in the Netherlands do not enjoy the same treatment dispensed to them elsewhere.

One client at a time gets full attention

Although service in the Netherlands is usually slow and may end in a bitter exchange of mutual complaints, there is an aspect that is clearly positive for the client. In shops, once it is finally your turn to be served, after a long wait, you will have the salesperson's full attention and exclusive dedication.

I'm not sure exactly which of the underlying value dimensions are more strongly at play here, but the fact is that most salespersons in the Netherlands will handle only one person at a time; they seem to be incapable of (or unwilling to) provide simultaneous service to two or more people, unlike what you may frequently see in other places like Brazil or France, for instance.

Giving simultaneous attention to more than one client is considered offensive, it shows a lack of respect to the person you are serving. If a sales clerk is attending to your request and another customer excuses himself and asks: "excuse me, what time does the shop close?" the typical response is: "I am busy with this client; wait for your turn!"

> *Once upon a Spring day, as I was purchasing a flight ticket at a Schiphol airport airline desk, a client came running to the counter, visibly upset and in a hurry, saying: "excuse me, where is the Lufthansa check-in?"*
>
> *The salesperson who was taking my order adopted a scornful expression and said flatly: "it's right behind you, sir!"*
>
> *She then turned to me, barely concealing her irritation, and complained: "Some people have no manners at all!"*

Therefore, whenever you are being attended by a salesperson, enjoy that person's complete attention, without interruption; and do not worry about the people standing in line behind you, as you carefully examine the different articles that the salesperson may show you. The people waiting will not mind that you take all the time in the world at the counter, comparing prices and chatting with the staff: they are not in a hurry… unless they are Americans visiting the Netherlands!

German on the outside, Brazilian hidden inside

Many of my friends, when talking about a Dutch person that they were about to introduce to me, would say things like: "you're going to like Piet; he is not your typical Dutchman." I heard this expression so many times, that I started to wonder… What is a typical Dutchman actually like? Most of the people I've met were introduced as "not typical Dutch people," so is there anybody who is typically Dutch?

I guess that the stereotype in many people's minds was that the Dutch would be rather strict, and direct to the point of being rude. Perhaps some Dutch people may give you that impression, at first. However, after a few minutes chatting, the Dutch turn out to be surprisingly flexible and friendly. I've come to say that the Dutch look like Germans (tall, blond, disciplined), but they have a Brazilian hidden inside (joyful and flexible).

Dutch people value organization and discipline, like the Germans; but unlike the Germans, when they have to decide between performance and quality of life, at a given moment, they tend to opt for quality of life. Another important aspect distinguishing the two cultures is how they deal with Uncertainty Avoidance (UAI). Although the Dutch score is significant (53), the Germans score even higher (65). And in terms of LTO, Germany (31) is more normative than the Netherlands (44).

Translating this combination of scores into laymen terms, what we have is that the German culture puts greater value in order and in complying with rules as a means to achieving better performance. By contrast, the Dutch culture puts less value on performance, to begin with, and it values flexibility and a bias towards making exceptions, in order to get better quality of life and care for "victims."

When Germans say "no," they mean "no" and sustain that "no" until the end, no matter the consequences; rules must be followed. If the rules are inadequate, then one should first change the rules, and then comply with the new rules.

By contrast, the Dutch will often begin by saying "*niet mogelijk*" (not possible) in response to most requests. But if whoever is making a request then tells a sad story that might justify making an exception to the rule, they might find a surprisingly flexible Dutch person quite open to making that exception, in contradiction to the initial apparent firmness.

The Dutch are proud of this and of their ability to analyze each case on its own specific merits and characteristics. In their view, doing this demonstrates intelligence, common sense and pragmatism applied in the interpretation of norms. This trait is also linked to the high degree of Individualism found in the Dutch culture, which is higher than in Germany.

To the Germans, this Dutch behavior shows that they lack character, they are not consistent, they are not as firm as they should be, and that they do not respect the rules. Germans see the Dutch as lacking in seriousness, and as being pushovers. The Dutch, in turn, see the Germans as stupid, lacking in the intelligence required to interpret the rules and apply them with wisdom to each different case.

Of course, I am exaggerating and referring to stereotypes. But these stereotypes are used on a daily basis and they lead to misunderstandings, disappointments and conflicts that end up escalating to the point of becoming business disasters and international diplomatic incidents.

Extreme Individualism

The Dutch culture puts great value in the freedom of expression and in taking individual responsibilities, in spite of the "leveling" that can be seen everywhere. In summary, this means that "we are all **equivalent**, nobody is better than anybody else; but we are all **different**, nobody is the same as anybody else. In these terms, equivalence is not the same as equality. The distinction is important, because people are used to speak of "equality" on a daily basis across cultures, when what is actually meant is "equivalence" (no one person having more value than the next).

This valuing of individuals leads to frequent discussions, which are Dutch people's favorite pastime: they love to argue. Someone has said that "armed with a cup of coffee and an opinion, a Dutchman can spend a whole afternoon at a café arguing with his friends."

This has important implications for work situations. The default stance of any Dutch person regarding any kind of proposal is to be against it. Expressing a contrary opinion is seen as a sign of a strong character and of assertiveness. The most frustrating response you can give to a Dutch person is to quickly agree, thereby avoiding discussion; this robs him/her of the opportunity to state his/her arguments.

> Once there was an ABN AMRO staff member whom I was mentoring. She came into my office looking very frustrated, right after having her performance review conversation with her boss.
> "What happened? Did you get a bad review from your boss?"

"On the contrary, it was very positive… My boss decided to give me a promotion."

"Congratulations! Aren't you happy?"

"Our meeting was very short… As soon as I came in, he said: 'I don't have much time, so let's skip to the conclusion: you did very well this year, so I'm giving you a promotion, effective at the beginning of next month!' *So I told him: 'But I had prepared all these arguments to discuss with you and to convince you that I deserved a promotion…'* He said: 'save them for next year… You just got a promotion!' *It was so frustrating…*"

It's worth noting that discussions many times do not lead to a conclusion… Often it happens that none of the parties involved are willing to change their opinion or make concessions; after a while, both decide that they "agree to disagree" and they just change the subject and move to a different topic. This means that many work discussions are dragged on for days with no conclusion in sight. To the Anglo-Saxons, the lack of a conclusion is extremely frustrating; to the Dutch, more important than reaching a conclusion is to be heard by the other party. "The final decision about what will effectively be done is secondary; but I want everybody to know what my opinion is!"

In work discussions, typically, the boss acts as a coordinator and tries to reach a consensus among the team: an option with which all can live with, even though each person might have certain different objections regarding certain specific aspects. This way, the team might "agree while disagreeing" and get into action. This process is usually quite time-consuming, requiring several meetings, to the dismay of the Anglo-Saxons eventually involved.

Re-discussions

Even more aggravating for Anglo-Saxons (and other cultures as well) is the fact that, once a decision is finally made by consensus, this same decision may be contested later and the discussion may be re-opened (this happens quite often). The reigning principle is that all stakeholders involved must **continue to be satisfied** with the decision made. If anyone re-thinks the issue and changes their mind, a week later, they have every right to re-open the discussion.

> Once upon a quarter, a team of internal ABN AMRO consultants had a series of meetings with the bank's management team in charge of the commercial business in Germany, consisting of five Dutch executives. Throughout these meetings, a new strategic business plan was designed, and a one-day seminar was planned for announcing the plan to an audience of 30 managers of the organization in Germany.
>
> On the evening prior to the seminar, the consultants and the five top-team executives met at the site of the planned event, a small village in Germany, to review details of the seminar planned to start on the following day. That was when one of the five executives stated that he no longer felt comfortable with a certain aspect of the plan, and therefore he could no longer endorse it.
>
> In a different culture, the other four executives (one of them being the Country CEO) and the consultants might simply remind this "late dissident" that it was now too late to change his mind, after all the discussions they had gone through, after they had all agreed to this version of the plan, and since it was going to be announced officially in a few hours!... But in the Dutch culture, they could not afford to do that.
>
> The consultants and the other executives spent a good two hours persuading the dissident team member to agree once again to that aspect to which he had already agreed previously. In case he did not accept their arguments, the seminar would be cancelled (in spite of the fact that the 30 participants were already at the venue) and the discussion would continue until they all reached a new consensus.
>
> Eventually the dissident did agree once again with the plan and the seminar was carried out with no other incidents.

I was a witness to many similar situations, in which a discussion that everyone considered to be concluded was reopened, sometimes two weeks later, because somebody changed their mind. The implementation of a project will only continue forward if all relevant stakeholders continue to be satisfied with the way it's going. One dissident voice is enough to stop the whole process and reopen a discussion, which will only end when the dissident is again on board. Until a new dissident appears…

Refugees

The fact that such high value is put on discussing issues and on ensuring that everyone deserves to be heard, makes the Netherlands a very inclusive culture. Leveling and caring for underdogs has led the Netherlands to give shelter to dissidents persecuted in their home countries. This has been going on for centuries and has come to the point that the Netherlands have become, by the late 20th Century, the country with the highest number of churches per inhabitant (one church for every one thousand people). There are large communities of Catholics, Jews, Muslims, Calvinists and many other branches of Protestants, as well as many other religious communities. This is supported by the basic Dutch cultural principle that everyone is entitled to express their religious beliefs.

Many religious communities that were persecuted in other parts of the world eventually found shelter in the Netherlands. This happened as early as the Pilgrims who went on to found what is now the United States of America.

Every American child learns at school that the Pilgrims left Great Britain on the ship "Mayflower" and founded the colony of Plymouth in Massachusetts, the first of the "Thirteen Original Colonies." The Dutch connection, however, began as part of that journey. The simplified story omits the fact that these Pilgrims fled from Britain and went initially to the Netherlands, where they stayed for about 11 years (1609-1620) and only then did they sail to America. Many families decided to stay in Holland, since after more than a decade living there, they had formed ties with the local community, married to form new families and felt integrated in Dutch life. On the other hand, the Pilgrims included several children born during the decade spent in the Netherlands.

By the time the "Mayflower" finally arrived in North America, in late 1620, there were other Dutch settlers who had preceded them to America since 1615, including a settlement on the Isle of Manhattan. It was only in

1667, after more than 50 years of Dutch colonization, that the island was negotiated with the British, who then changed the name of the existing Dutch village from Nieuw Amsterdam to New York.

To this day, a strong value in the Dutch culture is to allow dissident voices to be heard, whether from the extreme left or the extreme right, and whatever their religious conviction. Dutch culture gives room to each and everyone to express their opinion. There are not that many countries in which you see, on a given day, a demonstration against immigration; and on the following week, a demonstration in favor of more immigration.

Tolerant, except with loud noises

The Dutch enjoy an international reputation for being a tolerant society. In fact, this tolerance is driven by Individualism and by a certain pragmatic flexibility.

The Dutch tolerate differences, since the culture values freedom and individual responsibility. "You are allowed to be different from me, but stay on your turf and I'll remain on mine. We can live together in the same community, respecting each other's privacy and individuality."

The Dutch themselves say that "Dutch people are very tolerant towards everyone except their next-door neighbors." In a sense, tolerance is supported by keeping a certain distance from each other; mutual distance ensures that my own personal space is preserved. With neighbors, you have proximity. With that, the potential for conflict is increased. Perhaps someone next door is playing music too loud; or the neighbor's cat is jumping over the fence into your back yard. When they cook, does the smell of fried fish invade your dining room just as you are about to have your dessert of fresh strawberries?

In other cultures, such neighborly transgressions may be overlooked, when the culture values maintaining group harmony and cultivating relationships. For the Dutch these transgressions are especially annoying because they represent, in a sense, an invasion of privacy; and this is a serious offense.

A curious aspect is that Dutch people tend to be especially sensitive to loud noise levels, be it music played at a high volume, random sounds or people who speak with a loud voice. They see this as very annoying, also because it is difficult to block this kind of invasion of privacy. They can be quite tolerant to visual stimuli: if something offends you visually, all you need to do is turn your head and pretend that you just don't see (paraphrasing Bob Dylan), thus averting the offense.

In Amsterdam, many people dress in rather weird styles without attracting attention of passers by. You can even walk around naked on the streets without anybody giving you a second glance. However, all you need to do is raise your voice above a normal volume, and you will immediately attract angry stares. Soon you are bound to be scolded by someone, complaining about the noise…

Exclusive or inclusive?

There is a paradox linked to this value dimension, regarding being inclusive or exclusive as a culture. Forming groups in collectivist cultures is actually an exclusivist practice, especially when combined with high Power Distance (this combination happens in most hierarchical cultures, with a few exceptions, notably France, Spain and Italy).

Therefore, in collectivist cultures groups are proud of their members and they easily exclude (or consider as not belonging to their group) any people who do not fit the profile considered by them to be part of the group identity. What makes it more complicated is the fact that these standards are not always clearly evident, not even for the group members themselves. The standards are implicit, assumed and presumed.

Brazilians have an expression for this attitude, which is "go find your own tribe;" this is another way of telling someone that "you don't belong here!" Modern urban "tribes" are formed by people who share certain habits and preferences, and who tend to visit the same places: certain parks, bars, restaurants, shops and neighborhoods. People who attempt to break into these groups are rejected and excluded.

The term "exclusive" is used as a sales argument in advertising luxury items. Being exclusive has become a synonym for something desirable, sought after and wanted. The subliminal message is "this is only for a selected few, no one else can have it! You will be admired and envied by everyone else!"

These sales pitches have a strong bias about prestige, something that is quite strong in Anglo-Saxon cultures and also in all high PDI cultures. By contrast, in egalitarian and caring cultures (such as the Netherlands and the Scandinavian countries) who value leveling rather than standing out, we see that the effect is quite the opposite of the intention. People do not aspire to get something "exclusive," because this implies in excluding other people.

Dutch society is quite inclusive, compared to America or Brazil, both of which are exclusive, albeit in different ways.

Since the Dutch culture does not place great emphasis on performance, Dutch companies tolerate staff who in the US would certainly get fired after a couple of weeks on the job performing poorly. This aspect reinforces the Dutch culture's inclusiveness, where everyone deserves to have a place (more than just an opportunity, as in the US).

In the Netherlands there is no meritocracy (in the Anglo-Saxon sense); there is no hierarchy (in the Latin American sense) and groups are less important (although they do exist, of course). All of this makes the Netherlands a very inclusive society. Whoever shows poor performance is not pushed to the sidelines; there is some racial prejudice, but it is much more subtle than in other cultures; and social discrimination among social classes, based on purchasing power, is something blatantly condemned. Yes, it might exist in some social circles; but it will very subtle and not at all endorsed openly.

This is sometimes referred to in other cultures as "Dutch hypocrisy." The problem, as usual, is more in the eye of the beholder. When people from other cultures first make contact with the Dutch culture, they perceive it as being extremely egalitarian and tolerant. They might even think, mistakenly, that it is 100% egalitarian and tolerant. That is not the case, of course. In the Netherlands there is some hierarchy, some prejudice, some discrimination. It is less than what you see in most other cultures, but it is still there to be seen when you look carefully. The discovery of Dutch people showing prejudice and discrimination comes as a shock to the naïve observer, who then feels the initial perception has been betrayed. The reaction to that is typically somewhat exaggerated and expressed as: "they are actually hypocrites… they are not egalitarian and tolerant at all!"

Truth lies in the middle: Hofstede's research (and other's) has helped us to understand culture phenomena in their complexity and apparent contradictions. Using statistic measurements, we can now appreciate that the Dutch are indeed quite egalitarian, much more than the Chinese or the Brazilians, for instance, but perhaps no more than the Danes or the Swedes. No culture is devoid of discrimination. There is no such thing as absolute scores regarding culture.

Social Control

Dutch culture is quite stable and conservative. Historic traditions are treasured and equality (or rather, equivalence) is highly emphasized. Leveling leads to a high degree of social conformity, in terms of "*doe gewoon*" (do like the others are doing, do the usual, the ordinary).

This, in turn, breeds a counter-culture, supported by high Individualism. Conservative attitudes are strong and predominant, but it generates a rather eloquent counter-culture current, but a minority, still. This counter-culture is represented by a very creative art scene, where many youngsters (and also those not so young) express innovative, challenging and anarchic ideas. This can be seen in every form of artistic expression and also in Dutch architecture.

The general public enjoys this, they appreciate this diversity in artistic expressions and they are proud of them; but they soon return to the jobs they have kept for decades and to the homes in which they have lived since they were married.

Many Dutch people leave the Netherlands in search of greater adventures; the Dutch population living abroad grows year on year. These people complain that in Holland they felt there was too much social control and that hindered their sense of individual freedom.

Dutch society faces a certain tension between conformity and individual freedom. On one hand, people want to express themselves as individuals; on the other hand, standing out goes contrary to the notion of equality/equivalence. Since there is no pronounced hierarchy, what you see is that the common folk exercise social control, scolding those who seem to be violating behavior norms.

For instance: if someone parks in a no parking zone, the people around him/her will be the first to voice their disapproval, before a traffic warden shows up to issue a fine; if someone changes lanes without signaling, other drivers will honk their horns in protest (horns are rarely used in traffic; when it happens, it is usually to condemn a transgressor, never because they are in a hurry). This execution of social control by other citizens ends up annoying those less conformist individuals, who then decide to move elsewhere.

Working with the Dutch

Managers have a tougher job in the Netherlands than in many other places in the world; and expat managers, who come from a different culture, have a tough time adapting to the Dutch way of working with teams.

American managers in NL complain about the endless team discussions with no conclusion, about the little emphasis put on making deadlines, and about the poor differentiation in rewarding performance. In the US, outstanding performers in corporations earn significant bonuses and are admired as heroes by their peers. In the Netherlands people seek "leveling" instead of standing out; therefore, compensation schemes are designed with no intention of rewarding outstanding performance. When there is some differentiation linked to performance, it is the smallest possible, in order to avoid upsetting the notion of equality.

In America a good employee is praised in public and might earn twice as much as someone else doing the same job, if the staff member in question has noticeable better performance. In the Netherlands, public praise to individuals is usually avoided, because it might cause embarrassment to all parties involved. The employee who shows outstanding performance is likely to get the same amount of bonus as all others doing the same job. If there is a difference in reward, it is usually not bigger than 5% or 10%.

To managers, this means that they need to find other ways of motivating their staff, besides simply using financial incentives. They need to convince each and everyone in their team about how relevant and solid their business strategy really is. Since the Dutch have been brought up with a keen sense of criticism and they relish debates, managers have their work cut out for them. They know that when they present their ideas and intentions, there will be quite a discussion about them. This is the main challenge for managers coming from countries with a high PDI culture, such as Brazil, France or India. Such managers are used to being obeyed, no questions asked. In the Netherlands, they will need to persuade their direct reports of any proposals; it will not be enough to rely on the authority of their positions, since that does not mean much. In NL, the boss is in fact regarded more as a peer and he/she will need persuasion skills and solid arguments to convince their team of anything. Otherwise, the team might decide to go in a different direction from what the manager intended.

Managers need to be team coordinators and skilled at negotiating with their superiors and fellow managers. They need to respect each and everyone's autonomy and use arguments that will convince stakeholders that their proposals will benefit each and every party involved. Persuasion is a much more important management competence in the Netherlands than in other cultures like the Latin, Germanic or Anglo-Saxons. In these other societies, the position held by a manager in itself earns more respect, either due to higher PDI or because of the manager's status as an expert.

In the Netherlands people do not even show the kind of respect for expertise, as seen, for instance, in Germanic cultures. The Dutch consider the expert "just someone with an opinion," like anybody else. The "notorious wisdom" of specialists is simply not accepted as such. Curiously, this is also the case for Professor Geert Hofstede himself, who is widely regarded as the pioneer in measuring national cultures and considered a word-class authority on the subject. Even though he has been made a Knight by Queen Beatrix, he is generally more highly regarded by people outside of the Netherlands than by many Dutch businessmen, who think of him simply as "another guy with an opinion."

Assertiveness to engage in discussions is so much valued, that the lack of it is considered an actual illness. The Dutch National Health Service officially lists "lack of assertiveness" as an illness for which treatment can be obtained by applying for it through the public healthcare system.

Dutch Summary

The Dutch are egalitarian to the point of being annoyed by any kind of hierarchy; they are individualistic and value quality of life and caring, rather than performing. They have a very direct communication style, which they see as "honest and frank," but that others often find rude. They value leveling rather than standing out. They tend to be factual and rational; they struggle with handling emotions and feelings. They are pragmatic, respect privacy, and very much enjoy discussing and negotiating "on the same level" with other people.

They tolerate differences among people, but not if someone stands out over the others. They want to be heard, but reaching conclusions is secondary. They show little ambition and even less sense of urgency. They make a clear distinction between social life and work.

5. Brazil

The scores

These are Brazil's scores in the five dimensions:

- PDI – 69
- IDV – 38
- PER – 49
- UAI – 76
- LTO – 65

In summary, the Brazilian culture is hierarchical, rather than egalitarian: Power Distance is clearly on the higher part of the scale. Brazil is more collectivistic rather than individualistic, specially compared to the US and to most European countries. However, it is worth noting that Brazil is more individualistic than some of its Latin American colleagues, such as Guatemala, and also compared to many Asian cultures, such as China.

These two aspects (Power Distance and Collectivism) explain the major part of the eventual differences in perspective between Brazilian managers and their American and European counterparts. The American culture and the North-European ones are all egalitarian (low PDI) and individualistic. By comparison, Brazil is mostly hierarchical and collectivistic.

Regarding the third dimension, Performance Orientation (PER), Brazil scored right in the middle, between higher PER-scoring cultures such as the Americans, the British and the Germans, and the cultures more oriented towards quality of life and caring for others, like the Scandinavians, the Dutch, the French and the Spanish.

In this dimension, since performance is important, but also quality of life and caring for others, to an almost equal extent, what one may see is that both aspects are often expressed in daily life. This eventually supports contradicting stereotypes: on one hand, Brazilians are often described as "party animals" and "easy going." On the other hand, they may also be described as dedicated and hard-working, staying at work until late and over the weekend.

Since culture is always a statistical measure of a collectivity, in practice this means that some Brazilians can be workaholics, while others may be rather lazy. In some regions, like São Paulo, a lot of emphasis is put in working hard; while in others, like Bahia, there is more emphasis on enjoying life. This has led to regional stereotypes within Brazil, according to which "São Paulo can never stop," while people from Bahia are considered to be easy going and downright lazy.

In terms of Uncertainty Avoidance (UAI) the Brazilian score is higher, comparable to what has been found in Germany, Italy, France and Spain; it is much higher than what you see in the US and UK. However, the drivers of these scores can be quite different for each country, and the behaviors expressing them are also different. We will take a closer look at this, further on.

Long-Term Orientation (LTO) is high in Brazil. As described earlier in this book, although Brazil's score is much lower than China's, it is still much higher than all scores found in Europe and in the US. Brazil has a culture that is quite oriented towards flexibility; it is not normative. These values support the stereotypes of improvisation, creativity and of "finding a way" to get what you want (the famous Brazilian "jeitinho"). Most Brazilians are quite proud of these stereotypes. However, high LTO combined with high PDI give room for corruption, a stereotype of which Brazilians are not at all proud.

Paternalism

Management culture in Brazil is indeed quite paternalistic. This is reflected in the country's high score in Power Distance and in its low Individualism score (Brazil is collectivistic). Organizations are considered to be large families. Staff members are typically proud to be part of this big family and loyalty to the group is highly valued. The CEO (the boss, the chief) is a paternal figure: sometimes benevolent, sometimes strict. Performance Orientation is not high, so this gives room for paternalism over meritocracy. Although many Brazilian companies like to say that they are a meritocracy, it is a well-known fact that promotions and career progress are basically dependent on relationships and respecting the hierarchy.

"The boss' scrotum is the handrail on the ladder to success," goes the popular Brazilian saying (it sounds much better in Portuguese). This popular expression conveys the fact that if you please your boss you are on the road to being promoted. Everybody criticizes those who spend time flattering their bosses, but no one fails to do it whenever they have a chance. They know it works in this culture.

ABN AMRO in Brazil

The acquisition of Banco Real in Brazil by ABN AMRO from the Netherlands provided numerous interesting examples of the contrast between the Brazilian business culture, typically paternalistic, and the Dutch business culture, which is egalitarian, individualistic, caring, low on UAI and normative (by comparison). In other words: the Dutch culture is almost the exact opposite of the Brazilian one, in each of the five dimensions.

Immediately when the integration of the two organizational cultures began to unfold, the differences between the underlying national cultures became abundantly evident, from the very first day people started to meet with each other.

The Brazilians in Banco Real reacted to the news with typical sweet and sour Brazilian humor, capable of making jokes about the most tragic of events. One of the first remarks I heard from Banco Real staff was that "ABN" stood for "Aloysio 'Bandonou Nós" (Aloysio 'Bandoned Us), referring to the fact that Dr. Aloysio Farias (or simply Dr. Aloysio, as he was commonly referred to), the bank's major shareholder and CEO, had decided to sell the organization to ABN AMRO. Dr. Aloysio was a prime example of Brazilian paternalistic management, and selling his shares to another company was perceived as the father figure abandoning his children (the staff) to an uncertain future.

Pros and cons of paternalism

We all learn in Anglo-Saxon management books that paternalism is a "bad" way of managing people; it is totally the wrong way of doing things. Paternalism is perceived as condescending and amounting to a disguised form of oppression. It hinders people's growth, is an obstacle to merit-based career progress, it is an outdated practice that damages business and personal development.

This vision is biased by culture, notably by a culture based on low Power Distance, high Individualism and high Performance Orientation. There is no doubt that paternalism goes against many core values found in the Anglo-Saxon cultures and also in Germanic and Scandinavian cultures. However, we cannot say, in terms of overall intercultural understanding, that paternalism is inherently "bad," wrong or inefficient. In fact, paternalism can be quite effective and efficient, notably if it is inserted in a congruent national culture, that is: a high PDI and collectivist culture. Performance Orientation is actually less relevant here: there are paternalistic cultures oriented towards performance, while others are more caring-oriented.

In a paternalistic management system, power is concentrated at the top. The top incumbents have privileges associated with power, but they also bear great responsibilities, leaving the remainder of the organization often in a rather comfortable position. Middle managers need to worry but about one thing: keeping their boss happy, by demonstrating their loyalty. "If the company does badly, it's the boss who is responsible for that. He makes the decisions, and if the decisions turn out to be wrong, it's all his fault."

Hierarchy

In Brazil people say that "the boss is always right." The expression is used in other cultures, but in high PDI societies it is truer than anywhere else. In Brazil people also say that "the client is king," but if that is true, then "the boss is God." People behave as if the boss had the power of life and death over them. Respect for hierarchy is taken to the extreme.

At work, whenever you need to get anything done by somebody else, all you need to do is say that "the boss is asking for this." Immediately, all and any objections are laid to rest: if the boss is asking for this, then it's not a request, it's an order! This must be done at once! Drop everything and do what the boss is asking for!

Years ago, I was involved in a broad program aiming to emphasize client focus in a large bank. As part of this program, I joined a team that helped each staff member to identify who were their internal and external clients, as a starting point to discuss what could be done in order to better serve these clients.

Some people had great difficulty in making this identification: they did everything for their direct boss and could not see beyond that relationship with authority. "Everything I do is for my boss, it's because he asks me. I don't do anything for anybody else."

"And who are your boss' clients?" I asked.

"I don't care. I do everything for my boss, what happens afterwards is none of my business."

In a less hierarchical society, staff members might take more interest in the outcome of their work and what happens with it. In a hierarchical society, it's enough to satisfy your boss, the rest is not relevant. There is a Brazilian saying that goes: "Those who can, give orders; those who are smart, obey them!" *(Manda quem pode, obedece quem tem juízo)*. In other words: if you're smart, do as your told with no discussions. Otherwise, your bosses might use their power against you.

Sanctioned Initiatives

Popular sayings are great sample examples of cultural values. It is fascinating to observe how similar concepts are expressed quite differently in different cultures.

A Brazilian saying goes like this: "God will help those who wake up early" (*Deus ajuda quem cedo madruga*). The purpose of this saying is to stress that people should be awake early and take initiative. In English, the same intention is expressed differently: "The early bird gets the worm."

The difference is that in a hierarchical culture you expect that "God will help you" (a superior authority has the power and might help you); while in an egalitarian culture you are expected to help yourself (if you wake up before the others, you will be ahead in the competition of life and get what you need before the others do; no help from above is required).

In low PDI cultures, all you need is to take the initiative in order to get what you want. In Brazil (and in other hierarchical cultures) initiative is not enough; you also need "help from above." Your initiative needs to be supported, sanctioned or authorized, in order to be carried out. Many times people need to have an explicit authorization, before they allow themselves to dare take initiative. The attitude is one of "when in doubt, wait for instructions from the boss. He/she will tell us what to do."

The *mutirão* culture

As a collectivistic culture, Brazil emphasizes groups more than individual responsibilities. Belonging to a group and maintaining its internal harmony is more important than taking an independent position. This dimension expresses itself in Brazil in many situations: one of these is the *mutirão*, a very Brazilian expression that is hard to translate.

A *mutirão* is formed when a group of people get together to carry out a specific task, more or less spontaneously, believing that by doing so the task will be finished quickly. Brazilians don't need a lot of prodding to join a *mutirão*; the name itself sparks enthusiasm and people readily join simply because they've learned (since childhood) that it's great fun to do something together. Compared to individualistic cultures, Brazilians are easier to mobilize. They join because they relish opportunities to be in a group and further nurture relationships. If in addition to that, something gets done, that's a bonus.

The tasks at hand can be quite different: it might be building a small house over the weekend for one of the neighbors; it might be loading or unloading a truck; painting the neighborhood school; organizing a community feast to raise funds for charity. All of these things can be seen happening in other cultures too; what makes the *mutirão* distinctive is the fact that it is short-term and spontaneous, with no planning involved. Typically, a couple of people spread the word and the mutirão is formed for the next day, or for later on the same day.

What most Brazilians lack (and it's abundant in individualistic cultures) is critical thinking to challenge the orders given by a boss, or to go against the opinion of a group. In Brazil, if a leader has charisma, people are easily mobilized. If a group decides to do something together, it's easy to get people to join in; people prefer to be part of a group, rather than being on their own.

Privacy is relative

Brazilian Collectivism means that relationships are more important than tasks; and new relationships are rather easily formed.

In Northern Europe, the US and Canada, respecting privacy is a frequently discussed issue; and people defend their privacy fiercely.

By contrast, in Brazil people become quite intimate with other people that they have just met five minutes ago, typically while standing in line for something. They will tell you their whole life story after two minutes, without even knowing your name. Shop attendants engage in conversation with clients who they have never seen before in their lives, sharing tips on what to wear, how to raise kids and what you should be having for dinner tonight. They ask for advice and give it profusely, without a second thought.

Similar things may be observed in every collectivistic culture, such as most Latin American countries and also in Africa and Asia. For individualists, however, all of this constitutes invasion of privacy and they usually feel truly shocked. For Brazilians, they are just sharing a conversation. It is all natural and spontaneous, they never think twice about it.

Collectivism also leads to people easily having physical contact with each other. When talking to others, Brazilians frequently touch each other lightly on the arms, shoulders, back, whether touching clothing or exposed skin. In most individualistic cultures this is considered shocking and offensive; in some places, it is tantamount to sexual harassment. In Brazil this is simply a form of emphasizing whatever you are saying, even when talking to someone you have just met for the first time.

Whoever is on top gets the blame

In hierarchical and collectivistic societies like Brazil, control and discipline are "delegated upwards." That is to say: people tend to not take full responsibility for their own actions; they consider that power, authority and ultimate responsibility for controlling and maintaining discipline reside some place above their own position in social hierarchy.

The whole culture reinforces this attitude and looks to blame whoever is on top for whatever is happening in the economy, in politics and in society in general. If the economic situation is bad, "it's the government's fault." The mayors (local government) blame the state governors; and they blame the Federal Government.

Whenever there is a disaster or a tragedy, such as a big fire, a bridge falling down or a landslide, public opinion searches for "who is to blame" for this, on the higher ranks of public officials (who are regarded as ultimately responsible for everything that happens).

The Fire Department officials and the mayor are criticized for the fire that broke out; the person who inadvertently left a lit cigarette next to a paper wastebasket is off the hook. Focus is on whoever is the power holder, rather than on those directly responsible for what happened.

Criminality increases are blamed on the police, or on not having enough police on the streets; criminals themselves are not the focus of criticism. The bridge that collapsed is not the fault of the workers that built it; it's the fault of the engineer who designed it, or the government officials who should have inspected the construction. Landslides that destroy houses built on the side of hills are the responsibility of government inspectors who should have stopped people from building there; rather than of people who disobeyed the law and built their houses in a place that everybody knows is actually not legally allowed for construction; and so on.

This attitude indirectly encourages people to try to take advantage of others in all kinds of situation. If I do not regard myself as accountable for most things (because accountability lies with someone above my own position), it is only natural that I may try to bypass the law continuously, up until somebody above me actually stops me from doing so.

5. BRAZIL

In individualistic and low-PDI societies, each person takes responsibility for their own actions; in collectivistic and high-PDI societies like Brazil, responsibility lies with the boss. People don't think they are responsible; whoever has the power is responsible.

If you hold a position as a boss in Brazil, you need to exert control and maintain discipline, since this is expected from you. If you don't, you will not earn other people's respect.

Work and fun at the same time

Performance Orientation, in Brazil, has been scored at a mid-point, balancing between valuing quality of life and valuing performance. In practice, this means that one can observe situations in which behaviors lean towards performance, while in other situations behaviors are more directed towards preserving quality of life and caring for others.

In other words: Brazilians typically work hard and play hard. A notable difference from cultures in Northern Europe and North America is that they often to this simultaneously, rather than having a clear division between work and leisure.

Anyone working in Brazil will notice that people often make jokes as they do their work, on the job. While in other cultures the separation between work and leisure are clearly laid out, so that people behave seriously at work and during work hours, saving jokes and playful remarks for after-hours, week-ends or lunch breaks, in Brazil people are constantly playing and intersecting jokes even in the midst of serious discussions. Perhaps this has earned Brazilians a reputation for not being serious, or for playing too much or at improper times.

The fact remains that this is a culturally determined behavior. While in the US and Northern Europe companies regularly discuss "work-life balance," in Brazil people do not see these things as separate entities. Rather, they consider that work is an integral part of your life; and that you should have fun while you work, instead of keeping it apart and saving your funny remarks for later.

The mix of leisure and work, however, also means that people may accept doing work during their leisure time. It is quite common to take work home, to get things done in the evenings or on week-ends; and bosses may call their direct reports to discuss work matters also late in the evening or during week-ends. People often have conversations about their jobs at social events; and they may discuss their social life during their work at the office.

The mix can make working at the office more fun, compared to your typical corporate atmosphere in the US or in Germany. At the same time, American and German expatriates working in Brazil may find all that joking around at the office a bit annoying and lacking in professionalism.

For Brazilians, the jokes and playful remarks provide a kind of comedy relief in the otherwise drama of life. It helps them to work long hours, since the typical working day in Brazil lasts from 9 to 6 for staff in general, while managers at all levels tend to work from 8 am until 7 pm or later. Whistling while you work (as the Seven Dwarfs did in Disney's "Snow White") allows people to lighten the burden of working longer hours.

In terms of regional sub-cultures within the country, Brazilians will readily tell you that people in São Paulo work harder, while in Bahia "everybody is lazy." In the year 2000 an extensive research was carried out sponsored by José Carlos Teixeira Moreira's Industrial Marketing Institute (IMI), involving 10,000 respondents from every state. This project was coordinated by my wife Jussara Nunes Pereira de Souza and the statistical analysis was done by a Dutch team supervised by Professor Geert Hofstede himself. The study found that the regional differences within Brazil are, indeed, statistically significant. However, these differences are somewhat limited compared to the overall scores found for Brazil as a whole.

In other words: Performance Orientation is slightly higher in the South and slightly lower in the North, but the differences are not as large as the popular stereotypes suggest.

Joint Venture in Germany

A few years ago, a well-known Brazilian businessman was looking to expand his company's business in Europe and Germany appeared to be a good place to start. The organization had already an international reputation for quality and dedication to excellence; the company's founders were German immigrants, so it seemed that establishing a joint venture there would not be difficult it terms of culture differences.

5. BRAZIL

After a few months of scouting, a business development team identified a German organization with the right potential for a partnership: it was a company working in the same industry, knowledgeable about the local market, eager to expand and open to an international alliance.

> After a few contacts by mail and by phone, and an informal conversation in Frankfurt between executives from both companies, they set a first formal meeting for the two owners to get to know each other in person, along with senior advisors.
>
> The meeting was arranged to be held at the German company's head office, at 11 am. The Brazilian team arrived a couple of minutes early, determined to counter the stereotype that "Brazilians are always late." The Germans were expecting them and the meeting went according to the previously agreed plan; the atmosphere was cordial and objective.
>
> At precisely 12 noon, having covered all the points on the agenda, the meeting closed on a positive note. The German CEO made a point of accompanying the Brazilian delegation to the elevators and said goodbye looking forward to their next meeting, in order to pursue further negotiations.
>
> As they went down in the elevator, before reaching the ground floor, the Brazilian CEO said to his advisors: "We will never work with these people…" The team members were caught by surprise: "Why not, sir? I thought we had a great meeting…"
>
> "They had to invite us to lunch at the end of the meeting! How could they send us off, precisely at lunch time?"

To a less-informed observer, his reaction might appear to be exaggerated; but the Brazilian entrepreneur demonstrated that he placed great value on relationships, which he considered to be a fundamental aspect of forming a joint venture. The Germans, on the other hand, were focused on work and the tasks at hand. To them, having lunch together was something irrelevant to the business being discussed.

Vale in Canada

International media ran headlines, a few years ago, when Brazilian mining company Vale, one of the three largest in the world, acquired a smaller mining company in Canada. A Brazilian management team took over and a few months later the mineworkers went on strike... the first miners' strike in the company in twenty years! The strike lasted for months until finally the disputes were settled. What happened?

Undoubtedly culture differences were a major factor in the disagreement between management and the workers. When interviewed by the press, the union leaders complained strongly about the Brazilian managers. "They were only concerned with showing us who was the boss. They never sat down with us to discuss labor issues." The union leaders went on to stress that the company had previously a habit of sharing the mines' financial situation with the union, whenever it was time to negotiate a new collective agreement. To their amazement, the Brazilian managers refused to do so, despite knowing that this had been standard practice by their American predecessors for many years.

The Brazilians had attempted to employ the same leadership style that they were used to applying in Brazil (and in other hierarchical cultures where they also operated). But in Canada (egalitarian culture) that same style was perceived as authoritarian. The rift caused the company to lose millions while the mines were paralyzed.

Problems due to culture differences do not happen only when managers from the North are sent as expatriates to run businesses in emerging markets; they also happen when managers coming from emerging markets do not adapt their practices when faced with situations in cultures that are different from their own.

Uncertainty Avoidance in Brazil

Ever since Hofstede's research studies became better known in Brazil, at the end of the 90's, when we used that framework as a reference to integrate ABN AMRO and Banco Real's organizational cultures, some local academics questioned the scores found in Brazil for Uncertainty Avoidance (UAI).

The high score (76) seemed to go against the popular notion that Brazilians are skilled at treating situations where uncertainty abounds. This popular notion takes in consideration the fact that the average Brazilian faces many uncertain situations in his/her daily routine, due to a very dynamic labor market, frequent swings in the economic outlook, high inflation rates, and frequent changes in the political environment.

Betânia Tanure even published a research study carried out in several Latin American countries, in which the results pointed in the exact opposite direction: low scores in every culture where Hofstede had found high scores of UAI.

This study, however, used a totally different methodology compared to Hofstede's: different research tools, different sampling methods... no wonder that it got to different results. The problem lies in the differences in approach, which invalidates the comparison. Tanure's research measured something else, other than Hofstede's UAI.

The fact is that many people do not really understand this dimension and this leads to misinterpreting the scores. Hofstede's definition of UAI is far from simple, so such misinterpretations are perfectly excusable.

A common mistake is to consider that the actual social environment (stable or unstable) is part of the dimension (which it's not). UAI is not about the environment; it's about how people react to the environment. In other words: the environment might be stable and the culture might have either a low or a high score in UAI. Or the environment might be quite unstable, yet the culture could show either low or high scores in UAI. It's not about the environment; it's about how people cope with it.

In Germany, people deal with uncertainty by emphasizing planning and order. In Brazil, different mechanisms are used, notably superstition, religion, extensive legislation and clear expression of emotions (so that you know how people are feeling).

When you look at those aspects, it is quite clear that the Brazilian scores can be expected to be higher than, for instance, the score found in the United Kingdom (35). You can see examples all around you of Brazilians expressing those aspects. In addition to that, one can also observe still other behaviors that are correlated with high UAI: frequently reconfirming previously scheduled appointments; deeming everything as "urgent" at work; and frequent speeding and haste in urban traffic.

The only aspect of UAI that one does not see in Brazil is the emphasis on planning. Indeed, the culture does not stress that aspect.

Long Term Orientation in Brazil

This is another dimension that is frequently misunderstood because of what we normally consider to be "long term." This label can be quite misleading and there is a history behind it.

This dimension was identified through a research study carried out by Michael Harris Bond. This was reviewed and endorsed by Hofstede as a fifth value-dimension in culture.

What Bond uncovered was a complex dimension with many facets, not easily described. Initially he named it "Confucian Dynamism," a label that did not do much to facilitate understanding…

Taking a long-term perspective is indeed a key aspect of this dimension, but it does not explain it completely. Besides that, thinking in the long run does not only mean that you plan for the next ten years or more. As explained in the specific chapter dedicated to this dimension, it's more about an attitude that stresses the importance of seeking an ultimate outcome, more general in nature, compared to seeking an outcome that is more concrete and measurable, and obtained in the short term.

A good example is to consider a company that places more focus on positioning itself to gain market share over the next five years (high LTO) rather than dedicating its energy to reaching monthly or quarterly profit targets.

Another notable aspect of this dimension is relativism when applying norms (high LTO), versus the normative stance of following norms regardless of circumstances.

Both these aspects are clearly seen in Brazilian culture, starting with the pretty well known Brazilian *jeitinho*. This refers to a certain way of going around norms and regulations, in order to get what you want without blatantly confronting anybody or breaking the law. It also means applying norms in a flexible way, depending on the people and the circumstances involved, rather than doing that strictly. In Brazil, there are laws that are followed and other that are simply not followed… A certain circumstantial pragmatism prevails, instead of simply obeying the law as such.

It is true that some aspects of Brazilian culture reveal a somewhat short-term orientation: people want immediate gratification and they are often impatient. On the other hand, there is also a perennial feeling of hope, an idea that "everything will be all right, eventually." This attitude pushes the score upwards, along with flexibility and relativism.

Initially, Bond focused his attention on Asian cultures and comparing them with Europe and the US; the only South American culture to be included was Brazil, and he was surprised to find a rather high score there.

It so happens that this complex dimension involves some aspects that are not only Chinese or Confucian. It involves also this relativism that is found not only in Brazil but also in other Latin American cultures, and in some parts of Africa. More research is warranted to shed more light on what this dimension is measuring.

Some popular notions about Brazilian culture and how they relate to culture value-dimensions

Are Brazilians "nice guys" or "selfish con artists?"

Within Brazil these two opposite notions of the national character compete with each other. Some say that Brazilians are "nice guys:" they are kind, hospitable, enjoy helping others and show solidarity even to complete strangers. Let's explore this notion first, and later return to its competing opposite.

Anyone going to Brazil can see that helping others and being useful are things that the culture indeed values. Foreigners visiting Brazil often mention that people go out of their way to help foreigners who are asking for directions. They not only provide directions, but might even tag along and take the person to their destination. This is a kind of behavior that is more often found in collectivistic cultures, but seldom seen in individualistic ones.

Brazilians "buy into" other people's problems. They consider another person's challenge as their own and seek to solve the situation as if they were resolving their own problems.

A Brazilian taxi driver, when told that his passengers are late for an appointment, or risk losing their flight, will step on the accelerator and try to move as fast as possible, seeking alternative routes to avoid traffic jams, doing whatever they can to get the passengers to their destination on time. This is clearly collectivistic behavior: in that situation, driver and passengers are all part of the same group, trying to resolve an issue that belongs to them all jointly.

This seldom happens in individualist cultures. In such cultures, the prevalent attitude is that each person is responsible for their own actions, and not for the actions of others. If I am a taxi driver and you are running late, that is your problem, not mine. My accountability involves taking you to your destination, driving at a normal speed and following the usual route. You are running late? I'm awfully sorry, but there is nothing I can do. After all, this is not my fault and it's not my problem.

Volvo Ocean Race
In the 2005 edition of this well-known around-the-world sailing race that had previously had many editions, the main sponsor changed to Volvo (it was formerly known as the Whitbread Ocean Race and it has had other sponsors as well). On that year, for the first time there was a Brazilian sailboat in the competition, with the skipper and the crew of eleven being all also native Brazilians. The race lasted several months, split into nine different legs linking different seaports around the globe, so that a full circumnavigation of the planet was completed, starting in Spain and finishing in Sweden. The legs were extremely challenging, since they involved sailing in the open sea for many days, braving storms and all kinds of weather, to go from Spain to South Africa, for instance, or from South Africa to New Zealand.

At the end of each leg, the crews spent a few days on land, repairing damage on their boats, resting from the demanding days at sea, and preparing for the next challenging stretch. When the damage to the boat was significant, there was little time to rest: sometimes crews had to work day and night to get the boat ready in time for the start of the subsequent leg.

The Brazilian crew became rather famous for doing something unusual: they helped the other competing crews to fix their boats, during those days on land. As soon as the boats docked, each crew focused on their own boat, fixing the damage and doing required maintenance work; the Brazilians were no exception, they did the same. The difference was that, once they finished working on their boat, the Brazilian crew took walks around the marina and visited the other boats, offering to help them out, since some had suffered more extensive damage that required longer work to be done. This behavior is typically linked to Collectivism. Although they were all competing against each other, unconsciously the Brazilians saw themselves and the others as all belonging to the same group: that of the Ocean Race participants. Why not help out your colleagues from the same group?

Their behavior was welcome, but regarded as weird by the crews coming from individualistic cultures, who saw their own accountability as restricted to getting their own boats in shape. Why should you help your competitors from different boars?

The nasty Brazilian and "Gerson's Law"
This Brazilian willingness to help others goes against a widespread notion, in Brazil, that most Brazilians are actually selfish and self-centered. There was even a comedy sketch on TV, decades ago, where actors made fun of this issue: are Brazilians really so nice, or are they actually trying to take advantage of others whenever they can?

These conflicting notions about the Brazilian national character are linked to high Power Distance and low Individualism (Collectivism).

Assigning value to relationships and to maintaining harmony within groups is what drives Brazilians to be helpful, in unselfish ways (Collectivism). Assigning value to hierarchy and to exercising power over others are the forces that drive Brazilians to try to take advantage of others, because the assumption is that if they do not do it, others will exercise power over them. If I don't do it to them, they will do it to me.

In a way, high PDI leads people to have to choose between playing the victim or playing the bully. Since high PDI cultures start from the perspective that there are significant differences in the distribution of power among people, I need to position myself in relation to anybody I meet: is my position lower or higher (in the hierarchy) compared to this other person's?

This process, often described as "taking advantage" over the next person, became crystalized in Brazilian pop culture by a cigarette commercial on TV that promoted the Vila Rica brand. In that advertisement, the football player Gerson, one of the stars of the team who won the World Cup in 1970 in Mexico, was shown smoking a cigarette and describing the many advantages he got from smoking that brand: it had more flavor, yet it cost less, allowing him to take advantage of that so-called cost-benefit ratio. He finished by looking straight at the camera and saying, with a wry smile: "And you? You want to take advantage, right?"

That originated the expression "Gerson's Law," paraphrasing Murphy's Law ("If anything can go wrong, it will.") Gerson's Law states that "you should always seek to take advantage over others;" in any situation, including by acting dishonestly. To this day, fifty years after that commercial was aired, people still refer to "Gerson's Law" whenever they want to express their criticism about someone who acted unethically and took advantage over others.

Many people think of this behavior as being linked to Individualism, which in their perception tantamount to selfishness. However, that is not what Hofstede defined as Individualism. Gerson's Law, in Brazilian pop culture, is linked to high PDI and the unconscious need to put yourself above others, before they push you beneath them.

Impunity

Brazilians will often criticize their own culture and refer to "impunity," meaning: people not being punished for their crimes, large or small. The word is not commonly used in everyday English language, but the meaning with which it is used in Brazil would be equivalent to the American expression: "getting away with murder." In other words, not being punished when you have done something that deserves punishment.

The popular notion in Brazil is that there is little respect for rules and regulations in the country, while corruption is rampant. This is attributed to the fact that nobody gets punished. If nobody gets punished, this encourages people to continue with their wrongdoings. According to this line of thinking, if the country would enact more legislation, and laws that would be stricter, with more severe punishment, plus if these laws were then rigorously applied, there would be less crime and corruption.

This whole logic is directly linked to the Brazilian culture's value profile: high Power Distance, Collectivism, moderate Performance Orientation, high Uncertainty Avoidance and high Long-Term Orientation.

The high Power Distance means that some people have much more power and privilege than others. This concentration of power favors corruption. All over the world, countries with higher PDI show higher corruption indicators. Power corrupts. Absolute power corrupts absolutely.

High PDI also means that people perceive control as being something that happens outside of them, rather than self-control. Discipline, control, compliance, all these things are the responsibility of someone that has more power than I do.

When we combine this with Collectivism, we can see that there is less individual responsibility. It's not my responsibility, it is the group's, or it lies with whoever is the group's boss. Impunity, therefore, is not something that should be addressed by each and every member of society as responsible individuals. It's the Government who is to blame; or the police; or the faulty legislation. Or whoever has more power than me. Surely, it is not my responsibility.

Collectivism also supports the notion that "the law does not apply to my friends." Therefore, the law should not punish those who are in "my group of friends," and it should not punish the very powerful, who "are above the law."

Performance Orientation, since it is rather moderate in Brazil, does not contribute significantly for making people accountable or not. If anything, it might be regarded too high, because it does not support the reformation of criminals. Research shows that countries in which Performance Orientation is low (therefore, caring and quality of life are higher) such as the Netherlands and the Scandinavian cultures have a much lower crime rate and less corruption, when compared to other societies.

Uncertainty Avoidance is relevant because of its connection to the mistaken notion that impunity could be solved simply by creating more legislation. The practical experience of other countries points to the opposite. Having more laws, more severe legislation or more detailed regulations, none of these things lead to decreases in crime or corruption. It is the degree by which people obey the law (compliance) that influences crime and corruption.

The severity of established punishment is also not so important. Crime is lower in countries where laws are often less severe. What happens is that in these countries the laws are applied more often and more rigorously. It's the application of the law that makes the difference, not the fact that laws provide for long sentences and capital punishment.

This takes us to LTO; the dimension that measures how much value is attributed by a culture to applying norms. High LTO, as observed in Brazilian culture, means that compliance to norms is not regarded as something really important. Rather, it means that norms are relative. Their application depends on the circumstances surrounding each and every situation. It also means that "the ends justify the means." That is to say: my ulterior objective is more important than complying with legal and ethical norms. This aspect eventually supports crime and corruption, while PDI and Collectivism support impunity.

Facing this broad characterization of the Brazilian culture (which applies also to other cultures where corruption and crime are high, such as Russia, India and China), what could be done to change the situation for the better, in terms of reducing crime, corruption and impunity?

From a cultural point of view, basic values need to be changed; and this is something that requires multiple and simultaneous efforts, attacking on many fronts.

Too root out impunity, it would be necessary to reduce the factors that support relativism in applying the law (high PDI and Collectivism), and reduce LTO (away from flexibility and towards greater regard for compliance).

In practice, this means changing leaders' behavior (or even changing leaders). In high PDI societies, change only happens when leaders at the top of the hierarchies support it.

At the same time, every adult person's behavior needs to be influenced by intense public communication campaigns that emphasize the desired behaviors. Incentives should be created (financial and non-financial) to reinforce these behaviors.

In parallel, education (in its broadest sense) must change: for children, teenagers; at school, within each family, everywhere.

Positive and true examples of compliance and application of punishment should be broadly advertised, keeping in mind that it is not about punishing severely, but rather applying the law frequently and consistently, with abundant use of community services in sentences).

All of this is easier said than done, of course. The challenge is to support leaders who will champion these values and take action in very concrete terms. And to start with each person and each family, teaching values to children that will shift the culture in the desired direction.

6. China

Overview

Chinese culture is hierarchical, collectivistic and performance oriented. There is no major concern about uncertainty or ambiguity, and the culture has the highest score on the planet (among the thus-far researched cultures) on Long Term Orientation, a cultural aspect that is visibly dominant in most aspects of everyday life.

The Chinese scores in Hofstede's five dimensions are:

- PDI – 80
- IDV – 20
- PER – 66
- UAI – 40
- LTO – 118

Differences and similarities with American culture

Just by looking at the scores we can see many striking differences compared with the US culture, and a couple of equally striking similarities, the latter being with regards to Performance Orientation (US = 62) and Uncertainty Avoidance (US = 46).

Chinese culture is very different from America in terms of respect for hierarchy, Collectivism, and LTO (which is not just about time perspective, but also very much about flexibility and relativism (contrasting with American praise for following norms and applying them universally). This helps to explain why the US media is often excessively critical of certain aspects of Chinese culture: they are critical of those aspects that "rub them the wrong way," going directly against some of America's most treasured values, such as independent thinking, freedom of speech and complaining about the government.

It is probably no surprise to see that Performance Orientation is slightly higher than in the US. The media often highlights how the Chinese work hard and for long hours in factories that offer poor conditions. UAI is a different story: perhaps many would expect to see a bigger difference in this aspect.

Americans enjoy a reputation for valuing risk-taking. However, UAI is driven to a relatively higher score (compared to many European countries, for instance) because of the expression of emotions, planning and control, and frequent self-medication (plus: drugstores on every corner). The Chinese are often described as "sitting stone-faced" in meetings, but that happens mostly in formal business meetings with foreigners, and the drivers for such behavior are linked to respect for hierarchy. Amongst themselves and in informal gatherings, the Chinese are quite expressive.

LTO is where we can find the biggest gap in terms of the actual scores, and perhaps the most evident examples of difference. In the US, managers learn to think of short-term gains and quick wins for their businesses. By contrast, the Chinese learn to be patient and to think in terms of decades, rather than weeks, months and quarters. "Long-term" in the US means the next three years; in China, it means 25 years or more.

So when Chinese officials suggested that the US Dollar should be replaced in international commerce by a basket of currencies, American officials responded: "this is not going to happen." And they referred to an IMF meeting planned for the end of the year. The Chinese, however, explained that they expected their suggestion to be discussed "over the next ten years."

When Americans and Chinese do business or diplomacy with each other, there is potential for many misunderstandings. People unconsciously make a lot of assumptions about each other; their expectations are based on their own culture values. Yet, their time perspectives are very different; the Chinese assume that the ends justify the means; they believe contracts are but a mere formality easily overrun by ever-changing relationships; conflicts should be avoided; and they assume that hierarchy should never be challenged. Americans, on the other hand, feel that contracts are legally and morally binding; that rules are meant to be complied with; that conflict should be embraced; and that challenging hierarchy shows strength of character.

It's a wonder that so many cross-border venues have actually been successful between these two cultures. Such successes are a credit to the individuals involved on both sides, and their ability to adapt and learn about each other's values.

Differences from other Asian countries

China is not Japan, and it's not Korea either.

Japan scores very high on Uncertainty Avoidance and this can be seen in the many rituals that are found in their daily routine. Decision-making is also different in Japan: although PDI in Japan is higher than what can be found in North America and Northern Europe, it is still much lower than China's. In Japan decision-making involves a long strife for consensus at each level of its organizational hierarchy, at the end of which a decision is presented to the boss for sanctioning. A Japanese boss can influence the process during the consensus-building phase; in such a way that the final proposal coincides with his own opinion; or the boss might change his/her opinion to join the consensus. In Chinese culture, the decision lies clearly with the boss and not with the team.

Korea (South Korea, since North Korea was never researched) has a specific characteristic of emphasizing conflict between two opposing views. Discussions are frequent and appear, to foreigners, violent. They generally end in some kind of agreement that allows both sides to save face. Compared to China, Korea scores lower on PDI, lower on Performance Orientation, and higher on Uncertainty Avoidance. In this last dimension it is closer to Japan than to China, in terms of using rituals as a way of avoiding ambiguity and organizing the universe to feed a hunger for order. The Chinese deal better with ambiguity and uncertainty; they accept the co-existence of many truths, even in apparent contradiction.

There are other ethnic Chinese communities in neighboring countries, notably in Malaysia and Singapore.

In Singapore the Chinese community is predominant; the country's culture is basically Chinese formed by those who migrated there in the 19th Century. The culture received some influence from the Malay and the English colonists, who occupied the island for centuries. The resulting fact is that the present-day culture in Singapore is slightly less oriented towards performance (probably due to Malaysian influence), has lower UAI and LTO (probably English influence is accountable for these two aspects).

In Malaysia, the Chinese community is a minority. They are often perceived by the locals as individualistic and greedy. In fact, what happens is that the Chinese in Malaysia are very active in industry and commerce; they are entrepreneurs and their high Performance Orientation is mistakenly perceived by the Malay as greed and individualism. Actually, the Chinese are simply more work-oriented; they value hard work and are more willing to put in long hours and sacrifice their quality of life in order to achieve more.

Malaysia has the highest PDI score in the world (104). In the eyes of the Malaysians, the Chinese are perceived as unduly egalitarians lacking respect for authority. As usual, people judge other cultures according to the standards of their own society, not realizing that these standards are not absolute; they are always relative.

The Chinese community in Malaysia, on the other hand, tend to perceive the Malaysians as "not working hard enough," and "excessively hierarchical."

Power Distance (PDI) in China

This dimension is expressed in China every day and in every situation: within the family, at work, in the community.

Within the family there is a hierarchy in terms of seniority, in which the elder have privileges and deserve respect. It is true that all cultures value that one should show respect to the elder, but nowhere else is this stronger than in China. A son might be fifty years old and hold a high-ranking position in government, or he might be a hugely successful businessman; when facing his parents, who might be illiterate and poor, this son will show total respect and submission to their authority.

At school, teachers are never challenged on their authority. Pupils avoid asking questions, especially if they fear the question might embarrass the teacher. Students have as their duty to pay attention in class and make the most out of the wisdom that the teacher is spilling over them.

At work, everything revolves around the boss. Meetings will only start after the boss arrives. The boss leads all meetings and projects. People will only speak up when given permission by the boss; he/she controls the agenda (if there is one) and the meeting ends when the boss says it is time to stop.

At business dinners and power lunches people will sit at the table after the boss has done so and will only stand up to leave after the boss. In negotiation meetings with foreigners, only the boss speaks; unless he/she gives the floor to someone else, usually the second-in-command. All decisions are centralized and lie with the boss.

Decisions are not made during meetings; the purpose of meetings is simply to announce decisions previously made by the boss in private consultation with his closest assistants and direct reports.

If you are a foreigner meeting with the Chinese, you need to know that meetings in China are organized as a ritual, with a known desired outcome, which is usually simply to announce a decision already made by the boss, or to gather information that will be used by the boss to make a decision outside the meeting. If you wish to influence a decision, you must meet informally, in private, with the boss (or with his trusted advisors), many times, over several weeks and months, in order to develop a relationship of mutual trust. Collectivism is combined with Power Distance in these situations, and it is the only way for you to influence the boss' decisions.

Most foreigners do not have this required "Chinese patience." The Chinese are in no hurry during negotiations. They might show haste afterwards, during the execution phase of a project in order to meet a deadline. During the planning and negotiation phase, haste is relative (like everything else).

Among peers, the eldest has precedence over the others. If they are all the same age, precedence lies with the one who has been longer with the company. There is always a hierarchy among those present, whatever the setting. This hierarchy is readily identified by the Chinese, collectivists who have learned to read between the lines and spot body language hints in a group. Foreigners coming from individualistic societies have greater difficulty in reading these signs and perceiving the existing hierarchy.

Democracy in China

Most critical remarks made about China stem from Anglo-Saxon and Northern European value-systems, which are egalitarian and individualistic. To American, British, German and Scandinavian eyes, it is very disturbing to cope with China's collectivistic and hierarchical way of life. The tendency is to perceive China as being a society where the people are oppressed by authoritarian leaders, where people suffer continuously because they are not free to speak their mind against figures of authority or against what most others think.

This perception is distorted by the cultural filter of having been brought up in a society with different values. It causes people to judge Chinese culture based on the standards of the beholder, rather than based on Chinese standards. In China people believe that power is distributed unequally, and that is just a fact of life; it is the natural order of the world, and to deny it is foolish.

This begins in the typical Chinese family, where grandparents and parents have more power than children and grandchildren, and there is also a hierarchy among siblings, in which the eldest have more power.

It is extended to situations at work, at school, in public service, etc. Anyone who plays a leadership role, or holds a position as manager or supervisor, is regarded as an authority figure. They have "ascribed power," attributed to them due to the position they hold. This authority they have is very rarely challenged. It is not inherent to the person, but rather to the position held.

In egalitarian societies authority figures have "acquired power," (also known sometimes as "achieved power) which can be challenged and frequently is. In these societies, incumbents of positions of authority must reaffirm their merit and competence, from time to time, in order to keep their position; otherwise they might be replaced. Replacing incumbents, however, is not such a big deal in such cultures. It happens more often and does not imply greater consequences in a society where hierarchically linked privileges and status are not that big, to begin with.

In China, ascribed power is accompanied by privileges and responsibilities. People believe that power, privileges and responsibilities should always go in tandem. They consider the privileges to be deserved, for they reward the greater responsibilities borne by leaders at each of their levels in the hierarchy.

Power Distance begins to be seen already at the lower levels, with policemen on the streets, teachers at school, first line supervisors in factories. In fact, it is at these lower levels in the hierarchy that one can more often observe instances of power abuse. This happens to counter-attack (or pre-emptively attack) any kind of challenge to the authority of their respective positions.

In China, power is not only concentrated at the top of the Communist Party bureaucracy, contrary to what you might gather from reading American media; power is distributed across millions of positions of ascribed authority, each at their respective level in the social hierarchy. And each exerts power over those below it, respecting the power of the positions above.

The Dutch have a nasty expression for this, which they have coined, based on their own culture bias: they call this "the bicycle style of leadership." They say that "you keep your head down, submissive to those above you; and trample with your feet whoever is below your own position."

If there was suddenly a revolution that would by magic put at the top of Chinese society a European or American leader, this leader would be totally powerless to transform China into a European or American style of democracy. Resistance to such a change would not come from other top officials in government; it would come from the millions of Chinese people who treasure their hierarchical culture.

These members of Chinese society look at American society and say: "How terrible! Americans have absolutely no respect for authority! What a chaotic and sick society they have!" And they often add: "What America really needs is a truly strong and powerful leader, someone who is widely respected and who can put their economy on the right track! What good is this so-called 'democracy' that strips the president from the authority necessary to do what needs to be done?"

6. CHINA

Guanxi

One of the clearest examples of Chinese collectivism is the notion of "guanxi." The term refers to a network of friends that is developed by a person in childhood and that lasts for a whole lifetime.

In all societies people develop friendships in childhood. In most cases, such friendships tend to fade away with time; as people move to different neighborhoods, or change schools, new friendships in the new locations replace the previous. There is a tendency towards losing contact with the people who were left behind.

In adult life, friendships tend to revolve around work; and when someone moves to another job, new friendships replace the previous ones. In collectivistic societies friendships tend to last longer; and even when they started linked to a job, they may outlast employment in that job, especially if they are linked to a professional function, more than to employment in the same organization. For instance: Information Technology professionals might maintain friendships with like-minded I.T. professionals from many organizations; the same is true for Human Resources professionals, or for legal advisors. Friendships might survive many changes in employers or in home addresses, even more so because people can keep in touch through the use of social networks on the Internet.

All this pales by comparison to the Chinese "guanxi." It is a life-long network of friendships that endures from childhood to old age, regardless of changes in location, employment or professional activity. One must remain loyal to the friends that are part of that network, throughout one's entire life.

Such friendships turn out to be also quite useful when doing business, making commercial transactions, and in moments of financial and/or health need. The members of a "guanxi" must support each other at all times, whenever necessary, for the rest of their lives. It is a collectivist aspect taken to the extreme, and associated to the highest score in LTO, in terms of serving others and taking a long-term perspective.

The foreigners' illusion

Many foreigners live in China for a decade or more and think of themselves as "fully integrated" into Chinese society. I've had conversations with many and heard some say that they feel the Chinese are not, in practice, loyal to their friends. They've told me stories about their own experience, according to which they were suddenly abandoned by people with whom they had "a very close relationship."

These people, most of them coming from individualistic cultures, fail to realize that they are judging these situations based on their own original countries' cultural standards. For instance: for an American, having a friend for eight years is "a very long time;" for a Chinese, friendship is long if it lasts for decades.

What the typical Englishman considers "a very close relationship" is different from what a Chinese person feels as such. In China a close and lasting relationship among friends implies a much deeper degree of intimacy than what is typically found in individualistic cultures.

The relationships between the Chinese and people from foreign countries has always been (and will probably continue to be) more distant than it appears to be at face value. In the perception of foreigners, they are having long and close relationships. They are unpleasantly surprised when, in certain situations, their Chinese friends suddenly disappoint them.

In the eyes of the Chinese, these friendships are superficial and recent. As such, they do not compare even remotely to the *guanxi*. If a Chinese person has to choose between closing a deal with a fellow Chinese or with a foreigner, their natural tendency is to prefer his/her fellow Chinese. This is considered only natural and expected; and it is considered a demonstration of loyalty to their compatriots. To the foreigner, it is felt as betrayal to the friendship that they thought was very close.

Invasive intimacy

In Chinese culture the concept of privacy is quite different from what is known in individualistic societies. Often people touch each other's hair, arms or face. Frequently they will feel another person's clothing, to assess the texture of the cloth. None of these things is regarded as invasive or disturbing. An individualist would be absolutely shocked.

In China a person might rummage through the contents of someone's bags without a second thought, and this would be no cause for indignation. People who are friends, or even those who have only recently met for the first time, may share a degree of intimacy that is rarely seen in individualistic societies. They see Europeans and Americans, who have greater respect for privacy, as being cold, distant and insensitive.

Once, during a visit to Beijing, the sales attendants at a shop were intrigued by my wife's hair, very curly, which allowed her to hold it up in a bun simply by swirling it into a ball and inserting a pencil through it. As we entered the shop it was very warm inside and there was no air-conditioning; so after a minute or two she took a pencil from her purse and rolled up her long hair into a bun, holding it up by inserting the pencil through the bun. This was done in less than five seconds. Immediately a small group of three shop attendants formed around her, laughing and chatting excitedly in Chinese, and all of them spontaneously put their hands on her hair to feel its texture. They did not ask permission to do this, nor did they excuse themselves; my wife was amused, but not shocked, because she also has a keen understanding of the Chinese culture. However, we know that in Europe and in the US such behavior would be regarded as offensive and constitute a shocking invasion of a person's individual privacy.

These different reactions to physical contact contribute to define whether a relationship is perceived as close or distant. When a Chinese person touches a foreigner's clothing to feel the texture and praise its quality, and the foreigner reacts against it and pulls away, the Chinese feels rejected and hurt. He perceives the other's desire for physical distance as being also a desire for a distant social relationship. Therefore, in the eyes of this Chinese person, this foreigner does not deserve priority in business relationships if he/she is rejecting the well-intentioned attempts to come closer.

Chinese contracts

Many foreigners doing business in China complain that the contracts they have signed are not respected by their Chinese business partners.

In the eyes of the Chinese, contracts are but a mere formality, a ritual to celebrate a transaction. The relationship between both parties is far more important; it is fluid, dynamic and constantly evolving as each day goes by. The contract, by contrast, is a fixed and unchanging document. Two weeks after the contract was signed, the contract is already obsolete, since it no longer reflects the evolving relationship.

When the two are at odds, the relationship prevails over the contract. If there is mutual trust in place, both parties will do everything they can to nurture and develop the relationship further, going far beyond the ink set on paper. The contract is a limited document that restricts the relationship and reduces it to its most impersonal and superficial aspects. The relationship has much more value than that and it will determine if the business partnership will be successful or not.

When a foreigner complains that the contract is not being followed, the Chinese perceive this as a desire to break off the relationship.

When a Chinese businessman complains to his business partner about something, he does not refer to the contract; he refers to "what we had agreed on," or to "what we need to do, together, to make our business successful for the benefit of all parties involved."

Therefore, if foreigners have grievances to present to their Chinese counterparts, they should act like in a romantic relationship, when the couple sits down to "discuss the relationship." The conversation needs to be much more close and personal than is usually the case in the so-called Western World business culture. If foreigners do not behave that way, they will appear (to the Chinese) to be already paving the way for a break-up of the relationship.

Similarly, it is quite difficult to do audits in China according to the routines that are used as a reference in the US and Europe. In these other regions, signed contracts and written norms are the basic reference for an auditor, who will signal in his/her report the eventual divergences that may have been identified, in practice, when comparing reality with the referenced documents. In China this is considered completely inappropriate, because it is obvious that daily practice will always be different from what has been previously written. No document will ever be capable of mirroring the nuances and relativisms of real life. To the Chinese, it's a bit foolish to do audits based on documents.

The Chinese way of conducting audits involves assessing risks and divergences in subtle and imprecise terms, including several quite intangible aspects. It's not about comparing reality against documents and written norms. Rather, it is about comparing reality against a (somewhat subjective) notion of how the business being audited should be run, taking into consideration many surrounding circumstances. This is much more difficult and complex, because it involves aspects that are not objectively measurable.

Chinese auditors will handle all this quite well, and Chinese managers will also know how to interpret audit reports accordingly, feeling comfortable with all of it. By contrast, most American and European managers might consider this kind of an audit something far too vague and subjective to be really useful.

Mistaken notions about China

China's impressive economic growth and its gradual opening to the external world made it the focus of attention from media all over the world. However, the many journalists who report on the country, and even those who visit it in person, have done very little to really understand the Chinese culture. This greatly hinders their analysis and generally leads them to totally wrong conclusions.

Many economists have expressed very mistaken notions about China, basically because of their lack of knowledge about culture and due to their lack of awareness about their own culture bias. This is what generates the flawed analyses and leads to the wrong conclusions. Political and economic analyses are bound to go wrong whenever they fail to consider cultural aspects.

China will not continue to grow at the same rate that we have seen in the past ten years. It is only natural that the rate of growth will slow down, as their economy becomes larger. When pundits make linear projections of economic growth for China, they are showing blatant incompetence, or even worse: criminal intention to unduly influence financial markets.

China will not sink into chaos due to its authoritarian regime, and split into smaller nations. These forecasts are biased by the egalitarian cultures where they are generated. China has all the conditions it needs to hold itself together as a nation, since its hierarchical and collectivistic culture favors keeping their unity.

Migration from farming into large cities is not the only possible way forward for Chinese development in the next twenty years. China might be capable of controlling migration and adopt a different model of unique economic and social development. It is not necessarily condemned to repeat the patterns that have been seen in other countries. It could very well continue to grow, at lower rates, without excessive concentration in huge cities. Chinese culture allows the government to plan and control demographic distributions in ways that would be impossible to do in other cultures.

China does not intend to dominate the world through military might. Chinese culture favors domination through economic terms and through the dissemination of its values, rather than by using military force. The word "China" in Chinese means "the center of the world," and that is how they see themselves: the whole world revolves around China. They do not need to use force; they can dominate in economic and cultural terms, without firing a single shot.

The Chinese Communist Party does not hold on to power by force. As we've seen previously, Chinese culture reinforces the existence of a strong government. The people support this situation. The Chinese government is gradually allowing greater individual liberties and a better standard of living for everyone. Never in their thousands of years history have the Chinese enjoyed so much freedom as they do at present. The people also support this gradual opening towards greater liberty.

China is not concerned with competing against India; it focuses on competing against the United States. Some economists have highlighted the economic growth competition between China and India, but these competition analyses are only popular in India and in the United Kingdom. To the Chinese, India does not represent a standard against which they would like to compare themselves, while the US does represent that standard to which the Chinese aspire. They admire the American middle class' comfort levels and standard of living. This is what they want to achieve for their own society, someday.

China is not concerned with the global economic recession, which they see as a short-term event (even if it lasts for several years). The Chinese think in decades and not in quarters. They know that the world economy will eventually recover and grow at a steady pace again. Chinese culture values patience, persistence and following alternative paths in seeking to achieve long-term results. They are willing to endure sacrifices for decades, in order to obtain a better standard of living from 2030 onwards. They discuss what the global economy will look like twenty years from now, rather than two months from now.

China must be analyzed in the light of its cultural characteristics, and how these influence economic and political aspects. Any kind of analysis that does not consider Chinese culture will necessarily be flawed and incomplete.

Part IV – The Big Issues

Does Culture Change?

Yes, it does. But much more slowly than we think, regarding its core values; and quite quickly regarding the more superficial layers of culture.

National cultures are very persistent and perennial, when it comes to their core values. On the outer layers, regarding symbols, heroes and rituals, change happens faster. At the center, regarding the value-dimensions identified by Hofstede, change is very slow.

When we look around us, we see a lot of cultural change happening: people dress quite differently from what they used to 20 years ago. Come to think of it, people dress quite differently from what they did compared to last year!

Culture change does indeed occur, especially in the layers that are clearly seen on the surface, those aspects that Schein called "artifacts." The clothes considered to be "in fashion" change; food habits change, and so do popular language expressions. We see new TV and music idols (though The Rolling Stones insist to go through decade after decade being successful).

On the other hand, people find themselves behaving a lot like their parents, more often than they would like to admit. Interpersonal relationships in terms of hierarchies or equality, in terms of Individualism or Collectivism, in terms of emphasizing performance or quality of life; these aspects change less, and much more slowly.

We like to think that "things are changing" and especially we find it comforting to see that "things are changing for the better." Unfortunately, the core aspects of culture, its underlying values, change less and more slowly than many people would think. That is one of the reasons why we continue to struggle repeatedly with certain issues, time and time again. Things like urban violence, discrimination, inequality and corruption have been present in our societies for centuries.

In order to change the core values of a culture, it would be necessary to change how children are brought up in that culture. If kids' education changes (in the broad sense, both within families, at school and in the whole community), culture will change.

The new factor that emerged at the end of the 20th Century is the Internet. The worldwide web is influencing the way our children have access to information and it is surely influencing their education and their values.

How is this influence happening in practice? What are the culture values influencing our children, and how much influence are they experiencing? Will the Internet exert a bigger influence than other sources, such as family and school?

We do not yet have an answer to these crucial questions. Perhaps in another 25 years from now, when we have a second generation of people born into the Internet becoming adults, we might have a better notion of how values are changing in different parts of the world.

It is important to note that, even if we look forward into as far as 2050, we will probably still have millions of people in different parts of the world with no access to the worldwide web. What we see around us in our middle class communities is not the reality for the whole planet. If you live in an urban environment you might feel that everybody has Internet. It's a different reality in rural communities and still a different reality in many places in Asia, Africa and Latin America.

Yes, cultures change; but the core values change much more slowly than we think, and will probably continue to resist change for decades to come.

Is it possible to change culture deliberately?

As we've seen, culture changes very slowly in terms of its underlying values. Is it possible to deliberately influence the direction of cultural change? Is it possible to shape culture according to a desired vision, influencing its direction and velocity?

Organizational cultures are much more sensitive to planned change efforts than national cultures. Organizational cultures are shaped by the adults who work in an organization. They do not depend on changes made to the education of all children in a country's population; they only depend on the shared values espoused by the members of this organization.

The simplest way to go about changing the shared values of an organization is to change all the people working there. If you fire everybody and hire an entire staff body anew, different people with different values, you will get a different culture. If you select these new people based on a set of desired values, you will have a new culture in line with what you want.

In real life it is not possible to simply change all the employees of an organization over night. However, it is possible to drive gradual change, starting with the top management team. If the leaders of an organization change (or are changed), the culture will change, although not over night.

In practice, this is a very slow and difficult process; yet it does happen, and there are a few rare and beautiful examples of successful organizational culture planned change. Unfortunately, the examples of such initiatives going wrong are much more abundant.

ABN AMRO Bank in Brazil, in the period from 1992 to the end of 1993, was a good example (for a detailed case study description of this, see my book "*Clima e Cultura Organizacional: Entender, Manter e Mudar,*" 2017). I joined that bank in May of 1992 as Head of Human Resources, already as part of a planned change effort that had begun a few months before. We had a very favorable opportunity to change culture, because the bank had decided to move its Brazilian Country Head Office from Rio de Janeiro to São Paulo.

This physical relocation from one city to another 400 km away allowed us to change 80% of the Head Office staff in six months. We created a new Head Office in São Paulo, staffed with people who were hired according to a new set of values. 50 people were transferred from Rio to São Paulo; they were those who shared this new set of values and were willing to move to a different city in order to pursue their career in the new bank that was forming.

By the end of 1993, practically the whole top management team was different from the previously existing top team at the beginning of 1992.

At the start of 1994, ABN AMRO Bank in Brazil had a totally different culture, compared to a couple of years earlier. This was only made possible because of the physical relocation of the Head Office, which eventually led to renovating nearly its entire staff over a two-year period.

In principle, it is also possible to change the culture of a nation, although that is certainly more difficult and it takes more time. A successful example that can be referred to is that of Singapore. However, it must be noted that the culture change brought about in Singapore took several generations, it had its limitations, and there was also a social price to be paid (in terms of limiting individual freedoms). Besides that, Singapore has some unique characteristics: it is a city-nation, restricted to just over five million people living quite close to each other. The situation is quite different from that of other countries (such as the US or Brazil) that have hundreds of millions of inhabitants spread out over territories of continental proportions.

Still, David C. McClelland has demonstrated already in the 1950's in specific research studies, that there was a verifiable correlation between the content of primary school textbooks and the production and usage of electric power in the same countries 20 and 40 years later. Those countries that had textbooks highlighting stories about achievement motivation, winning competitions and reaching measurable targets, brought up generations of people who decades later had a greater positive impact on their economy than a control group of neighboring countries.

Therefore, it is possible to plan and implement culture change in larger countries, by changing education, as long as one is willing to wait for a generation until the results are visible. Generally speaking, politicians are not ready to wait that long; their time perspective is much shorter than that. But in China, a culture with the highest LTO (Long Term Orientation) in the world, we might be soon seeing the results of planned change efforts that started decades ago.

Are we putting people in boxes?

Whenever we classify cultures as "hierarchical" or "egalitarian," as "individualistic" or "collectivistic," we must remind ourselves always that such classifications are simply an artificial tool used to increase our understanding of culture differences.

Each person is a universe to be respected as being unique. Whenever I interact with someone who I just met, I need to approach this person with an open mind.

Hofstede's value dimensions framework aims to help us in understanding people's behavior, by looking at it from the perspective of a frame of reference. The framework is of little use when trying to **predict** an individual's behavior; using it for that purpose is likely to result in failure. Each person is uniquely unpredictable. We need to get to know people and allow them to get to know us, in order to establish a relationship of mutual respect that can also become mutually gratifying.

Any model, by definition, is a reductionist representation of reality, which in turn is infinitely richer and more diverse than any model can be. Hofstede's framework is certainly useful, but it must be used responsibly and with moderation.

Ultimately, "putting people in boxes" is something that some people do because they have that in their mindsets, but it is not in the model itself. Keep your mind open and nurture your curiosity to find out how people really are, each in his/her personal richness.

Is happiness a cultural value?

Certainly the definition of happiness is something influenced by culture; and surveys about happiness are also influenced by culture.

It is one thing to be happy. It is a different thing to feel happy. A person could be happy without realizing it; or someone might feel happy without actually being happy. It all depends on how you define happiness and how aware one can be of one's own happiness.

Most international surveys about happiness are conducted by social scientists who come from egalitarian and individualistic cultures, and who are based in Northern Europe or North America. The operational assumptions of these surveys are all influenced by the original cultures where these scientists come from.

For instance: all these surveys begin with the assumption that the best way to find out whether people are happy is to simply ask them if they are happy. Their responses will provide the answer about how happy they are.

This assumption implies that people are aware of their own level of happiness and that their statements about this provide sufficient evidence regarding this. Serious research studies have demonstrated that this assumption is false: people in general do not have an accurate level of objective awareness about their own feelings and values. This is the reason why psychologists invented "projective tests" to assess personality traits. These tests assess personal characteristics indirectly, instead of accepting the subject's responses to objective questions.

Direct questions and responses may be relatively more valid as a research approach within egalitarian and individualistic cultures, which represent approximately 10% of the world's population; but it is certainly less valid in for collectivistic and hierarchical cultures, which represent 90% of the world's population. In these societies, the notion of individual responsibility is different and the expression of opinions is severely affected by whatever is considered to be socially desirable.

Some social researchers believe that by formulating questions in a certain way they might obtain answers that are closer to "the truth." The actual truth is simply that no matter what the method you employ; it will always be affected by the cultural bias of whoever is using that method, unless the method is scrutinized for cultural bias before it is applied.

Up until this book was being written, surveys were only capable of measuring whether "I am content with what (little) I have," and this reveals a typical Northern European bias. Surveys have not attempted to measure "joy," for instance, which is something more typical of Southern Europe, the Latin cultures and India. The curious conclusion has been that Scandinavian countries appear on these surveys as having the highest levels of happiness, while Mediterranean, Latin American countries and India appear in mid-level positions.

Meanwhile, the Scandinavian cultures show some of the highest suicide ratios; and when vacation times come, people flock to the Latin and

Mediterranean cultures "to enjoy life." Something tells me that these surveys about happiness are severely biased.

Does religion precede culture or it the other way around?

Religion is a cultural manifestation that belongs to the outer layers, linked to the rituals. Culture values are at the core of culture, and as such they precede religion.

Popular opinion usually places religion as one of the main drivers of culture, influencing a population's values and culture, but actually it works the other way around. It is a population's shared values that determine what kind of religion will blossom in that community and how it will be practiced. Even when a certain religion is adopted in different nations, one can see how the culture of each nation shapes the rituals of that religion, resulting in different styles regarding the rituals and behaviors of the faithful. One can be a Catholic or a Muslim anywhere in the world; but being a Catholic in Spain is different from being a Catholic in the United States; and being a Muslim in Brazil is different from being a Muslim in Saudi Arabia. The religious dogmas might be the same, but the way they are followed and put in practice differs according to the local culture.

For example: priests tend to be more authoritarian in hierarchical cultures, and less so in egalitarian communities. Parishes might be more inclusive or less, depending on whether the culture is more collectivistic or individualistic; and so on.

People used to think that Protestant religions were the drivers of American culture; today we know that it is actually American culture values that drive the growth of Protestant religions in America, and the same goes for every country. It is no coincidence that the Christian Reformation began in Germany and flourished in Northern Europe: these are egalitarian cultures that rebelled against the hierarchy of the Catholic Church and the obedience to the Pope. Meanwhile, the Catholic Church resisted the Reformation and remained strong mostly in hierarchical societies.

Are multicultural teams better or worse?

A research experiment conducted by Doctor Carol Kovach at UCLA, published in 1997, revealed that the performance of multicultural teams tends to lie on the extremes of a bell-shaped curve (see figure 8).

Multicultural teams either have an excellent performance, well above the average of other teams, or they show very poor performance, well below the average. Monoculture teams, in which all members come from the same culture, regardless of which culture they are from, tend to perform at the level of the overall average, not too far above nor below that average.

This occurs, basically, because the higher diversity of a multicultural team enhances the team's capabilities to understand complex issues, approach these issues in a creative manner, and solve problems.

However, a multicultural team must be aware of its own diversity, and of the different expectations, assumptions and working styles of their members; and they need to agree on a way of working together that will be efficient and effective.

Figure 8: Performance of multicultural teams

Multicultural groups

Monoculture Groups

Low Performance   Average Performance   High Performance

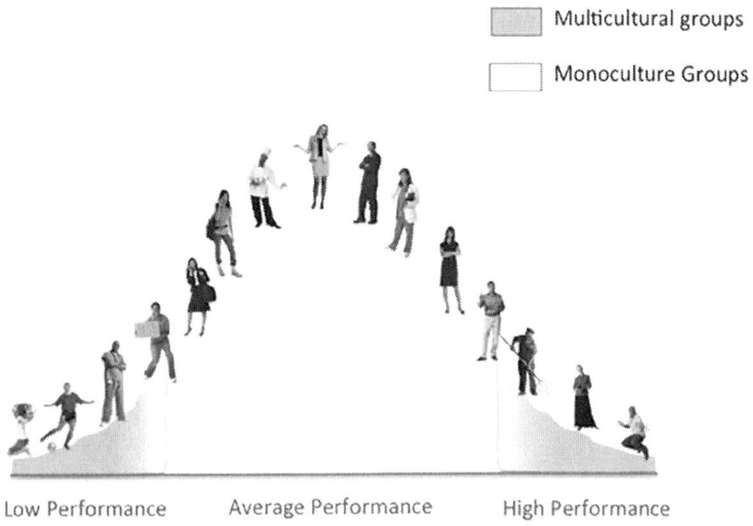

When a multicultural team does not share a clear way of working together, performance falls on the opposite side. Expectations are frustrated; assumptions are unclear, communication breaks down and productivity plummets. The team performs worse than a typical monoculture team.

Within a multicultural team, understanding and capitalizing on diversity is a pre-condition to maximize potential and achieve top performance. If the team's diversity is not acknowledged and managed, the team will drift towards the opposite end of the spectrum and performance will be very poor.

Society's Great Dilemmas

Among the six value dimensions identified in Hofstede's frameworks, four of them are clearly connected to archetypical dilemmas faced by humanity in every society. These dilemmas are related to the dimensions Power Distance, Individualism, Performance Orientation and Long Term Orientation.

That is not the case for Uncertainty Avoidance, because this dimension is a bit more complex. There are several different drivers affecting the scores in this dimension, in such a way that it does not seem attached to a single primary dilemma. This dimension has many facets.

The sixth dimension (Indulgence versus Restraint), as we have seen, is still somewhat contentious among cross-culture specialists. The very definition of this dimension includes two distinct aspects (feeling in control of one's life and allowing yourself to enjoy the simple pleasures); therefore, it does not appear to be connected to a single basic dilemma. Perhaps in the future the issues about this dimension will be more clearly defined.

Equality versus Hierarchy

Each primitive social community, each tribe, must face the issue of Equality (or Equivalence, a more accurate term that is not so widely employed). Within each social group people ask themselves, unconsciously or consciously, how much of a hierarchy should be considered valid among the group's members.

In practice, all social groups have some kind of hierarchy. However, in some groups this hierarchy is quite subtle and appears to have little differentiation (we say that in these groups there is low PDI). In other groups, the hierarchical differentiation is quite clear and evident, shown in a very explicit and intense way.

Through the centuries, different nations found different solutions to this dilemma. Some migrated towards the side of high Power Distance; while others moved towards the side of low PDI. Which of these would be ideal, in a utopic world? It's impossible to say without confessing to a bias towards one of the two extremes in the dilemma.

Perhaps then ideal might be in a position of balance between the two more extreme positions. But even this choice for balance might be influenced by some potential bias; we cannot say objectively that there is a certain stance regarding this dilemma that is actually "better" than others.

In our present-day world, the issue of Power Distance is behind political regimes that are either less or more authoritarian. In every country there is some form of government and there is some form of hierarchy; but some regimes are more liberal and others are totalitarian, with many varying degrees between the two extremes.

It is important to note that the popular discussion between the virtues of Capitalism and Communism is actually on a more superficial plane than the core value dilemmas of culture. Communism became strong for many years in Russia and in China, both of them cultures with high Power Distance. Because of that, many people developed the impression that Communism is a totalitarian regime, which it is not.

Russia tends towards a totalitarian regime because of its high PDI. This supported totalitarian rule during the era of the Czars, during Communism, and now it continues in the age beyond Communism. Similarly, China had centuries of totalitarian rule under the Emperors; this continued under the Communist period and now continues although the regime at present is a unique blend of Communism and Capitalism.

At the same time, the Netherlands and the Scandinavian countries have political regimes with many socialist components, yet they are not totalitarian. This is because of the low Power Distance found in these cultures.

Individual Freedom versus the Common Good

This issue regarding the conflict between preserving an individual's freedom versus acting for the benefit of the common good is one that has been explored multiple times along the history of mankind, clearly and explicitly, by many philosophers and thinkers.

The notion that "a person's freedom ends at the beginning of another person's right" is a central issue in Western philosophy that serves as a reference to legislative and judicial debates all over the world to this very day. It has also become a central part of the debate around political regimes, lying at the core of the perennial discussions about the merits and setbacks of Capitalism and Socialism.

As we've just seen in regards to Power Distance, we can say that the issue of Individualism precedes the choice about a Capitalist or Socialist regime.

Where lies the best balance position regarding this issue? Wherever the culture is strongly individualistic, such as in the US, UK and the Netherlands, we come closer to the Anarchist Movement's ideal of having "no government at all," a combination of low PDI and high IDV. Everyone is free, and nobody can tell them what to do; this would be aligned to the ideal of self-governance. In practice, we can observe that, indeed, it is rather difficult to govern highly individualistic societies, because they position themselves in a way that tests the limits of individual freedom at the expense of the common good.

On the other hand, the collectivist extreme leads to the cancelling of the individual as a person, removing differentiated identity. Where is the ideal point of equilibrium? Is it possible to find a position that is equally distant from both extremes? Should the ideal be situated a bit to the right or a bit to the left?

Each community must discuss these questions, become aware of their own culture bias and seek their own point of equilibrium to serve as a guide for their future.

Work Hard versus Enjoy Life

The dilemma between performance and quality of life also exists in every society and is resolved in each one as a matter of degree.

Obviously, in every society people need to work. It is also obvious that in every society it is necessary to have moments of leisure to enjoy life. Each culture emphasizes one of these two aspects a bit more than the other.

There are cultures that emphasize performance and work to such a great degree that they dedicate very little time to enjoy even the small pleasures that life has to offer, and spare only moments for having fun or caring for those around them. In these cultures one finds many who are addicted to work, the so-called workaholics; they are people who "live to work" almost exclusively and end up dying without really enjoying life.

Other cultures put greater emphasis on quality of life and caring for others. Of course, in these societies people also work hard, but here they see work as a means to an end; and this end is being able to enjoy life more comfortably.

Paraphrasing the fable of the grasshopper and the ant, it is as if in the performance-oriented societies the ant went to the extreme of working during the whole year, finally dying without ever enjoying life. While in the quality of life oriented societies the grasshopper worked daily from nine to five and then played his/her guitar in the evenings. When winter comes, she has enough accumulated during the summer to still survive through the winter, and she is content enough with that.

Where is the point of equilibrium, the magic Goldilocks point that is not too high and not too low? In fact, this depends also on how much makes you feel content. Working more means accumulating more. Working less means accumulating less. If you work too much for too long, you leave yourself no time to enjoy what you have accumulated. And if you spend all your time enjoying life and not working hard enough, you may not have much to allow you to enjoy life with comfort.

Each society may have its own point of equilibrium tending slightly more towards performance orientation, as long as it does not turn people into workaholics, or a little more towards the enjoyment of life, as long as that does not turn everyone into free-loaders, and people work enough to allow them to enjoy life with comfort in a modest way.

Absolute Truth versus Everything is Relative

In this case the archetypical dilemma can be expressed in terms of being normative versus being relativistic.

On one hand, it is important to have clear and solid parameters regarding what is right and what is wrong; on the opposite extreme of the dilemma lies the practical application of these parameters in concrete cases, in such a way that good decisions can be made to the satisfaction of all parties involved.

In all societies there are written and unwritten norms of conduct. In every society the application of these norms to concrete cases requires some degree of interpretation and adaptation to the case in question.

Harris Bond's research found that in most European countries and in North America cultures tend towards being more normative, that is: they value the establishment of clear rules and rigorous compliance to those rules.

In many other cultures of Asia and Latin America, the scales pend towards the opposite side. What is given greater value is relativism when obeying and applying norms in practice. Who are the people involved? What is the background to this situation? What will be the practical consequences of applying this norm?

Every society faces this dilemma; some cultures have decided towards one side, others opted to follow a different path. Each group also faces this dilemma and seeks to find a balance that will reflect their specific conclusion, and that might tend towards one side or the other. The choices agreed by one group, very likely will be severely criticized by a different group that chose to pend towards the opposite side.

Reconciling Dilemmas

The purpose of studying cultures is to help people understand the different value-logics behind all these dilemmas. By doing so, it may be possible to reconcile the dilemmas, seeking to find the positive aspects of both opposite poles and bringing them together to find a resulting optimal combination of both.

All this is not easy. The first step is to seek the understanding of differences, the comprehension of the opposite poles. The next step is to seek reconciliation possibilities. For this, one needs to abandon the dogmatic position of siding exclusively with one of the poles in detriment of its opposite.

Instead of perceiving each dilemma as a straight line with two opposing poles, it is necessary to consider each dilemma as two axes placed next to each other at an angle of 90 degrees. By doing this, we can form a matrix consisting of four quadrants (Figure 9).

The first quadrant refers to the meeting point of the two axes in the angle they share in common, "point zero." The second quadrant refers to the maximum point of the horizontal axis "x;" the third quadrant refers to the maximum point of the vertical axis "y." What we strive for, in theory, is to reach quadrant four, in which reconciliation is possible by keeping the maximum values of both axes.

This is certainly not easy and in some cases may not even be possible. It is worth trying, to avoid misunderstandings that lead to the extreme of resorting to violence. We should strive to reach mutual understanding, dilemma reconciliation and mutual collaboration. By doing so, we can make this a better world, richer in its diversity, more fair and more productive for the next generations.

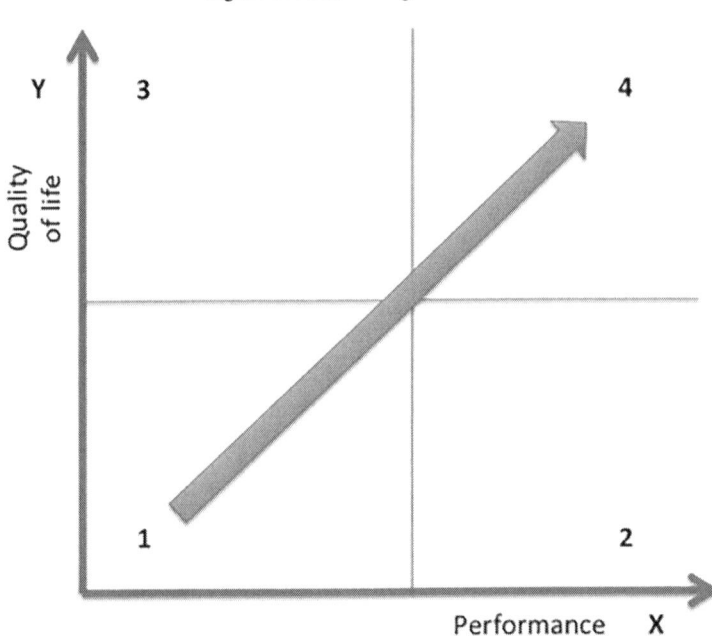

Figure 9: Reconciling Dilemmas

Skepticism

There are those who criticize Hofstede's work; the criticism can (and should) be separated in terms of the different aspects towards which they are directed.

The notion of the very existence of culture

Incredible as it may seem, there are still people who in the 21st Century challenge the existence of national cultures or even organizational cultures. These people consider that individual people's behavior varies due to personality differences and not due to culture differences.

We need to clarify, to begin with, that these two concepts (personality and culture) are not mutually exclusive. Actually, they complement each other.

Hofstede himself has always stressed that his research has always targeted culture and not personality. In order to distinguish one thing from the other, the Professor further emphasized that his research findings should not be applied to individuals, since individual personality is totally different from culture, which is a concept referring to collectives.

Those who deny the existence of culture usually do so because they consider "culture" a very abstract concept, difficult to understand and difficult to measure. They end up concluding that "what I fail do understand, does not exist;" or they consider that whatever is difficult to measure, has no relevance or does not deserve to be taken seriously.

I once met an American Human Resources manager of a multinational corporation who stated that "companies don't have culture, they have an image." After many long conversations about the topic he eventually came to better understand the concept and he at least accepted that culture exists. His initial disbelief was based on ignorance, that is, on the fact that he did not really know much about the topic.

In a similar way, I've met some Hofstede critics who challenge his findings because they do not understand the concept of culture. Their criticism is summarized as "I don't understand this and therefore I disagree with it! Besides, there is no such thing as culture!"

Professor Hofstede's work is not perfect, as certainly no studies on social psychology may be considered perfect. However, the existence of national and organizational cultures is no longer a matter of opinion or personal preference, at least for most people. Yes, culture exists, and there are countless research studies demonstrating its existence. One may disagree about the description of this or that culture, or whether addressing culture as an issue should be a priority among the many actions necessary to manage an organization or a nation. Depending on what is considered important to discuss or to do, the discussion about culture might be set aside to be addressed at another time; but to deny its very existence is to ignore a crucial factor that might be influencing in a decisive way the very issues that you are trying to solve first. You may be wasting time by ignoring the root cause of those issues.

A common criticism to the existence of a "national culture" is linked to the notion of cultural diversity within the same country. In the United States you often here statements like: "America is such a diverse country… it does not have a single 'American culture;' what you have are many different cultures in this huge country. People from the South are completely different from people in the East Coast, and so forth."

I usually argue that looking at national cultures is like Google Maps: if you zoom out to a distance equivalent to 30,000 feet altitude, local differences disappear; you see the region as a whole, but you can no longer see the differences between different neighborhoods in the same city.

Likewise, if we look at America as a whole, it is entirely possible to describe certain American culture characteristics, common to all regions and different, for instance, from German common characteristics. And if we come closer to each region, we will see the differences among them, among different states and towns. Ultimately, at the close-up level, we will see differences among individuals, and those are personality differences and not culture differences.

This holds true not only for America and is not only due to the fact that it is almost the size of a continent. The same comments about "our diverse culture" are heard in every country, regardless of its size. The Netherlands, which is about the size of New Jersey, considers that their cultural diversity is huge… "People from Groningen, in the North, are completely different from people from Maastricht, in the South!"

Differences exist, and so do similarities. Statistically speaking, it is possible to identify and measure these collective similarities and to name them as cultures and subcultures.

What happens is that behind this kind of criticism there is usually a certain feeling and a set of underlying personal values. People criticize the notion that it is possible to "classify people" or groups of people and "put them in boxes." Actually, there is nothing wrong with that, as long as you allow people to get out of the boxes, or rather, that you allow yourself to simultaneously see people outside of the boxes, or in different boxes, or as totally unique and free individuals. "Boxes" can be useful, as long as you don't think of them as absolute, deterministic and permanent. The box is not necessarily the problem; the problem might be how you make use of them. If you use them to better understand people, it's fine. If you use them to imprison people forever, that is not a good thing.

The counter argument to explain the existence of culture is to start with the individual. Do you believe that an individual has values, certain things that he or she believes in, that an individual has a notion of what is right and what is wrong? If you can accept that, can you also accept that a group of two, four or six people, although they are very different as persons, may have certain values in common (and many other values that are different)? These common values are what we describe as "culture." You might say that culture is a concept based on the statistical study of large groups of people. The "large groups of people" might be organizations, towns, regions or nations. Looking at large groups does not detract from the appreciation of individuals or personality; it is simply a different way of looking at people, like Sociology is different from Psychology.

It is worth noting that the notion of culture is useful to the understanding of human behavior, more than to predict people's behavior. Each individual must be recognized as such and should be approached with an open mind. The concept of culture should be used to dismiss stereotypes and understand the values logic that influences (but does not determine) people's behavior.

Culture exists; but it should not be used in a deterministic or preconceived way. It must be used with caution, for the purpose of mutual understanding and authentic interpersonal interaction.

Also, culture is not an imposed set of norms that everyone in a group is obliged to follow. Cultures are norms that a group follows, whether they have been imposed or not.

Usually, what we find is that certain leaders try to impose a culture, but it is always up to the group to accept that or change the norms and create a modified version of them, unconsciously. The imposed norms are not culture, they are propaganda. Culture refers to the values that people actually adopt and practice, regardless of what a leader says.

The definition of culture being used

When Hofstede says that "culture is the collective programming of the human mind," this concept is undoubtedly disturbing. We don't like to hear that we are not completely autonomous and independent; when B. F. Skinner said something similar in other words, in the 50's, people did not like it either. We don't even like to hear that our mind has a part that is unconscious and that this influences our behavior without we realizing that it's happening. Freud revealed that over one hundred years ago and there are still people denying it.

The expression "collective programming" immediately refers us to George Orwell's "1984", about a society in which there is no individual freedom; it also reminds us of Skinner's behaviorism and the concept of operational conditioning, according to which people do whatever they are rewarded for, devoid of a moral notion of what is right or wrong.

We may not like the term "programming", but the fact is that the values we learn in childhood do influence our behavior for the rest of our lives. It is also a fact that we are influenced by the behavior of other people around us. We all have a need to feel accepted by the community in which we live and we suffer group pressure from those around us. Our notion of what is "right" and "wrong" is influenced by the values of the groups to which we belong.

When our group's values coincide with the values that we learned in childhood, all these values reinforce each other and strengthen our sense of identity. When group values clash with our individual values, we feel discomfort. We may cope with this feeling of discomfort rather well or rather badly.

It's important to differentiate between "I don't like this concept" and "I don't agree with this concept." It is one thing to think that Hofstede's definition of culture makes us feel uncomfortable, although it might be true and valid. It is a very different thing to say that the definition is not true or has no validity.

The framework of culture dimensions
There are those who disagree with the specific dimensions that Hofstede identified. Usually this criticism stems from the lack of understanding each dimension, or from an erroneous interpretation of the labels chosen by Hofstede.

When we hear terms such as "Individualism" or "Masculinity", we immediately associate them to our previous understanding of these words; and our disagreement and criticism stems from that.

In order to understand Hofstede's framework you need to let go of your previous notions about these labels. There are language and translation issues involved in using them.

If we try to understand what each dimension is really describing, regardless of the label used to refer to it, most criticism is dissipated.

I once had an argument with a Dutch international business consultant who disagreed with Hofstede about the concept of Uncertainty Avoidance. This consultant asserted that the people of Thailand should have a much lower score in UAI (the score was 64) because Thai people seldom buy home insurance, while in the Netherlands the score should be higher (it was 53), since everybody buys insurance for their homes. Actually, UAI has nothing to do with home insurance!

Buying insurance does not decrease the risk of having an accident or insurance incident; it merely offers financial compensation for someone whose home has been damaged by a fire, flood or any kind of disaster. Insurance does not avoid uncertainty, and what Hofstede describes as UAI has nothing to do with buying any kind of insurance.

It is absolutely important to understand what each culture dimension is describing, in terms of underlying values. If you take a dimension according to your own interpretation of its name, you are most probably misunderstanding it.

One might certainly criticize Hofstede for his choice of labels; in that sense, suggestions are welcome. In my professional life I have often used slightly different labels compared to the ones originally published by the professor; I would also welcome suggestions. What is most important is to go beyond the labels and seek to understand the application of each dimension to intercultural communication.

The specific scores of certain countries
This is one of the most contentious aspects of Hofstede's work; the criticism also stems from not understanding what the scores actually mean.

On one hand, the use of numeric scores was greeted positively as an advancement in the study of culture. On the other hand, differing opinions were expressed, insisting that such a complex concept, as culture could never be reduced to figures.

Sometime you can be criticized for wearing a hat and criticized for not wearing a hat… For some, numeric scores were progress; for others, it was a step backward. In any case, it's important to put things in perspective.

First of all, we must once again state what Hofstede himself has said countless times, but has been often overlooked among many comments about his research: the scores are comparative and not absolute.

One of the distinctive aspects of the Professor's methodology is that the culture values of different countries should always be taken two (or more) at a time, that is: comparing two or more cultures among themselves.

When we say that the US scores 91 in Individualism, this number should not be interpreted as something isolated and absolute. The US score in Individualism only makes sense when compared to another country's score, such as Brazil's 38.

Looking at these two scores we can say that the American culture is much more individualistic than the Brazilian; there is a 53 point difference between the two. The US score also happens to be the highest score found so far, among 103 countries; however, that does not mean that it is not possible that another culture might score higher, one that has not yet been the subject of a research study. The lowest score found so far in this dimension is Guatemala (6). Again, it is possible that there is a culture out there scoring lower, among those that have not yet been researched.

Let's look at how we should interpret the scores of these three countries, to avoid misunderstandings.

The American culture is more individualistic than the Brazilian, and even more than the Guatemalan. However, we must bear in mind that Hofstede's original scores were not meant to be percentage points. It is wrong to think of the US as having 91% Individualism; the original scale was not designed as going from 0 to 100. In fact, some countries had scores above 100 in certain dimensions. For instance: Portugal scored 104 in UAI and China scored 118 in LTO.

When Hofstede calculated the statistical differences among comparable samples of different countries, he created a numeric scale to display those differences, but he did not establish "a priori" that the minimum should be "zero" and the maximum should be "100." In theory, it's possible that a culture might have a score below zero in a certain dimension. In practice, that has not yet been found. Only 103 countries have scores so far, there are many countries that have not been researched yet.

Therefore, when you see that Pakistan has a score of "zero" in LTO, this does not mean that in this culture you will not find any expression of flexibility or orientation towards ultimate objectives (rather than immediate ones). The "zero" means simply that, when compared to other cultures, Pakistan has the lowest observed frequency and intensity of these behaviors among the countries researched so far. Even in this culture, however, one can find flexible and ultimate-objective oriented behaviors.

In a similar way, when we say that USA has the highest Individualism score in the world, that does not mean that in American culture there are no expressions of Collectivism to be found.

The most individualistic cultures also have behavioral expressions of Collectivism; the most collectivistic cultures also have expressions of Individualism. What happens is simply that in very collectivistic cultures Individualism is observed less often and with less intensity.

The same is true for all dimensions: an extreme score does not imply the total absence of the opposite kind of behavior.

Getting back to our "ABG" examples (America, Brazil and Guatemala): when we compare these three cultures we can say that, to a

Guatemalan, Brazil seems to have an individualistic culture; however, to American eyes, Brazil is collectivistic.

Cultures are always observed through an observer's culture-tinted glasses; we must always remember that when trying to facilitate cross-culture interaction.

Hofstede himself alerts to the fact that we should not take the dimensions' numeric scores too strictly. If in his original study he found a score of 91 in Individualism for the US, he might find a score of 92 or 93 in a repeat study, or perhaps 89 or 90. Statistics is a science, but it does not have the same millimetric precision that you see when you are working with metal materials in industrial manufacturing.

Besides that, the scores do not have the intention of reflecting everything about a certain culture; they are merely a measurement taken of a certain dimension of culture values. In their outer layers of symbols, rituals and heroes, cultures are infinitely more diverse and complex than at the core, where we find the underlying value dimensions.

I have mentioned previously the comparison with weather phenomena. Hofstede scores are akin to measures of temperature. If I know that the average temperature in Holland is 9 ºC in November, this is an important piece of information to adjust my expectation and plan what to pack in my suitcase for my upcoming trip. However, knowing something about the average temperature tells me nothing about rainfall or winds. On the day of my arrival, it may very well be that the temperature will be 5 Celsius in the morning and 12 degrees in the afternoon.

Hofstede's scores are valuable information to understand culture, but they do not intend to reduce the richness of culture to a mere figure, nor do they purport to explain its complexity by using a ruler.

The spinning onion

A misinformed critic once said that Hofstede's framework was "static, ignoring the dynamic nature of cultures." Apparently this person had not bothered to read what the professor had written about the topic; if he had done so, he would have realized that nothing could be further from the truth. Hofstede has described the complexity and dynamism of cultures countless times, so it is quite puzzling to observe that some people fail to see that the professor has expressed this. Perhaps these critics have looked at a very superficial summary of Hofstede's work and perceived it to be as shallow as their own mindsets.

In order to convey some of the basic concepts about culture using language that simple minds can understand, I have added a couple of aspects to Hofstede's "culture as an onion" metaphor, introduced in page 30. This new version of the onion combines it with the work of Edgar Schein, who wrote about culture using an inverted triangle as a metaphor.

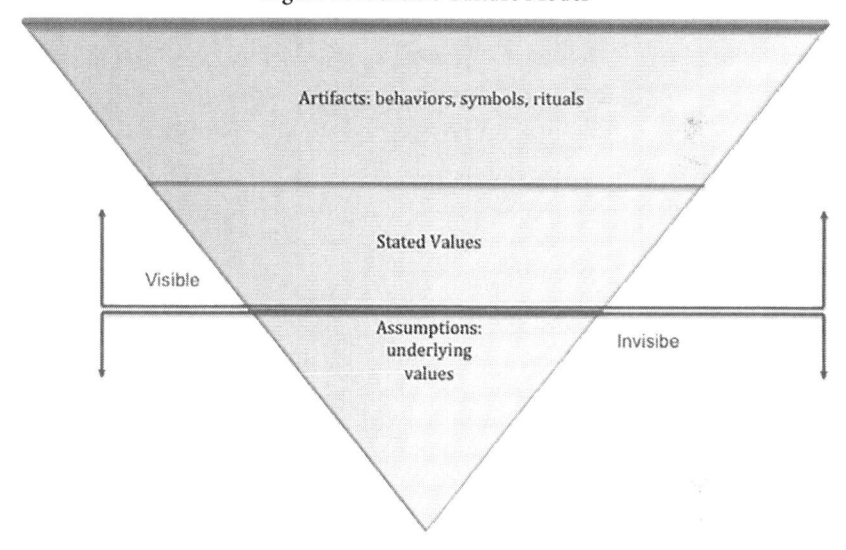

Figure 10: Schein's Culture Model

According to Edgar Schein, culture has two visible parts (the artifacts, such as behavior, symbols and rituals; and the stated values) and an invisible part, made of underlying values or assumptions. This invisible part determines how people behave and perform (Figure 10).

The stated values do not necessarily represent the real culture: most likely they describe a desired culture, which may or may not be really influencing people's behavior in practice.

In terms of organizational culture the stated values are usually referred to as "The Corporate Values," and are displayed prominently in a company's advertising material, in posters and billboards at the company offices, and often at the lobby of the corporate headquarters building.

Corporate values are always socially accepted versions of values, the product of the desired culture as defined by a company's top leaders. You might say that they represent what leaders say in their speeches and presentations, but not necessarily what they show through their behavior in daily situations. Therefore, there is often a significant difference between the stated values and the underlying values, which are typically unwritten and often difficult to identify without specific diagnostic tools used by trained professionals.

It is important to know the difference between stated values and underlying values, because the latter are part of the "real culture" of an organization, while the earlier are simply part of what Hofstede referred to as symbols and rituals, the more superficial layers of culture. It's comparatively easy to change a company's stated values: all you need is a specialist in institutional advertising and the involvement of the CEO or top management team. These people can agree on a set of values to be articulated in an attractive format, and on a communication campaign to broadcast them to target audiences.

Changing the "real" culture is much more difficult, since it requires involving all of the company staff in one way or another, and changing actual behavior of every staff member is quite a complex endeavor.

The stated values of national cultures are typically part of the national flag, and the national coat of arms (if the nation has one). They may also be featured in the country's currency or be part of its national anthem. If you are trying to understand a nation's culture, however, you need to go deeper than these superficial symbols. Very often, the actual national culture is quite different from the national motto or the more socially acceptable versions of national ideals.

For instance: France has a well-known motto of *Liberté, Egalité, Fraternité* (Liberty, Equality, Brotherhood); yet, the underlying values differ a bit from that. Liberty is a value that is consistent with France's scores in Individualism; but the high PDI score (68) tells us that it is actually a hierarchical culture (lower equality) and the high Individualism score (71) is clashing with Brotherhood. The point is simply that, if you want to understand French culture, you need to go beyond its stated values and look at its underlying values (which Schein referred to as assumptions).

To integrate Schein's ideas into the onion metaphor, I have added a layer on the inner side of the superficial layers: the stated values. In doing this, we can combine Schein's and Hofstede's metaphors as depicted in Figure 11.

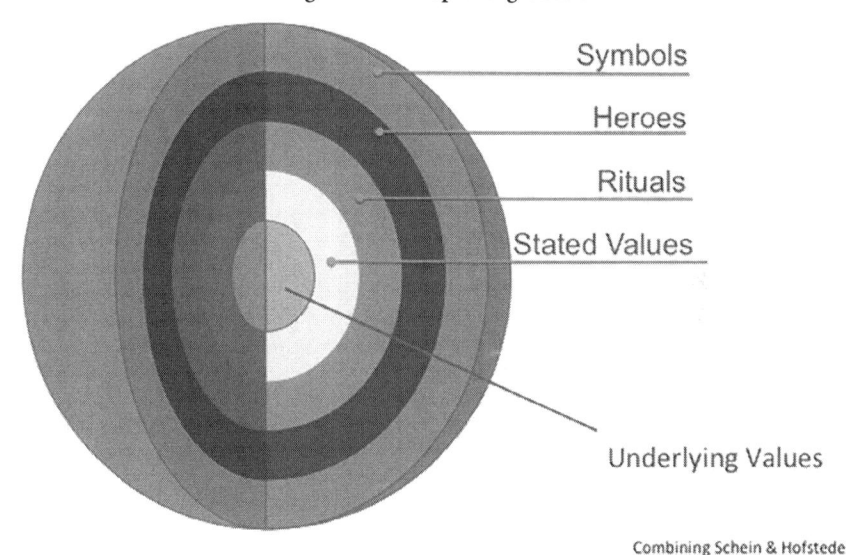

Figure 11: The Spinning Onion

- Symbols
- Heroes
- Rituals
- Stated Values
- Underlying Values

Combining Schein & Hofstede

The second aspect added to the onion metaphor is to think of it as an object that is spinning: this is why we refer to it as "the spinning onion."

The rotating motion represents change. Representing culture as a spinning onion means that the linear speed of the outer layers is much faster than the linear speed near the core of the onion. In other words: change in the outer layers (symbols, rituals and heroes) happens much faster than change at the outer core (stated values) and the inner core (underlying value dimensions).

Think of culture as a very large onion, as large as the planet Earth. The linear speed at the Earth's surface is an amazing 1,047 miles an hour; but at the planet's core, within a 4-mile radius of the absolute center, the linear speed is just 1 mile an hour.

This metaphor symbolizes the fact that the core values change very slowly, almost unnoticeably; while the layers on the surface, such as eating habits, clothing and music, change a thousand times more quickly.

If you think of culture as a spinning sphere (or onion) with many layers and a radius of 4,000 miles such as the planet Earth, you can see that it is complex and dynamic. At the same time, you can see that the speed of change on the outer layers of culture is immensely faster than change at the core, where the underlying value dimensions are found.

In conclusion

The Culture Dimensions Framework might be seen by some as being excessively "labeling", "putting people in boxes" or "deterministic." Still, others might be disappointed to learn that the scores are not absolute and that they do not really allow you to predict people's behavior with precision.

The numeric scores represent an objective measurement, catering to those who believe that "only what can be measured has scientific value." On the other hand, these scores have so many implicit relative aspects that they end up disappointing those who would like to see culture values subject to the same precise rules of mechanical engineering.

The world of culture values is far more complex than simple engineering; it is more diverse than classifying metals as "ferrous and non-ferrous."

Hofstede's framework is just a framework; it helps us to understand cultures and to explain the logic of underlying values existing beneath the surface in every culture. It should not be used to form stereotypes, but rather to dismiss them. It should not be used to predict an individual person's behavior, but rather to understand it.

It should be used with caution in every situation; and with the purpose of facilitating mutual understanding.

Mastering the culture values framework can also be compared to learning how to play a musical instrument, such as a guitar. A guitar teacher can show anyone how to play a guitar in less than an hour, and in that period you can learn how to hold the instrument, strum the strings to produce sounds, press the strings with your left-hand fingers to play two or three different chords. In an hour, you might even learn how to play a simple song. However, if you really want to learn how to play the guitar, you will need many lessons and you will need to practice for hours on end and for several years.

IN CONCLUSION

The same holds true about culture. It is easy to learn about the six dimensions in less than an hour. Yet, to apply the framework on a daily basis, in order to improve the effectiveness of your cross-culture interactions, you will need to practice regularly. The more you practice, the better you will know how to use the instrument.

Never lose your curiosity, your interest in learning and understanding other cultures! This is what will bring you the greatest satisfaction when interacting with people who are like you and who are unlike you. Remember that we all tend to learn more from people who are different from us.

In cross-culture interactions, you first need to perceive and understand differences; this allows you to become aware, subsequently, of the existing similarities; and that will lead you to building a more efficient, effective, and mutually gratifying relationship.

Bibliography

ANDRADE, Mário de – *Macunaíma* – Rio de Janeiro: Editora Agir Sinergia, 1963.

BARBOSA, Lívia – *Igualdade e meritocracia* – Rio de Janeiro: FGV Editora, 1999.

BERNE, Eric – *Games people play: the basic handbook of Transactional Analysis* – New York: Vintage, 1969.

BERNE, Eric – *What Do You Say After You Say Hello?* – London: Corgi Books, 1975.

BERNE, Eric – *Sex In Human Loving* – New York: Simon & Schuster, 1970.

BURKE, W.W.; HORNSTEIN, H.A. – *The Social Technology of Organization Development* – Fairfax: NTL Learning Resources, 1972.

BURKE, Peter – *What is the History of Popular Culture?* – History Today, London, v. 35, n. 12, p. 5-6, December, 1985.

Cathcart, Thomas and Klein, David – *Plato and a Platypus Walk Into a Bar* – Harry Abrams, 2007.

CHOCKALINGAM, V. – *Mind Your Heart* – 2nd ed. Delhi: Elsevier India Pvt. Ltd., 2010.

Cummings, Tom and KEEN, Jim – *Leadership Landscapes* – London: Palgrave MacMillan, 2008.

Damásio, Antonio R. – *O erro de Descartes* – São Paulo: Companhia das Letras, 1996.

DAVIS, Stanley M. – *Managing corporate culture* – Cambridge, Massachussets, USA: Ballinger, 1984.

FOGUEL, Sérgio; SOUZA, Carlos César – *Desenvolvimento Organizacional: uma resposta aos desafios de mudança* – São Paulo: Editora Atlas, 1976.

Frankl, Viktor – *Man´s Search For Ultimate Meaning*, Basic Books, 2000.

Freud, Sigmund – *O mal-estar na cultura*, Porto Alegre: L&PM, 2011.

FREUD, Sigmund – *A interpretação dos sonhos* – Porto Alegre: L&PM, 2012.

FREUD, Sigmund – *Sobre a psicopatologia da vida cotidiana* – Rio de Janeiro: Imago, 2006.

FROMM, Erich – *Meu encontro com Marx e Freud*, Rio de Janeiro: Zahar, 1971.

GILLIAN, Terry – *The Life of Brian* – film produced by Columbia Pictures, 1979.

HALL, Wendy – *Managing Cultures: making strategic relationships work*. Chichester, England: John Wiley & Sons, 1995.

HAMPDEN-TURNER, Charles – *Creating Corporate Culture: from discord to harmony*. Reading, Massachussets, EUA: Addison Wesley, 1990.

HILLMAN, James – *The Thought Of The Heart And Soul Of The World*. London: Spring Publications, 1992.

HILLMAN, James. *The Soul's Code: In Search of Character and Calling*. New York: Bantam, 1997.

HOFSTEDE, Geert – *Cultures Consequences*. London: Sage, 2003.

HOFSTEDE, Geert – *Cultures and Organizations*. London: McGraw-Hill, 2010.

HOFSTEDE, Geert – *Masculinity And Femininity: The Taboo Dimension of National Cultures* – London: Sage Publications, 1998.

HOFSTEDE, Gert Jan; HOFSTEDE, Geert; PEDERSEN, Paul B. – *Exploring Culture: Exercises, Stories and Synthetic Cultures* – Yarmouth, Maine, EUA: Intercultural Press, 2002.BLIK

JUNG, Carl Gustav – *O homem e seus símbolos*. Rio de Janeiro: Nova Fronteira, 2008.

JUNG, Carl Gustav – *Os arquétipos e o inconsciente coletivo* – São Paulo: Vozes, 2011.

KOTTER, John P.; HESKETT, James L. – *Corporate culture and performance* – New York: MacMillan, 1992.

LANZER, Fernando – *Take Off Your Glasses*. Amstelveen: LCO Partners, 2012.

LANZER, Fernando – articles in *Revista de Marketing Industrial*, Cotia, São Paulo: Escola de Marketing Industrial, 2009 to 2015.

LANZER, Fernando – *Clima e Cultura Organizacional: entender, manter e mudra*. São Paulo: LCO Partners, 2017.

Lanzer Pereira de Souza, Edela – *Desenvolvimento Organizacional: Casos e Instrumentos Brasileiros*. São Paulo: Ed. Blucher, 1971.

MARLIER, Didier e PARKER, Chris – *Engaging Leadership*. London: Palgrave MacMillan, 2009.

MARTIN, James – *The Meaning of the 21st Century* – London: Eden Project Books, 2006.

MAY, Rollo – *O homem à procura de si mesmo* – São Paulo: Vozes, 2004.

McKEON, Richard – *The basic works of Aristotle* – London: Modern Library, 1941.

MEAD, Margaret – *Growing up in New Guinea: a comparative study of primitive education* – London: Pelican Books, 1970.

MINTZBERG, Henry – *Designing effective organizations* – Englewood Cliffs, New Jersey, EUA: Prentice Hall, 1983.

MORGAN, Gareth – *Images of organization* – London: Sage, 1986.

ODNANREF, Reznal – *Concepts of Culture* – White paper presented at the 14th Global Forum on Executive Development, Shanghai: 2007.

OXFORD Dictionaries – *Oxford English Dictionary*. Oxford: Franklin Watts, Publisher, 2012.

PERLS, Frederick S. – *Ego, Hunger And Aggression: A Revision of Freud's Theory and Method* – New York: Random House, 1969.

PETER, Laurence J. – *The Peter Prescription* – New York: Bantam, 1973.

Price Waterhouse Europe – *International assignments: European policy and practice* – London: PWC International Assignment Services Europe, 1998.

REDDIN, William J. – *Managerial Effectiveness*, London: McGraw-Hill, 1970.

SCHEIN, Edgar H. – *Organizational Culture and Leadership* – Second Edition, San Francisco, California: Jossey-Bass, 1997.

SCHNEIDER, Benjamin – *Organizational Climate And Culture* -Rolling Meadows, Illinois: CEB Valtera, 2012.

SOUZA, Edela Lanzer Pereira de – *Clima e Cultura Organizacionais: como se manifestam e como se manejam* – São Paulo: Editora Edgar Blucher, 1978.

SOUZA, Edela Lanzer Pereira de – *Desenvolvimento Organizacional: Casos e Instrumentos Brasileiros* – São Paulo: Editora Edgar Blucher, 1975.

SOUZA, Edela Lanzer Pereira de – *Treinando gerentes para o future* – São Paulo: Editora Edgar Blucher, 1992.

STEVENS, John O. – *Awareness: Exploring, Experimenting, Experiencing* – Lafayette, California: Real People Press, 1971.

TORBERT, William R. – *Managing the Corporate Dream: restructuring for long-term success* – Homewood, Illinois, EUA: Dow Jones-Irwin, 1987.

TROMPENAARS, Fons and ASSER, Maarten – *The Global M&A Tango*, London: Infinite Ideas, 2010.

UNDERWOOD, RON. *City Slickers* – film distributed by Columbia Pictures, 1991.

WITTGENSTEIN, Ludwig. *Lectures And Conversations On Aesthetics, Psychology And Religious Beliefs* – Berkeley, California, USA: University of California Press, 1973.

WITTGENSTEIN, Ludwig – *Culture and value* – Chicago: University of Chicago Press, 1984.

About the Author

Fernando Lanzer Pereira de Souza is Dutch and Brazilian, born in 1952.

He started writing at age seven, but the reaction of others to what he wrote was never again so enthusiastic as then in those first days.

He earned a degree as a Psychologist at PUCRGS in 1975 and began his career working in a team of consultants, in which he had the longest hair and the shortest experience. Soon he was absorbed by a client and became a Human Resources Manager at the now defunct Sulbrasileiro Bank.

Unable to get a real job, he was stuck in HR and in organizational consulting, alternating between these roles for many years until he acquired 23,000 reasons for an ulcer as Human Resources Director of ABN AMRO/Banco Real in Brazil.

Eventually he moved from São Paulo to Amsterdam, as Global Executive Vice-President for the ABN AMRO Group, in charge of Leadership Development & Learning. He left that organization after completing 15 years of service and returned to his roots as a consultant, this time based in Amsterdam.

He founded LCO Partners as a consulting firm dedicated to Leadership and Organization Development; in parallel, from 2008 ro 2016. he also collaborated with ITIM International, a firm now based in Helsinki.

Fernando lives in Amstelveen, the Netherlands, with his wife Jussara who is also a Psychologist and consultant. He travels all over the world serving his clients and visiting his four daughters who live in different Continents.

He is a former member and Chair of AIESEC International's Supervisory Group, the world's largest student-led organization dedicated to arranging cross-border internships. He sits on the Board of Trustees of ISA – the International School of Amsterdam.

Printed in Great Britain
by Amazon